D1353796

ABERDEENSHIRE LIBRARIES
1943775

NATURE EXPLORER

Authors
David Burnie, Ben Morgan,
Richard Walker, and John Woodward

DK

LONDON, NEW YORK,
MELBOURNE, MUNICH, AND DELHI

Senior Editor Shaila Brown
Senior Art Editor Spencer Holbrook
Managing Editor Linda Esposito
Managing Art Editor Diane Thistlethwaite
Publishing Manager Andrew Macintyre
Category Publisher Laura Buller
Senior Production Controller Angel Graef
Production Editor Andy Hilliard
Picture Researchers Anna Bedewell, Celia Dearing, Liz Moore, Sarah Pownall, and Frances Vargo
DK Picture Library Claire Bowers, Rose Horridge, and Sarah Mills
Photography Dave King
Jacket Editor Joanna Pocock
Jacket Designer Yumiko Tahata
Jacket Manager Sophia M Tampakopoulos Turner
Consultants Kim Bryan, Lisa Burke, Dr Jacqueline Mitton, and Dr Douglas Palmer

First published in Great Britain in 2010
by Dorling Kindersley Limited, 80 Strand,
London WC2R 0RL

Contains content from Birdwatcher (2005), Bug hunter (2005), Stargazer (2005), Rock & fossil hunter (2005), Nature ranger (2006), and Weather watcher (2006)
Dorling Kindersley Limited
A Penguin Company

Copyright © 2010 Dorling Kindersley Limited
2 4 6 8 10 9 7 5 3 1
177890 – 02/10

All rights reserved. No part of this publication may be reproduced, stored in a retrieval system, or transmitted in any form or by any means, electronic, mechanical, photocopying, recording, or otherwise, without the prior written permission of the copyright owner.

A CIP catalogue for this book
is available from the British Library.
ISBN 978-1-4053-5404-2

Colour reproduction by MDP, United Kingdom
Printed and bound by Leo, China

**Discover more at
www.dk.com**

BE SAFE! IMPORTANT NOTE TO PARENTS

Some of the activities in this book require adult supervision. Symbols are used to indicate where an activity must only be done with the help of an adult. An "Important" box gives further information about any risks involved and appropriate safety precautions to take. Please carefully check which activities require adult supervision and supervise your child where indicated.

Activities shown with this symbol must only be done with the help of an adult.

Take extra care when doing this activity.

IMPORTANT
Provides safety information and indicates whether an activity can be messy. Follow the guidance notes on those activities that are messy and should be carried out only in suitable places.

Always ensure that your child follows instructions carefully. The authors and the publisher cannot take responsibility for any accident or injury that occurs because the reader has not followed the instructions properly, and will not be responsible for any loss or damage allegedly arising from any of the activities in this book.

ABERDEENSHIRE
LIBRARY & INFO SERV
3014153
Bertrams 02/06/2010
J508 £9.99

Contents

Remember!
Show respect to wild creatures and make sure you don't disturb animals' environments.

CHILDREN – BE SAFE!
READ BEFORE STARTING ANY ACTIVITIES!

1 Tell an adult before you do any of the activities in this book as you will need an adult to supervise these activities.

2 Pay attention to the following symbols:

Take extra care with an activity.

You need an adult to help you with an activity.

3 Read the "Important" boxes – these provide safety information and let you know which activities may be messy and should only be carried out in suitable places.

4 Follow the instructions carefully.

Bird watcher

The world of birds

If you ask anyone to list their favourite animals, birds often come out on top. It is easy to see why. Birds are wonderful to watch, both on the ground and in the air. You don't have to go to the countryside to see them because birds live everywhere, from seashores and mountains to gardens and city streets. But before you head off, find out here what birds are and how they fit into the animal world.

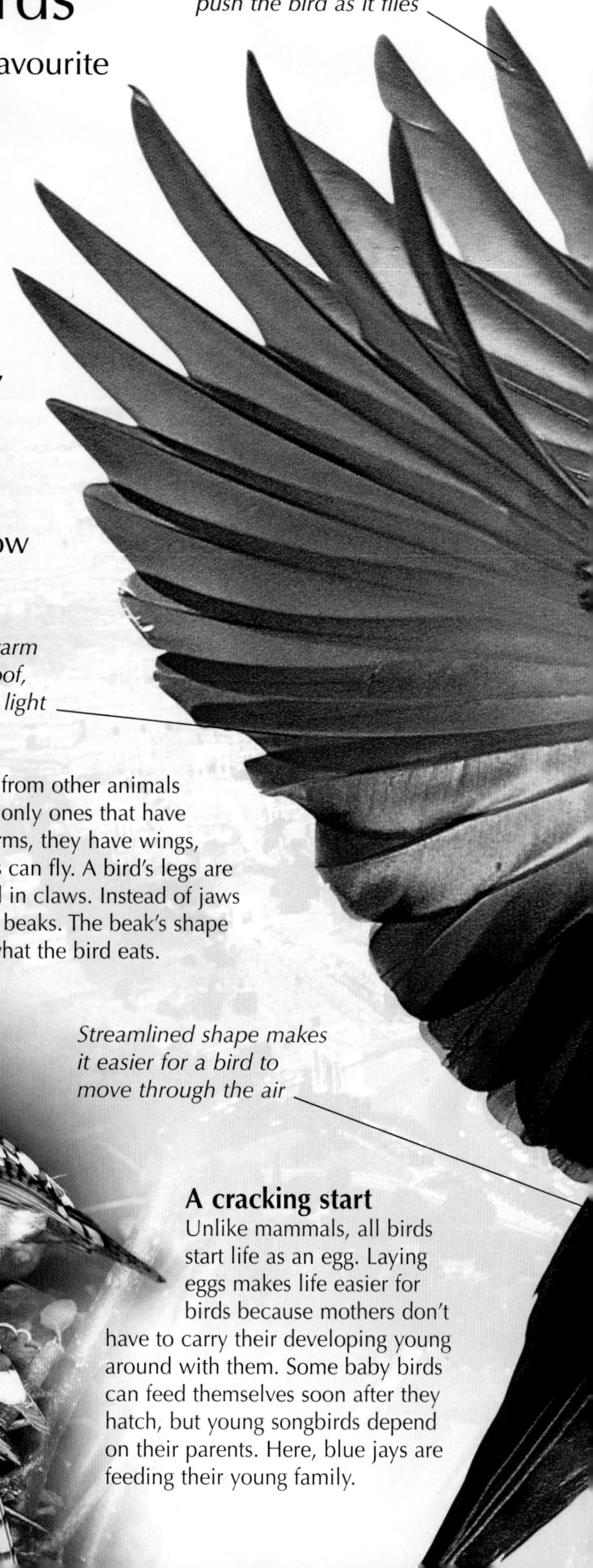

Long flight feathers push the bird as it flies

Plumage is warm and waterproof, but also very light

Streamlined shape makes it easier for a bird to move through the air

Lift-off!

It is easy to tell birds from other animals because they are the only ones that have feathers. Instead of arms, they have wings, although not all birds can fly. A bird's legs are scaly and its toes end in claws. Instead of jaws and teeth, birds have beaks. The beak's shape varies according to what the bird eats.

Nestlings beg for food whenever a parent bird appears

A cracking start

Unlike mammals, all birds start life as an egg. Laying eggs makes life easier for birds because mothers don't have to carry their developing young around with them. Some baby birds can feed themselves soon after they hatch, but young songbirds depend on their parents. Here, blue jays are feeding their young family.

ORNITHOLOGY

People who study birds are known as ornithologists. Professional ornithologists work all over the world, studying the way birds live and their habitats. Many are involved in bird conservation. Amateur ornithologists enjoy watching birds and seeing how many types they can spot. Some champion birdwatchers have seen more than 6,000 different kinds of birds.

◂ Getting a good look
Birdwatchers use telescopes and binoculars to study birds without frightening them away.

Superb eyesight for finding food
Beak designed for catching and holding food
Legs stow away close to the body after take-off

Wild and tame

Birds are wary of people. If they are disturbed, they usually fly away. But with patience, wild birds can sometimes be tamed. This is a great way of seeing birds close up and watching how they behave. To get friendly with a robin, try sitting in the same place every day and offering it some food.

Essential equipment

Birdwatching is something you can do almost anywhere, whether you have a few spare minutes or the whole day. But to get the most out of your birding, it helps to have the right equipment with you. Binoculars are really useful, and so is a bird guide and a notebook and pencil. If you're going on a long outing, it's worth packing some collecting equipment in case you find anything you want to bring home.

BIRDWATCHER'S CODE

When you go birdwatching, do not harm any birds or other wildlife. Follow these four golden rules:

- Try not to disturb the birds you are watching.
- Don't get too close.
- Don't approach birds that are on their nests or with their young.
- Leave baby birds alone. Their parents are almost certainly nearby.

WHAT TO PACK

For birdwatching, you must have some binoculars so that you can study birds from a distance. Tweezers, containers, and a magnifying glass are useful for studying and collecting interesting feathers and bones.

Binoculars ▸ Choose binoculars that magnify between eight and ten times. Avoid large, heavy ones.

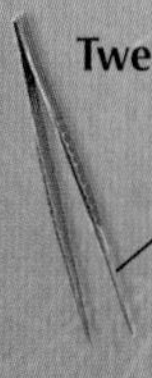

Tweezers *Use tweezers with pointed tips*

Self-sealing plastic bags *Use these for feathers*

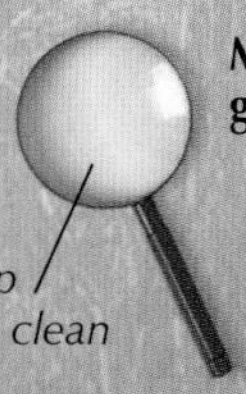

Magnifying glass *Keep lens clean*

Small plastic box with lid *Useful for bones and pellets*

IDENTIFYING BIRDS

When you first start birdwatching, don't be disappointed if you can't identify birds straight away. With practice, you will soon learn what to look for so that you can tell different birds apart. Check the key features below – you can also use a bird guide.

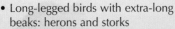

◀ Herring gull
It is easy to spot gulls, but harder to tell the species apart. The herring gull has a yellow beak with a red spot and grey wings with black tips.

- Long-legged birds with extra-long beaks: herons and storks
- Waterbirds with flattened beaks: ducks, geese, and swans
- Daytime hunters with sharp claws: birds of prey
- Night-time hunters with sharp claws: owls
- Coastal birds with sharp beaks and slender wings: gulls and terns
- Birds with hooked beaks and colourful plumage: parrots
- Tiny birds that hover in front of flowers: hummingbirds
- Birds that perch vertically on tree-trunks: woodpeckers
- Small birds with musical songs and calls: songbirds

Out in the open
Birdwatching can take you to some exciting places. Coasts are great places, especially in spring, when seabirds come back to land to breed. Hillsides and open country are good places for spotting birds of prey.

Hide and peep

Birds are very good at spotting movement, which is why it's so easy to scare them away. But unlike us, they don't pay much attention to things that keep still. If you watch birds from a portable hide, they will quickly forget that you are inside. Lots of bird reserves have permanent hides that give visitors an ideal view. But you can make your own portable hide with some netting and bamboo. It's easy to put up and dismantle, so you can take it on all your birdwatching trips.

WHAT YOU WILL NEED

- Four strong bamboo canes about 1.5–2 m (5–6½ ft) long
- 3–4 m (10–13 ft) plastic garden netting
- Ball of strong string
- Leafy twigs. Select these when you are ready to use them

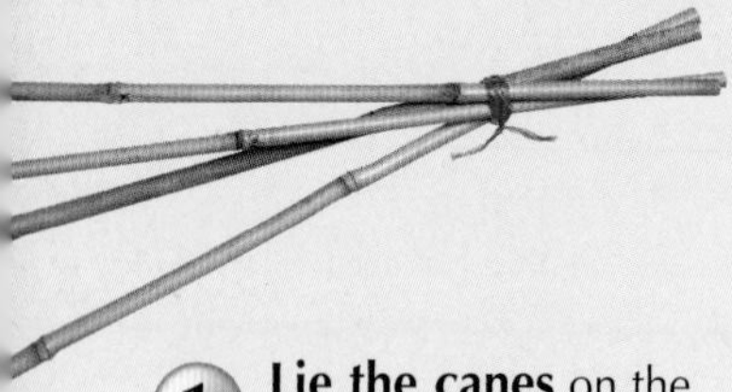

1 **Lie the canes** on the ground. Then tie them together tightly about 25 cm (10 in) from one end.

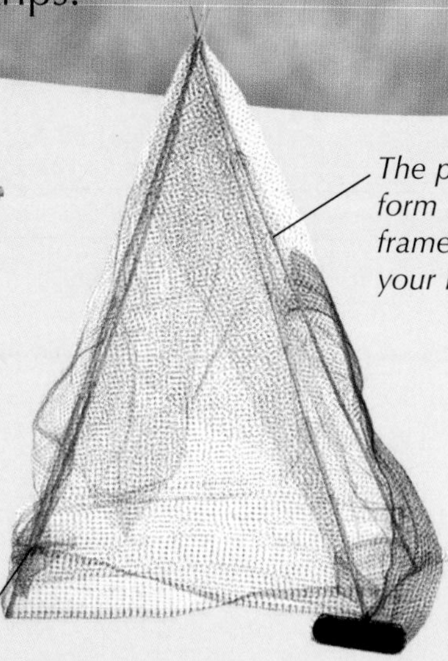

The poles form the frame of your hide
Spread the netting out over the poles

2 **Stand the canes** on end, and spread them out to make a wigwam shape. Lay the netting over the frame, leaving a gap between two of the canes to make your entrance.

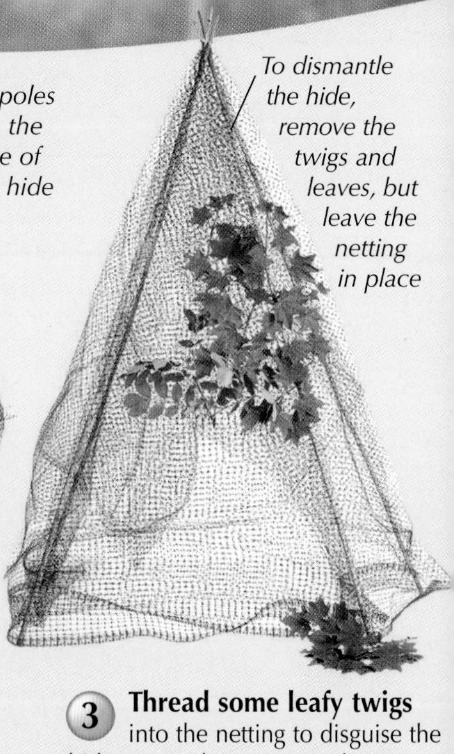

To dismantle the hide, remove the twigs and leaves, but leave the netting in place

3 **Thread some leafy twigs** into the netting to disguise the hide. Leave the entrance clear so that you can get in and out easily.

IMPORTANT

Ssshhh! Birds have very good hearing. Be careful what you pack to eat in your hide. The sound of crackly wrappings will frighten them away.

BIRD EYESIGHT

Your eyes look straight ahead, so you can see only part of what is around you – to see the rest, you have to turn your head. But most birds have eyes that face out to either side. This means that they can see all around them, so they're hard to creep up on. Their eyesight is sharper than ours, too, enabling them to spot tiny insects amongst leaves and grasses.

◂ **All-round view** A pheasant's eyes look out to each side, and take up nearly half the space in its skull.

4 **Your hide** is now ready for use. It will provide an excellent base for you to observe some of the many species of birds in your area. In the hide, you can use binoculars, and you can also photograph and sketch the birds that you see to help you identify them.

Making a bird table

If you want to attract birds and watch them feed, a bird table is hard to beat. You can buy bird tables ready-made, but with an adult to help you, it's good fun making one yourself. The bird table shown here is simple to make, and easy for birds to use. The table sits on a square post, which needs to be hammered into the ground. It has a rim to stop food falling off, and small gaps to let rainwater drain away.

WHAT YOU WILL NEED

- Weatherproof plywood to following sizes: 30 x 40 cm x 15 mm (12½ x 15½ x 1/16 in) for tray; 1.5 m x 1 cm sq (5 ft x ½ in sq), cut into 4 strips, 2 @ 40 cm (15½ in), and 2 @ 26 cm (10 in) for tray rim; 50 cm x 4 cm sq (19 x 1½ in sq) for postholder; 1.5 m x 4 cm sq (5ft x 1½ in sq) for post
- 20 mm (1 in) nails
- 55 mm (2 in) screws
- Tape measure • Pencil
- Saw • Hammer
- Electric drill

You will need an adult to help you as this activity requires sharp tools.

1 Make the rim by nailing the four strips to the edges of the tray. The gap at each end of the two short strips lets rainwater flow away.

2 Cut the timber for the postholder into four pieces. Drill pilot holes through them, and screw them to the base of the tray. This makes a square holder for the post.

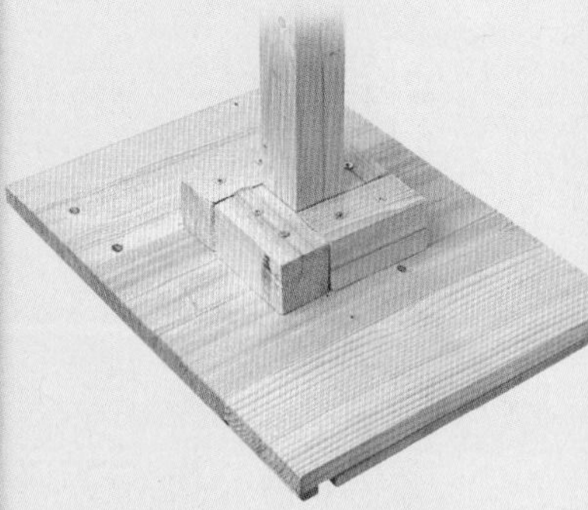

3 Saw one end of the post to create a sharp point. Push the other end into the postholder, making sure that it fits tightly.

FEEDING IN WINTER

If winters are cold where you live, feeding birds helps them to get through a difficult time of year. Birds need food to keep warm – if they don't eat enough, they can die of cold during the night. Don't forget to put out water as well as food, because birds can get dehydrated when ponds and puddles are frozen up.

Robin in the snow ▲
Snow makes it harder for birds to find food on the ground.

FEEDING TIME

Once your bird table is ready, don't be tempted to put out too much food. Instead, put out small amounts of different foods, and brush the table clean at least once each week. Instead of putting out large pieces of food, it's best to use ones that are chopped up, or finely divided. This will stop large birds from snatching the food and flying off with it.

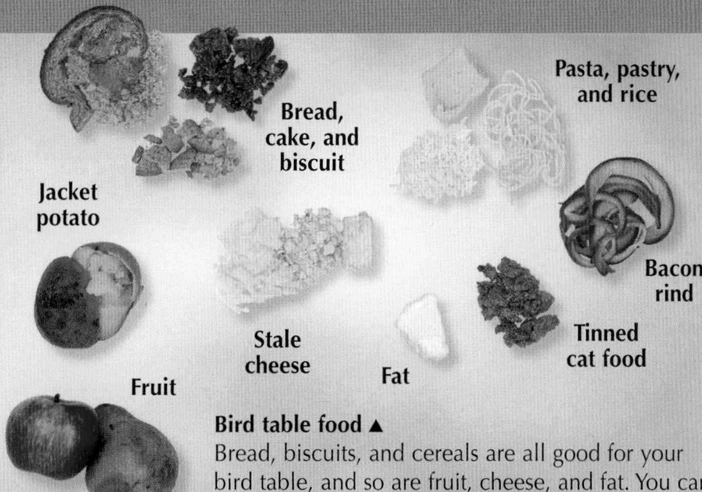

Bird table food ▲
Bread, biscuits, and cereals are all good for your bird table, and so are fruit, cheese, and fat. You can also try pet food – but only in very small amounts.

Birds feel safe on a bird table, because they have an all-round view while they feed

Screw in here to fix post

IMPORTANT

Birds can carry germs. Always wash your hands after you have put out food, or after cleaning away leftovers.

4 **Drill one** or two pilot holes sideways through the postholder, and insert screws to fix the post firmly in place.

5 **To put up** the table, choose a suitable spot and hammer the centre of the tray, driving the post into the ground.

Feeding signs

When birds feed in the wild, they often leave tell-tale signs behind them. Many birds peck at seeds or fruit, but some specialize in the trickier task of opening nuts or cones. A few are expert at smashing open snails, or digging out grubs that bore their way through wood. With a bit of detective work, you can find out where these birds have been feeding. If you're lucky, you may also spot the private larders that some birds make – they use these when fresh food is hard to find.

Scattered scales
This crossbill is extracting seeds from a cone. Its beak works like a pair of cutters, levering the seeds out of the cone, and dropping the scales on the ground. Crossbills often feed in flocks, so you may find lots of scales in one feeding place.

WHERE TO LOOK

- Pecked nuts, cones – woods, hedges, parks
- Shrike larders – thorny hedges, barbed wire
- Broken shells – flat rocks near the shore, rocky places inland
- Woodpecker holes – woods, parks, gardens

Skewered snacks
If you are out in the countryside, keep an eye open for insects or small lizards spiked on barbed wire or on thorns. These gruesome remains show that a shrike is in the area. Shrikes skewer their prey to make it easier to eat, and to keep it for later.

Stone "anvil" for crushing snail shells

Smash and grab
Many birds feed on hard-bodied animals, such as crabs, mussels, and snails. To get at their food, they often have to break it open first. Some drop it from the air, but this thrush is smashing snails against a hard stone.

Beak chisels a hole and spear-like tongue stabs prey

Storing food

Instead of eating their food straight away, some birds store it for later. This jay has collected an acorn, and is about to bury it in the ground. Jays bury hundreds of acorns during autumn. Later, in the winter, they dig them up for food.

Breaking and entering

Woodpeckers chisel holes in trees to get at wood-boring grubs. To see where they have been at work, look out for rotten wood that is covered with peck marks, and check the ground for fresh wood chippings. Large woodpeckers also break their way into other birds' nest holes, so they can eat their eggs or chicks.

BEAK CLEANING

When a bird has finished eating, it often flies off to a perch to clean its beak. Unlike mammals, birds cannot lick themselves clean – instead, they wipe their beaks on a twig or a branch. A bird's beak has a base of bone, but the main part is made of the same substance that is in hooves and nails. Just like a fingernail, the outer part grows all the time, so a bird's beak never gets worn down.

A quick wipe ▶
This crow is cleaning its beak after a meal. It perches on a branch and then wipes each side of its beak. When birds do this, you can sometimes hear a hollow sound as the beak hits the wood.

Feathers and flight

Birds often have thousands of feathers, but their flight feathers, which are on a bird's wings and tail, are the most important of all. These feathers are strong but light, and they lift a bird and let it steer as it speeds through the air. Feathers are interesting to study and fun to collect. Flight feathers are easy to find because most birds shed or moult them at least once a year. They replace the old feathers with new ones to make up for wear and tear.

MAKING A FEATHER COLLECTION

Good places to find feathers are under trees, along the sides of lakes and reservoirs, and on the shore. Remember to wash your hands after handling feathers. One of the best ways to store your feathers is to slide them into pieces of corrugated cardboard. You can then paste them in a scrapbook, or put them in a box.

◀ Safely stored
Keep your feathers in the dark. Daylight will make them slowly lose their colour.

Macaw flight feather

Feather types

Most birds have four different types of feathers. Flight feathers grow on the bird's wings and its tail – beside the tail feathers. They keep birds airborne, and help them to steer. Body feathers give them a streamlined shape, so they slip easily through the air. Beneath these, fluffy down feathers keep them warm.

Flight feather ▲
These have strong shafts, or quills. The quill is nearest to the feather's front edge.

Down feather ▶
These have small quills, and are soft and fluffy. They trap air next to a bird's body.

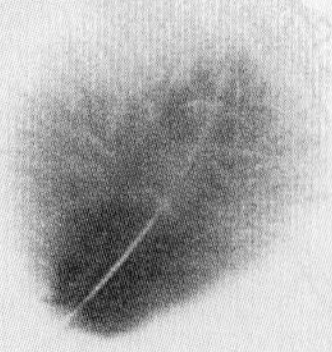

Soft fringes muffle the sound of the owl's wings as it hunts

Silent flight

If you find a flight feather, try working out what kind of bird it came from. Owl flight feathers are easy to identify because they have a fringe along their leading edge. These fringes work like silencers, letting owls catch their prey by surprise.

Moulting

In late summer, watch out for birds that have gaps in their wings. These birds are moulting their flight feathers, and replacing them with a new set. Most birds moult their flight feathers gradually, so that they can still fly.

Magpie tail feather

Pheasant tail feather

◄ Body feathers
These are soft and fluffy at the base, but smooth at the tip, giving the bird an even outline.

Tail feathers ▲
These sometimes look like wing feathers, but they have a quill running down the middle, instead of to one side.

Bath time

Birds love taking baths because it keeps their feathers in top condition. They sometimes bathe in dust, but really enjoy a splash in water. Birds don't like a long soak. They prefer a quick dip in shallow water in case they need to make an emergency getaway. If you can find a dustbin lid and a few bricks, you can make the kind of bath that they like. Then you can watch how birds go about washing, and how they preen their feathers afterwards.

WHAT YOU WILL NEED

- Dustbin lid (metal or plastic)
- Some small pebbles
- Three bricks or blocks of wood
- Water

1 **Choose a spot** on open, level grass or bare ground and arrange the bricks in a triangle.

2 **Put the upturned lid** on the bricks and adjust it until it is stable. Spread the pebbles over the deepest part of the bath.

3 **Pour cold water** into the bath until the level is about 2 cm (3/4 in) below the rim.

Clean the bath and replace the water regularly

4 **Watch the bath** from indoors or from an outside hideaway. If you have binoculars, train them on the bath so you are ready to watch when the first birds arrive.

DUST BATHS

In dry weather, birds often use dust to keep their feathers clean. They crouch down on the ground and fluff themselves up so that the dust gets deep into their plumage. The dust acts like talcum powder, cleaning the bird's skin and feathers. Game birds such as chickens, grouse, and partridges enjoy taking dust baths and never take baths in water.

◀ **Dust bath**
This partridge is taking a dust bath to clear away parasites and flakes of dead skin from its feathers.

IMPORTANT

Make sure that you put the bath in an open place so cats cannot ambush the birds as they wash.

Birds flutter their wings to splash water all over their bodies

Nesting time

Before birds can raise a family, most of them have to make a nest first. Even if they have never built a nest before, they know exactly what shape to make it and what building materials to use. You can lend them a hand by putting out some of these materials in your garden or backyard. If you stand back and watch the birds arrive, you'll be able to see what they choose.

IMPORTANT

Don't disturb nesting birds during the breeding season. Watch them from a distance, but never try to get close up to their nests.

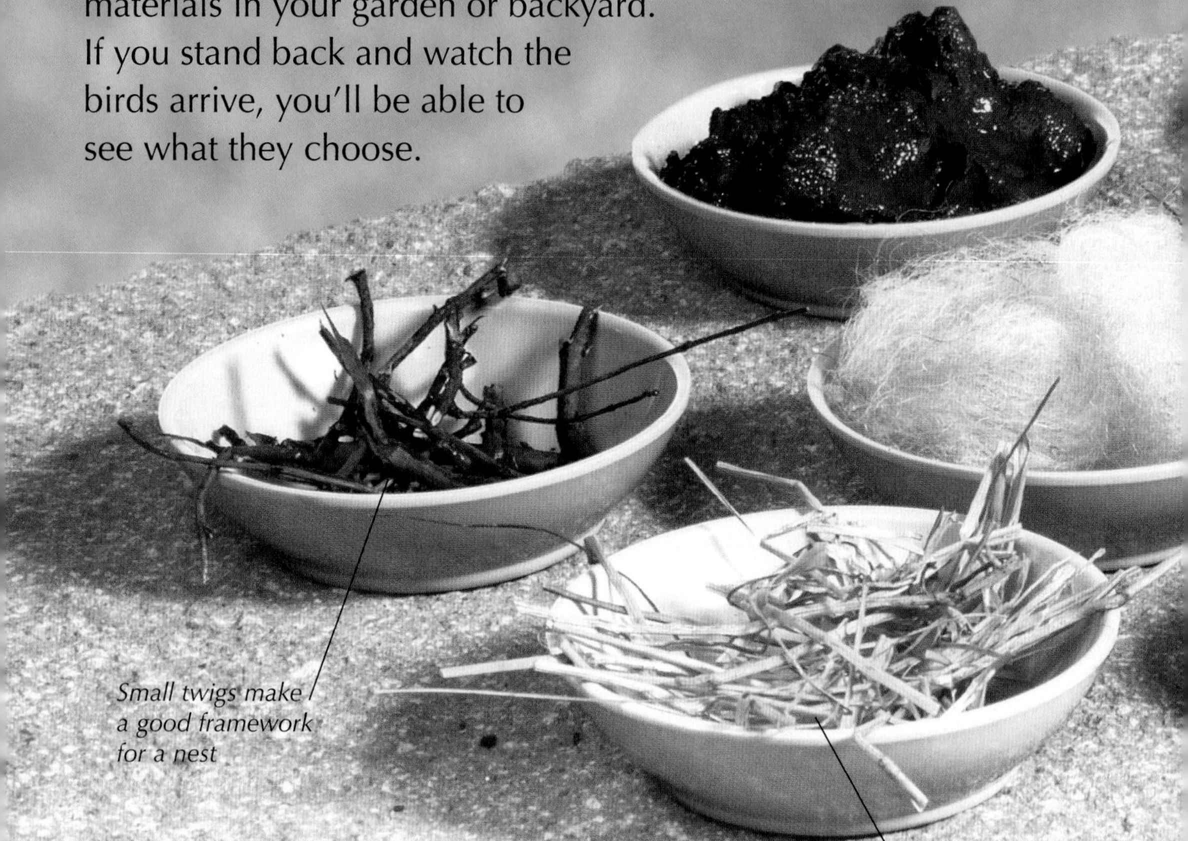

Small twigs make a good framework for a nest

Straw is an ideal nesting material

WHAT YOU WILL NEED

- 6 shallow dishes
- Wet mud • Moss
- Small twigs
- Straw
- String cut into short lengths
- Sheep's wool collected from a farm, or short lengths of knitting wool

1 **Put the materials** into dishes and out in the open where birds can spot them – near the edge of a lawn is ideal. Make sure the mud is soft and moist. Leave the dishes alone for at least 24 hours, so your local birds have time to get used to them.

2 **Watch from** a distance to see which materials they take and how they carry them. Who does the collecting? The male, the female, or both?

Blue tits and their relatives line their nests with mud
Small songbirds use moss to insulate their nests

NEXT DOOR NEIGHBOUR

For some birds – including sparrows and starlings – houses make good nesting places. If you check out the buildings in your neighbourhood, you can often spot places where birds have moved in. Nesting materials poking out of holes or beneath roofs, and splashes of white droppings are signs that birds have set up home.

Sparrow ▲
Thriving house sparrows nest on buildings all over the world, and eat the food that people drop.

BIRDS WITHOUT NESTS

Instead of building a nest, some birds lay their eggs straight on to the ground. Many seabirds lay their eggs directly on rocky ledges, and terns lay theirs on shingle. Lots of desert and grassland birds are ground-nesters, because their habitats contain very few trees. Ground-nesting birds often have camouflaged eggs and chicks, which makes it harder for predators to find them.

Hollow home ▶
Terns lay their eggs in a hollow, called a scrape, which they dig out with their feet.

Nesting together

Most garden and backyard birds like their privacy and nest on their own. But if you go birdwatching in the countryside or on the coast, you will sometimes see birds that nest together in groups. Birds nest together for safety or because good nesting spots are few and far between. Some nesting groups, or colonies, contain 20 or 30 birds, but the largest can contain more than a million. The sight of so many birds can be an unforgettable experience, as can the noise – and sometimes the smell!

Living on a ledge

For humans, cliffs can be very dangerous, but for seabirds they are often a safe place to nest. High up on rocky ledges, these kittiwakes and their chicks are very hard for predators to reach. Kittiwakes make cup-shaped nests from seaweed and mud, but many other seabirds lay their eggs directly on to the rocks.

WHERE TO LOOK

Coastal cliffs and offshore islands are the best places to see seabird colonies. Visit in spring or early summer. At other times of the year, most of the birds will be out at sea.

Parent bird spreads its tail to brake

Housemartins make bowl-shaped nests, with a small entrance at the top

Under the eaves

Some colony-forming birds nest close to our own homes. Swallows nest in outbuildings and barns, while housemartins often build their nests underneath eaves. These birds usually choose the same place year after year. They make their nests from wet mud, so they need to have damp ground nearby.

IMPORTANT

Take great care when watching cliff-nesting birds. It is easy to lose your balance when you are watching birds in flight. If you are using binoculars, sit down.

TETCHY NEIGHBOURS

Gannets often nest on rocky islands a long way offshore. Here they are safe from most of their enemies, but they have to be careful of each other. With so many birds crowded together, every pair jealously guards its small patch of rock. If a bird lands in the wrong place, it risks a vicious peck. Young birds must be careful, too. Neighbours will attack them if they wander within pecking range.

Touchdown ▶
Gannets recognize their mates by their calls. When a gannet comes in to land, it listens for its partner and then drops down next to their nest.

Starting life

When their nests are ready, female birds get on with the important task of laying eggs. Then the mother sits on her eggs to incubate them. With some birds, the parents take turns at this job, but for most it is a task for the female alone. Inside the eggs, the warmth does its work, and soon the baby birds are big enough to hatch. It's time to keep your distance because nesting birds must not be disturbed.

Incubation
This kestrel has laid a clutch of six eggs and has settled down to incubate them. Every few hours, she rolls the eggs around with her beak to make sure that none of them get cold. While she is sitting on the nest, her mate keeps her supplied with food.

Shell detective

When nestlings hatch, parent birds often pick up the shells and carry them away from the nest. It's a good security system because it makes it less likely that predators will spot the nest. During the nesting season, you will often see pieces of broken shell on the ground. By looking closely, you can sometimes tell what kind of bird laid the egg.

American robin ▶
Like many other birds in the thrush family, the robin lays blue eggs. They make cup-shaped nests lined with mud.

Sparrowhawk ▶
The sparrowhawk lays camouflaged eggs, like most birds of prey. It makes a platform-shaped nest out of sticks.

PERFECT PACKAGING

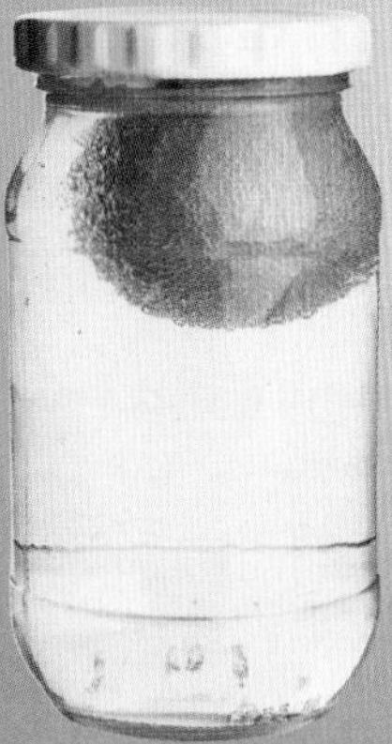

Eggs have a hard outer shell and a flexible inner lining. The shell gets its strength from calcium, a mineral that birds eat in their food. You can see how calcium works if you leave an egg in vinegar overnight. Some of the calcium will dissolve and the egg will become soft and rubbery.

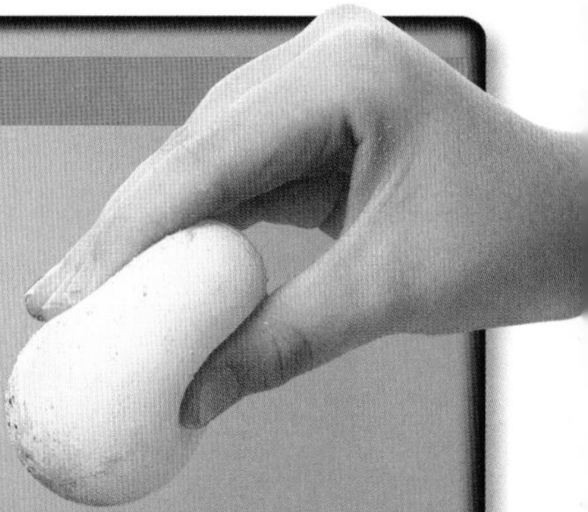

1 **Half-fill** a jam jar with vinegar and put a chicken's egg inside. Loosely screw on the cap and leave the egg for at least eight hours.

2 **Pour away the vinegar** and try squeezing the egg with your fingers. Instead of cracking, the egg will bend.

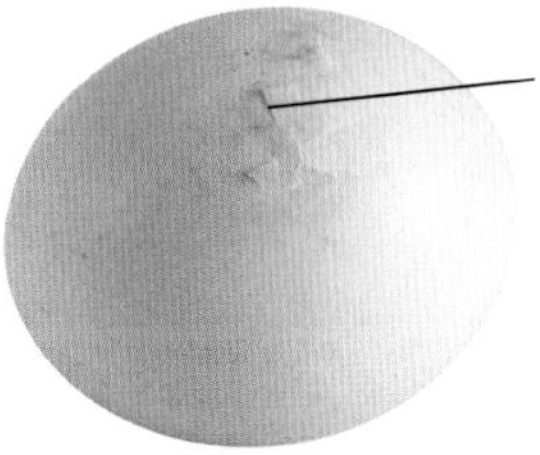

Tiny crack shows that the chick has started to hatch

Hatching

When a baby bird hatches, it has to break through its eggshell and into the outside world. Like many birds, this tawny owl chick uses its egg tooth, a hard bump on the tip of its beak. After each peck, the chick turns inside the egg so that it cuts a crack right around the shell. Eventually, one end of the shell breaks away and the chick tumbles out into the nest.

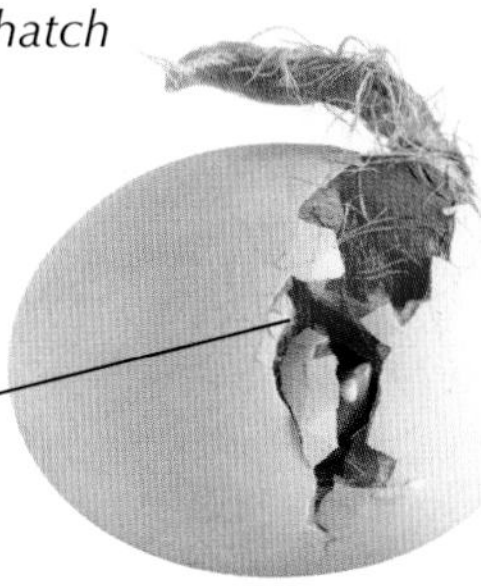

Chick pushes with its feet to widen the crack

IMPORTANT

It is against the law to take eggs from wild birds' nests. Don't be tempted to go near nests because the parents may abandon their young.

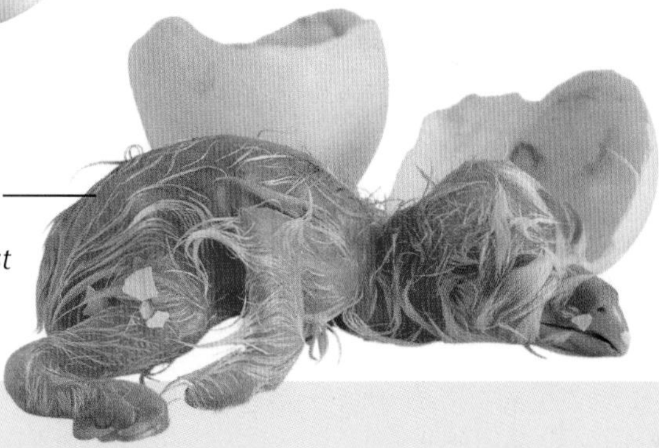

Newly hatched owl chicks are blind and almost featherless

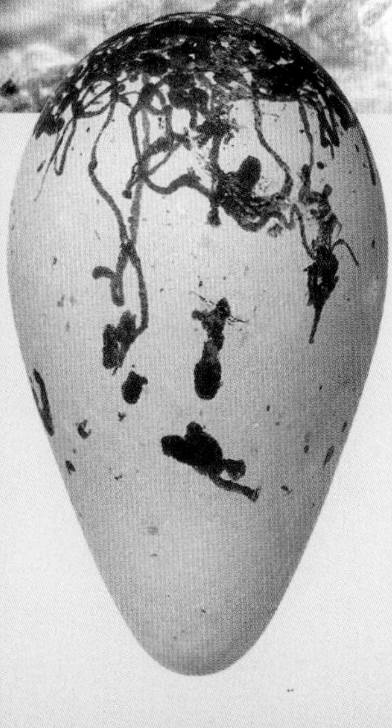

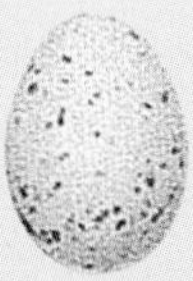

◀ Long-tailed tit
Tits lay up to 12 eggs in a cup-shaped nest. Their shells are white with a pattern of darker speckles or blotches.

Wood warbler ▶
Songbirds often lay speckled eggs. Most songbirds nest in bushes, but the wood warbler nests on the ground.

◀ Guillemot
Guillemots nest on bare rocky ledges. Their eggs have a sharp point, which helps to stop them rolling off.

Growing up

If you have a nestbox in your garden, you will be able to see just how quickly birds grow up. Most people get by on just three meals a day, but baby songbirds need many more. Their parents have to work flat out to keep them fully fed. By watching them for just 15 minutes, you can estimate how many times they bring food to the nest in a day.

WHAT YOU WILL NEED

- Binoculars
- Timer or wristwatch
- Notebook
- Pencil • Calculator
- Calendar or diary

It is essential that you find a nest you can observe without disturbing the birds in any way.

1 Pick a place where you can watch parent birds at work without disturbing them. They should not even know you are there.

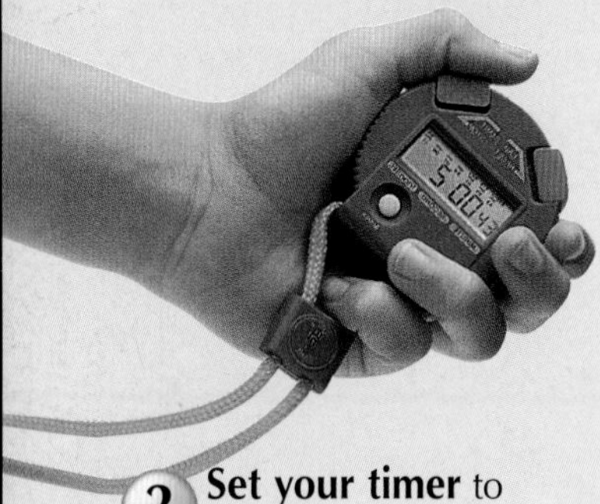

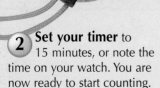

2 Set your timer to 15 minutes, or note the time on your watch. You are now ready to start counting.

3 Make a mark in your notebook each time one of the parents arrives at the nest with food. Keep counting until the 15 minutes are up.

4 Use a calendar or diary to work out how many hours there are between sunrise and sunset. The parents are busy from dawn to dusk, so this will give you the length of their working day.

A QUICK START

Birds that nest on the ground grow up even faster than ones that nest in bushes or in trees. You can see this by watching ducklings or goslings in your local park. They can swim and feed when they are just three hours old. They instinctively follow their mother wherever she goes – even if it means crossing busy roads.

◀ **Close family**
Goslings keep close to their mother, but they find their own food.

PARENTS ON GUARD

Some birds go to great lengths to defend their eggs or young. Crows croak noisily if you get too near their nests, and terns and gulls often dive-bomb people to scare them away. If you are in an open, grassy place or on the shore, look out for any bird that seems to be trailing a broken wing. The chances are that it is playing a trick and trying to distract you from its nest or young.

Follow me! ▶
This killdeer is pretending to be injured so that predators will be distracted and ignore its nest.

5 **Add up** the number of marks in your notebook and multiply the total by four. Finally, multiply this figure by the number of hours in the birds' day. The result is the number of trips the parents make in a day.

Parent blue tit arriving with a caterpillar in its beak

Nestlings' brightly coloured mouths attract their parents

IMPORTANT

If you find a baby bird on its own, don't pick it up unless you are certain that it is injured. Its parents are probably close by, waiting for you to go away.

Ducking and diving

Wherever there is freshwater, there's a good chance that you will find ducks, and perhaps geese and swans. These birds are often used to humans, which makes it easy to watch them feeding. Ducks and their relatives have different ways of finding things to eat. You can observe their feeding techniques by throwing them a mixture of food that floats and food that sinks.

WHAT YOU WILL NEED

- Two glasses of water
- Breadcrumbs
- Rice soaked overnight and drained

HANDY TIP

Make ducks gather around by pretending to scatter some food before you start the test.

1 To see how the feeding test will work, put some dry breadcrumbs in a glass of water. The food is full of air, so it will float near the water's surface.

2 Soak the rice overnight, then drain it. Mix it with some more dry breadcrumbs and put a bit of the mixture in a glass of water. The weight of the rice will make the food sink.

3 Take some dry breadcrumbs and soaked rice mixture to a local pond or lake and scatter them into the water. Watch how the ducks collect bread from the surface and rice from the bottom.

FEEDING OUT OF WATER

Geese have webbed feet and are very good swimmers. They often spend the night on water but, unlike ducks, they usually feed on land. Geese have strong beaks that are ideal for feeding on plants. Instead of biting off their food, they grip it tightly, and then pull it off with a sharp tug. In winter, geese often feed in large flocks in fields and marshland.

Snow geese ▶ These geese breed in the chilly tundra of northern Canada and spend the winter in warmer places, such as California, USA.

FEEDING STYLES

Some ducks collect food from the surface of the water. Others tip up on end to reach food on the bottom in shallow water. Diving ducks plunge beneath the surface and swim down to get food.

This mallard has up-ended to reach food beneath the surface

Beaks and feeding

Ducks, geese, and swans have the same overall shape, but their beaks and necks are different. This helps them to get at different kinds of food. A few of them feed on fish, but most eat plants or small water animals such as insects, snails, and worms. Their beaks have sensitive tips, so they can feel food they cannot see – a great advantage if the water is muddy.

Dabbling beak ▸
A mallard's beak is long and broad – the ideal shape for collecting food on the water's surface, or for feeling for it in the mud on the bottom.

Mallard

Sifting beak ▸
Shelducks collect food on mudbanks at low tide. They sift through the mud with their beaks, moving their heads from side to side and walking forwards, leaving zigzag tracks in the mud.

Shelduck

Gripping beak ▸
Geese and swans use their beaks to tug at their food. They have strong jaw muscles that can clamp their beaks tightly shut.

Black swan

Fishing beak ▸
A merganser's beak is unusually narrow, with serrated edges and a hooked tip. This bird dives to catch fish, and the serrations give it a good grip.

Merganser

Birds on the shore

The shore is a great environment for spotting birds and for seeing how they get their food. Gulls are natural scavengers. They search the shore from the air, swooping on dead remains and anything edible that people leave behind. Other shorebirds, such as oystercatchers and turnstones, search the shore on foot. They like molluscs, shrimps, and worms, and they each have their own ways of dealing with their food. The best time to watch shorebirds is at low tide, when they are busy looking for a meal.

WHERE TO LOOK

- Oystercatchers – on rocky and muddy shores, sometimes in damp fields a little way inland
- Turnstones – on sandy and muddy beaches
- Avocets – in shallow bays with muddy bottoms
- Gulls – on shores of all kinds, also in city parks
- Terns – on sandy and rocky shores, also near lakes inland

Oystercatchers use their beaks to open shells and to probe for worms

Cracking open a meal

With their pencil-sized beaks, oystercatchers have just the right equipment for eating animals that live inside shells. To open small shells, an oystercatcher often uses its beak like a hammer, smashing open a hole. With larger shells, it uses it like a screwdriver, prising the two halves of the shell apart. Oystercatchers are noisy birds – listen out for their loud "kleep-kleep" calls.

IMPORTANT

If you go birdwatching along the shore, remember to check the time of high tide, or you could get cut off when the tide comes in.

Tideline food

When the tide drops, a line of seaweed is often left on the shore. Some birds, like the turnstone, flip over the seaweed to find animals underneath. If you try it for yourself, you will see tiny sandhoppers scatter across the beach. Gulls also search the tideline, looking for the remains of fish and crabs.

The turnstone uses its short beak to flip over seaweed, or to prise open shells

Its plumage becomes more colourful in summer, when it migrates to the far north to breed

FEELING FOR A MEAL

On low-lying shores, lots of small animals hide away in mud or move about in muddy water. Birds cannot see these tasty treats, but they can find them by using their beaks. Most wading birds have beaks with sensitive tips. They probe the mud or sweep their beaks through the water, feeling for anything that might be food. The moment they touch something tasty, their beaks snap shut and they pull their catch to the surface.

Sweeping up ▶
These American avocets use their up-curved beaks to catch animals in muddy water. They wade through the water, sweeping their beaks from side to side.

Birds about town

You don't have to be in the countryside to go birdwatching, because some birds are perfectly at home in cities and towns. Compared to country birds, they are often quite tame. Their favourite haunts include gardens and parks, but some live right in the middle of town among buildings and on busy streets. Try making a habitat map of your nearest town. Once you have done that, you can visit each habitat to find out which birds use it as their home.

WHAT YOU WILL NEED

- Large piece of white paper
- Coloured pencils
- Small pieces of white card for notes
- Noticeboard and pins
- Selection of bird pictures from magazines

Pond
Heron standing on edge of pond catching fish. Ducks chasing each other across the water.

1 **Draw a map** of your local area, showing various different habitats, such as houses, gardens, woodlands, and ponds. Pin the map to the noticeboard. Visit each habitat and make notes of any birds you see and what they are doing.

2 **Make a card** for each habitat. Write some information about the birds you saw at the top of each card. Then look in magazines for pictures of the birds you saw. Cut them out and stick them to the cards. Pin the cards in the correct places on your habitat map.

CITY SCAVENGERS

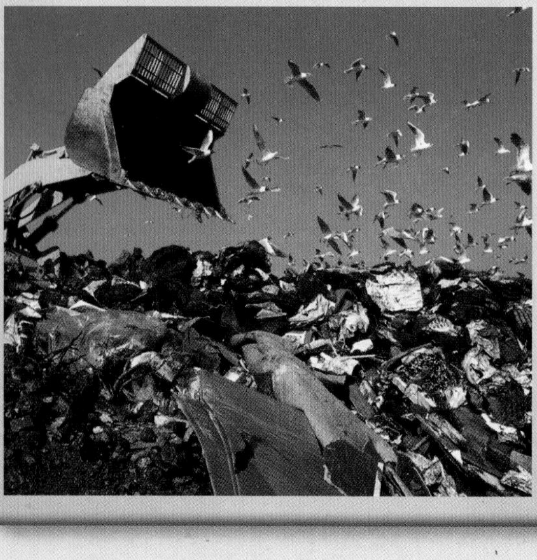

Cities are great places for birds that eat what we throw away. Gulls and crows are some of the most successful urban scavengers. They are inquisitive and aggressive, and this helps them to get meals. Pigeons and starlings are not quite so pushy, but they are experts at spotting food the moment it hits the ground.

◀ **Easy pickings**
Scavenging birds often gather at rubbish dumps. Here, scavenging gulls are being frightened off by a bulldozer, but they will soon return.

Marsh
Lapwings in a flock on marshy ground near river. Warblers calling among the reeds.

River
Kingfisher diving into water, and then sitting on perch to eat fish.

Houses
House sparrows nesting in a wall. Often come to the bird table to feed.

Woods
Spotted woodpecker climbing up trees. Keeps behind the tree to stay out of sight.

Grass
Flock of starlings feeding in grassy field. Crows sometimes chase the starlings away.

River

Pond

Marsh

Grass

Woods

House and garden

Nightwatch

The owl uses its wings and tail as brakes when it nears the ground

When the sun sets, most birds roost, or go to sleep. But some do exactly the opposite. For owls and nightjars, dusk is the start of the day. To see these birds, or to hear them, you need to be in the right place at the right time. The best time to start your nightwatch is just before sunset. This will give your eyes plenty of time to get adjusted as the light fades away.

IMPORTANT

If you plan to go birdwatching after sunset, make sure that you take an adult with you. Pick somewhere in the open, well away from roads.

Feeding in the dark

This owl is swooping down on its prey with its claws outstretched. Owls catch most of their food on the ground, but they also snatch small birds that are roosting on the branches of trees. Some owls even feed on frogs and fish.

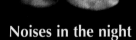

Noises in the night

If you listen quietly after sunset, you may hear birds calling. Owls hoot and screech, while nightjars make purring or buzzing sounds as they fly through the air. In summer, these birds are sometimes joined by songsters like this nightingale, which stays awake all night long.

A safe night's sleep

These pigeons are settling down to roost on a branch. By sticking together, they get a safer night's sleep. Most garden birds roost on their own, but many other kinds stick together. If you watch the evening sky, particularly near reservoirs, lakes, and parks, you will often see birds flying in before night falls.

Flying tonight

It is difficult to spot birds with a torch because they are often on the move. Instead, a better way to spot them is to find a place with a clear view of the setting sun. Just after sunset, you will see birds, and often bats, silhouetted against the sky. To tell which is which, look carefully at their shapes, the way they fly, and their path through the air. Binoculars work well just after sunset because they gather up light and make things easier to see.

Owl ▲
Barn owls fly slowly, with a dipping motion and steadily flapping wings. They criss-cross fields and verges, listening for sounds from small animals on the ground. Other owls fly more quickly, and stop more often to settle on perches.

Nightjar ▲
Nightjars start to feed at dusk. They fly close to the ground in wide circles, scooping up insects in their beaks. Males sometimes touch their wingtips together – a call sign to the females – which makes a sharp slapping sound.

Bat ▲
Bats chase individual insects, and their flightpath is full of sudden twists and turns. Their wings flap much more quickly than a bird's. Bats often hunt over water, sometimes dipping down to drink.

Brainy birds

Birds do not have a great reputation for being brainy, but they can be smart when they are trying to get at food. You can see this for yourself by offering them a tasty snack. The snack is in two pots. One pot is open, so the food is easy for birds to reach, but the other has a lid. Humans know that lids have to be opened, but can your garden birds work this out?

WHAT YOU WILL NEED

- Two small, transparent, flat-based plastic pots
- Bird seed
- A small piece of stiff cardboard or paper
- Sticky tape or masking tape
- Small pebbles
- Scissors
- Pen or pencil

1 Put one pot upside-down on the piece of card and draw a circle around it. Put the card to one side. Next, half-fill both pots with pebbles – these will stop birds knocking over the pots when they feed.

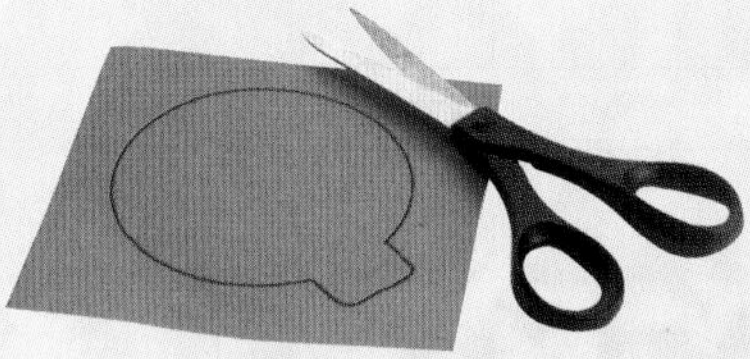

2 Make a lid for one of the pots by cutting around the circle on the card. Leave a small tab sticking out. Fasten the lid in place by making a hinge with sticky tape.

3 Put a small quantity of seeds in both pots and close the lid. Put the pots outside, close together.

BIRDS WITH AMAZING MEMORIES

In late summer and autumn, watch out for jays burying seeds and nuts in the ground. They dig up these again in winter, when other food is hard to find. They can remember the exact location of hundreds of nuts, even when the ground is covered by snow. Many migrating birds also have good memories and return to the same nest site from thousands of kilometres away.

BIRDS THAT TALK

If you've been to a zoo, you have probably heard birds that can talk. Parrots are experts at imitating human speech. Budgies, which are small parrots, often learn many words. But talkative birds aren't quite as brainy as they seem. They don't understand what they are "saying". They are just copying sounds.

Stopping for a chat ▸
Budgies are best at learning words when they are young. They can even be taught to whistle tunes.

HANDY TIP

Try repeating the experiment a day later, to see if birds remember how to get at the food.

4 See what happens when the birds arrive and start to feed. To begin with, they will feed from the open pot. When that one is empty, see if any of them are brainy enough to open the lid of the other pot.

Starlings are some of the brainiest garden birds

All birds will eat from the open pot first

Migration

If you get to know your local birds, you will notice that some are permanent residents – you can see them all through the year – and others are migrants. Migrants usually arrive in spring and stay throughout the summer, but when autumn begins, they disappear. Migrating birds often travel huge distances, but the effort is well worthwhile. They breed in the summer, when there is lots of food for their young. When they have raised a family, they fly to somewhere warm for the winter and return the following year.

Migrants on the move
Snow geese migrate up to 4,000 km (2,500 miles) between the Arctic and the southern USA. Like most migrating birds, they follow routes called flyways. Each flyway has "refuelling stops", where the geese take a break and feed.

FORMATION FLYING

Big birds, such as geese and cranes, often fly in V-formation when they migrate. This saves energy because each bird is helped by the swirling air from the one in front. The leading bird has to work hardest, so each bird takes a turn at the front. Birds migrate by day and by night. On clear nights in spring and autumn, look at the full moon through binoculars. You might be lucky enough to see migrating birds silhouetted as they fly past.

Long-distance travellers

In many parts of the world, spring is an exciting time for birdwatching because that's when most migrants arrive. Some migrants, including swallows, are easy to spot because they spend a lot of their time on the wing. Others stay well hidden. The best way to recognize these is by their calls.

Common cuckoo ▲
Throughout Europe and northern Asia, the cuckoo is a well-known migrant famous for its two-note call, which is impossible to miss.

Scarlet tanager ▶
This bird breeds in North America and winters in South America. Males are bright red in spring and summer, but they turn greenish-yellow once the breeding season is over.

GETTING READY TO GO

Departure lounge ▲
Before swallows migrate, they fly about restlessly, settling on roofs and wires and frequently preening their wings.

As summer draws towards an end, watch out for birds getting ready to migrate. Swallows often perch on telephone wires waiting for the big day when they set off. On the return journey, the males usually arrive first, often to the very same nesting site that they used the year before. Some migrants, including swallows, migrate in scattered groups, but many birds travel on their own. Amazingly, young birds find their way, even though they have never made the journey before. They are guided entirely by instinct.

▲ Ruby-throated hummingbird
This tireless migrant travels all the way from Central America to Canada, flying non-stop across the Gulf of Mexico.

Chiffchaff ▼
This common insect-eater arrives in northern Europe just as the trees are coming into leaf. Its "chiff chaff" call is a sure sign that spring is underway.

Swallow ▶
Swallows breed right across the Northern Hemisphere, arriving in mid-spring when the first insects are on the wing. North American swallows spend the winter in South America, while European ones head for Africa.

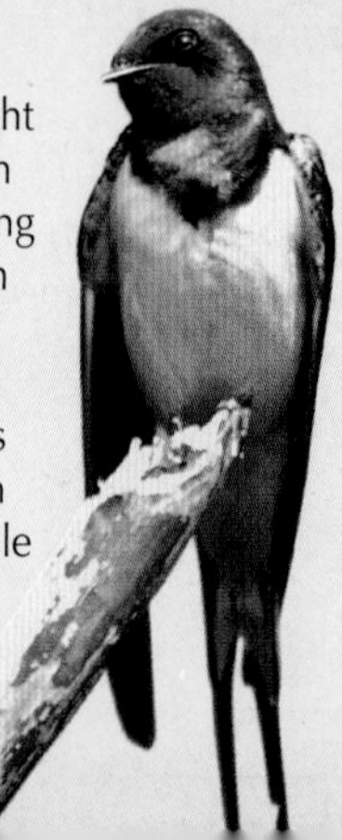

Bird lifespans

Compared to humans, birds have very varied lifespans. Small songbirds often live for less than three years, while larger birds can survive well into their forties. But before a bird can reach old age, it first has to get through the early months of its life. This is a dangerous time for birds. Many young birds are caught by predators, while others die from hunger or cold. But because birds have large families, enough usually survive to raise young of their own.

Bird ringing
This young oystercatcher has been fitted with leg rings so birdwatchers can check its progress as it grows up. If you find a dead bird with a ring, look to see if it has an address on it. Your find could provide useful information about survival in the wild.

The female calls softly to keep the ducklings in a group

Against the odds
If you watch ducklings during the spring and summer, you will see how tough life is for young birds. This female eider has lots of ducklings, but by the time summer arrives, she will probably have only two or three left.

BIRD BOOM

If all baby birds survived to become parents, birds would crowd out the skies. If you have a calculator handy, an easy sum will show you why. Starting with two adult blue tits, how many would there be after ten generations if all their young survived? Blue tits lay about six eggs a year. To get the answer, just multiply six by itself ten times.

Fast families ▼
Blue tits have one family a year, but many songbirds have two or even three. They raise lots of young because only a few survive.

Ducklings' fluffy down helps to keep them warm

Success stories

Once a bird is fully grown, its chances of survival get much better. Compared to young birds, it is better at finding food and at keeping out of harm's way. How long it lasts will depend partly on luck, and partly on what kind of bird it is. Here are some examples of how long birds live in the wild.

Grey heron ▶
Herons can survive to be more than 20 in the wild, and even older in captivity.

Tawny owl ▶
For their size, owls are long-lived birds. Tawny owls live to about 15. They start breeding at one year and, like most birds, keep breeding until they die.

House sparrow ▼
Compared to owls and herons, house sparrows have short lives. They rarely survive to be more than five, but have up to three families a year.

Bird classification There are about 9,500 different species of birds in the world. Scientists classify them into 30 different groups, called orders, based on key features that they share. The largest orders contain thousands of birds, while the smallest contain fewer than 10. On these two pages, you can find out about 12 of the most important orders of birds. Each order has two names. One is its scientific name. The other is its everyday name, which is the one normally used by birdwatchers.

BIRD	NAME OF GROUP	SPECIES TOTAL	KEY FEATURES	EXAMPLES
 **Heron**	HERONS AND STORKS **Ciconiiformes**	119	Tall birds with long legs and long beaks. Herons and storks usually feed in or near water, but they roost in trees.	Grey heron White stork
 **Duck**	DUCKS, GEESE, AND SWANS **Anseriformes**	149	Waterbirds with broad, flattened beaks and webbed feet. These birds are all good swimmers, but most are also fast and powerful fliers.	Mute swan Mallard
 **Eagle**	BIRDS OF PREY **Falconiformes**	307	Predatory birds with hooked beaks and powerful feet with sharp claws. Many birds of prey search for food by soaring high into the air.	Golden eagle Kestrel
 **Chicken**	GAMEBIRDS **Galliformes**	281	Plump, ground-dwelling birds with small heads and rounded wings. Instead of flying away from danger, they often run.	Chicken Common pheasant
 **Gull**	SHOREBIRDS, GULLS, AND TERNS **Charadriiformes**	343	Birds that feed on the coast or in damp places inland. Some of these birds dive for fish, but shorebirds search for food by the tideline.	Curlew Herring gull

BIRD	NAME OF GROUP	SPECIES TOTAL	KEY FEATURES	EXAMPLES
 **Pigeon**	PIGEONS AND DOVES **Columbiformes**	309	Plump birds with small heads that bob backwards and forwards as they walk. Pigeons often feed on the ground, but are strong fliers with powerful wings.	City pigeon Diamond dove
 **Parrot**	PARROTS **Psittaciformes**	353	Colourful and often noisy birds with hooked beaks and fleshy toes. Parrots are good climbers, and often feed in trees.	Cockatiel Rainbow lorikeet
 **Owl**	OWLS **Strigiformes**	205	Predatory birds that hunt after dark, using keen eyesight and hearing. Owls have camouflaged plumage, which helps them to hide during the day.	Tawny owl Barn owl
 **Hummingbird**	HUMMINGBIRDS AND SWIFTS **Apodiformes**	424	Superb fliers with stiff, slender wings. Hummingbirds feed on nectar by hovering in front of flowers. Swifts hunt insects in mid-air.	Ruby-throated hummingbird Common swift
 **Kingfisher**	KINGFISHERS, BEE-EATERS, AND RELATIVES **Coraciiformes**	191	Birds with compact bodies and large beaks that often swoop on their food. Kingfishers dive into water, but bee-eaters feed in the air.	Common kingfisher European bee-eater
 **Woodpecker**	WOODPECKERS AND RELATIVES **Piciformes**	380	Good climbers with strong toes that spend most of their lives in trees. Woodpeckers chisel into wood with their beaks to find food and to make nesting holes.	Great spotted woodpecker Yellow-bellied sapsucker
 **Thrush**	SONGBIRDS **Passeriformes**	5,000+	A huge group of birds that often sing loud songs. Songbirds tend to be small in size.	Wren Blue tit Common cardinal House sparrow

Bug hunter

The world of bugs

Whether you live in the countryside or in a city, bugs are never far away. Most of them live outdoors although, given the chance, quite a few will flutter, hop, or scuttle into people's homes. But what exactly is a bug? Why are they such successful animals? And what is the difference between bugs and other creepy-crawlies? To find out the answers to all these questions, the place to start is right here!

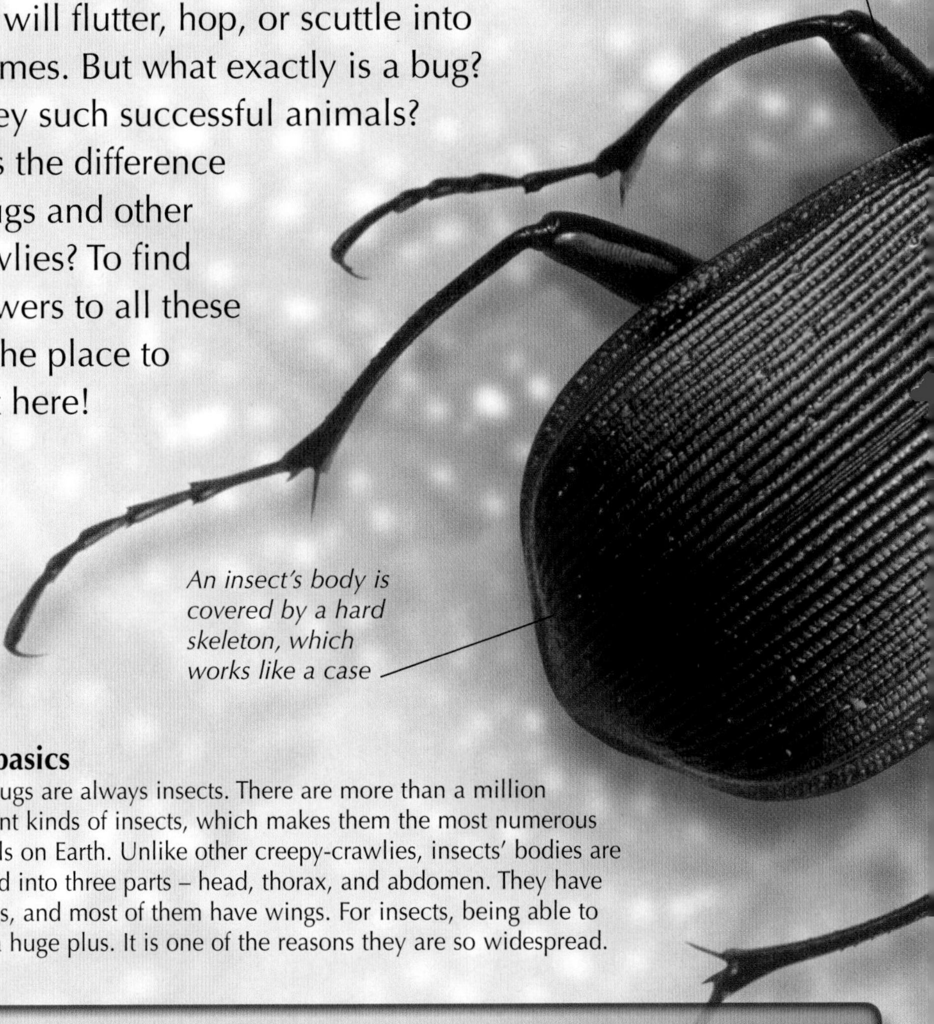

The legs and wings are attached to the insect's middle part, or thorax

An insect's body is covered by a hard skeleton, which works like a case

Bug basics
Real bugs are always insects. There are more than a million different kinds of insects, which makes them the most numerous animals on Earth. Unlike other creepy-crawlies, insects' bodies are divided into three parts – head, thorax, and abdomen. They have six legs, and most of them have wings. For insects, being able to fly is a huge plus. It is one of the reasons they are so widespread.

STUDYING INSECTS

Scientists who study insects are called entomologists. They work all over the world, identifying new species and investigating the way insects live. Some entomologists study farmland insects, particularly those that pollinate plants or feed on crops. Medical entomologists study insects that spread diseases as they feed.

◀ Bug research
This entomologist is investigating insects from the tropical forests of Costa Rica. Every year, entomologists identify thousands of new insects from all over the world, but lots more are still waiting to be discovered.

Identity parade

Lots of animals look like insects, but are built in different ways. Crustaceans have lots of legs, spiders always have eight, and centipedes and millipedes can have hundreds. Of all these animals, insects are the only ones with wings.

Insects have a pair of antennae, or feelers, on their heads
This beetle's abdomen is covered by its wings
This ladybird is in proportion to the huge beetle above
Ladybird

Crustacean

Spider

Centipede

Millipede

Insect

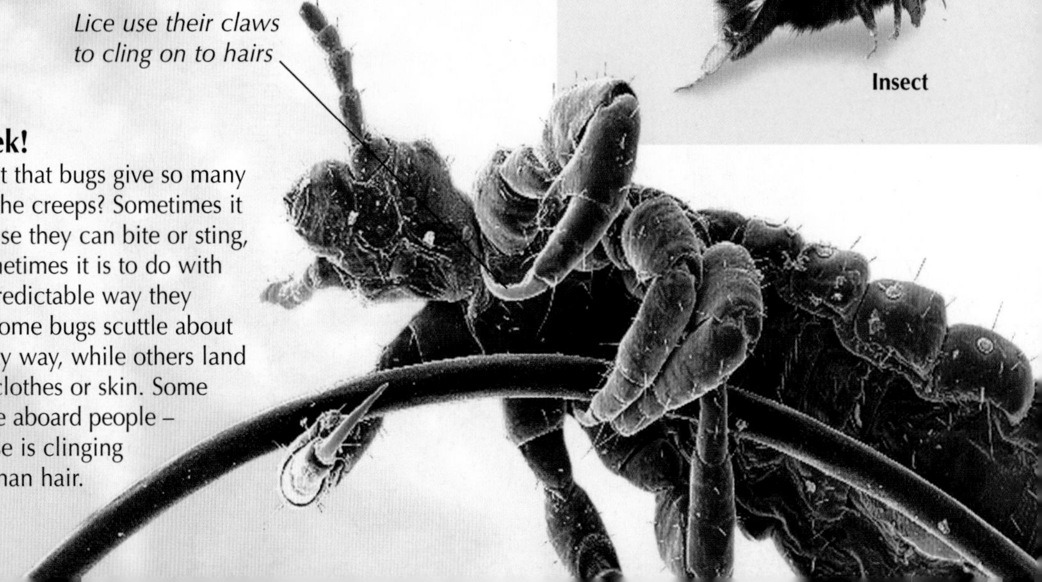

Lice use their claws to cling on to hairs

Eeeeeek!

Why is it that bugs give so many people the creeps? Sometimes it is because they can bite or sting, and sometimes it is to do with the unpredictable way they move. Some bugs scuttle about in a jerky way, while others land on our clothes or skin. Some even live aboard people – this louse is clinging to a human hair.

Essential equipment

Insects are small, so you need to get close to see how they work. One way to do this is to collect them – see below to find out what to pack in your collecting kit. To get a good look at most bugs, you will need a magnifying glass or hand lens. A magnifying glass enlarges by about two or three times, which is enough to see lots of extra detail. A hand lens is even better, because it magnifies by about ten times, but is small enough to fit in a pocket.

BUG HUNTER'S CODE

When you go bug hunting, it is important that you do not harm any bugs or yourself. Stick to these three rules:

- Don't touch any bug with your bare hands unless you know that it is harmless.
- If you collect a bug to study it, release it when you have finished.
- If you go bug hunting at night, make sure you have an adult with you.

COLLECTING KIT

The most important part of a bug-collecting kit is a set of containers for living animals. Jam jars are good, if you make air holes in their lids. You can also use empty margarine tubs, as long as you give them a thorough wash and rinse. Use a drawing pin to make air holes in the lid, put in some kitchen roll as padding, and your bug box is ready.

Use this for live bugs

Jam jar

Use these for dead bugs only

Self-sealing plastic bags

Sketch the bugs that you find

Notebook, pencils, coloured pencils

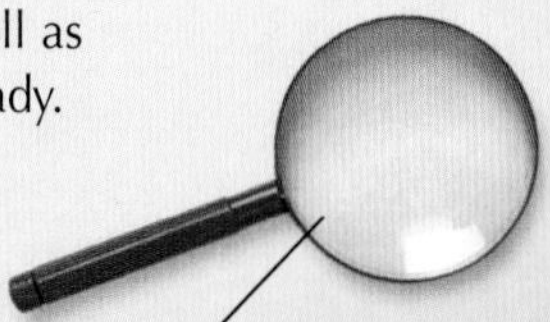
Keep lens clean

Magnifying glass

Use tweezers with pointed tips

Tweezers

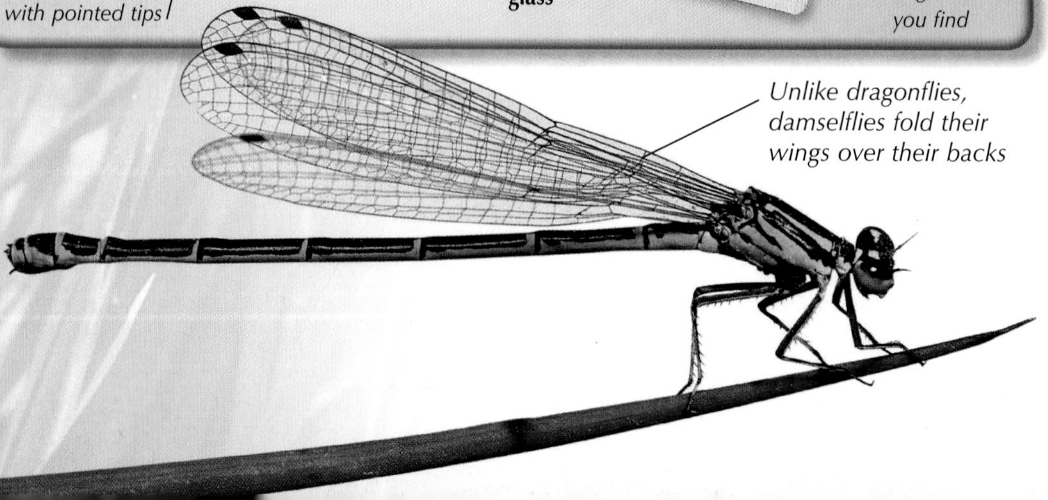

Unlike dragonflies, damselflies fold their wings over their backs

IDENTIFYING BUGS

When looking at bugs, run through the list of features below, and then check a field-guide. You'll soon be able to tell one type of insect from another.

Hardened forewings
Beetle

Soft brush for nudging bugs

- Long, slender body and four wings that stick out sideways: dragonfly
- Long, slender body and four wings that fold back: damselfly
- Long body and extra-large back legs, with, or sometimes without, wings: cricket or grasshopper
- Broad body and mouthparts that pierce and suck: plant bug
- Hardened forewings that fit over abdomen like a case: beetle
- Two-winged flying insect: true fly
- Big colourful wings held above body at rest: butterfly
- Narrow waist, slender wings, and bright stripes: bee or wasp

Magnifying glass clearly shows the dragonfly's eyes
Wing veins vary between different types of dragonflies
A dragonfly's colour helps to identify it

Using a magnifying glass

Hold the magnifying glass close to the insect, then gradually pull it away until the insect is in focus. Use a soft cloth to keep the lens clean.

Bug habitats

When you start bug-watching, you'll soon notice that different bugs live in different places. For example, bees and butterflies stay close to flowers, while dragonflies prefer ponds and streams. Woodlice live in leaf litter – a layer of dead leaves under shrubs and trees. These different places are called habitats. A habitat is more than just a home. It gives a bug everything it needs to survive, including food and the right conditions for breeding.

Freshwater ▸
Lots of bugs live in freshwater, so ponds are good places for bug-watching. Some insects live on the surface, while others swim below it. Dragonflies speed through the air, catching other insects on the wing. If you have a dip net, you'll find that swimming bugs are easy to catch. Be careful not to touch them, because some of them can bite!

◂ Leaf litter
One of the best places to hunt bugs is in leaf litter – the crumbly compost that forms when dead leaves rot down. Leaf litter is home to many kinds of insects, and other creepy-crawlies as well. Many leaf litter animals, such as this woodlouse, like surroundings that are dark and damp.

IMPORTANT

Take care when lifting up branches or stones, because animals beneath them can sometimes bite or sting. It's best to lift stones with a stick.

▲ Trees and shrubs

Many insects live in trees and shrubs, because there is plenty for them to eat. Caterpillars and crickets feed on leaves, while aphids suck up sap. Many of these insects are well camouflaged, because they need to hide away from birds.

Leaves are ideal places for bugs to hide

◂ Grass and flowers

Flowery places are perfect for spotting butterflies, bees, and hoverflies. These insects visit flowers to feed on nectar – a sugary liquid food. Sunny days are best, because nectar-feeders like to be warm as they work.

Walls and paving ▲

In warm weather, walls and paving are good places to spot mini-animals on the move. Wall wildlife includes tiny red velvet mites, and also jumping spiders, which leap on to their prey.

WHERE TO LOOK

- Dragonflies and damselflies – ponds
- Woodlice, centipedes, and millipedes – leaf litter and under trees
- Moth caterpillars and sap-sucking bugs – trees and shrubs
- Butterflies, bees, and hoverflies – gardens and flowery grassland
- Beetles – on the ground and in leaf litter
- Spiders – grassy places and under stones

BUGS INDOORS

You don't have to go outside to see bugs, because some kinds live indoors. Indoor bugs include temporary visitors, such as flies and mosquitoes, and long-term residents, such as spiders. Spiders are useful animals to have indoors, because they keep insects under control.

Kitchens

In summer, houseflies and bluebottles often fly into kitchens through open doors and windows. They come indoors to look for food or for somewhere to lay their eggs.

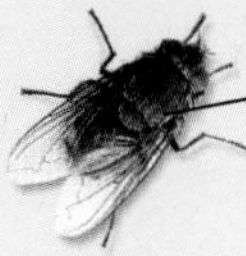

Flies often leave sticky spots when they land

Attics, cellars, and bathrooms

Spiders often lurk in quiet corners in attics and cellars, but some wander about after dark. House spiders sometimes get trapped in baths, because they cannot climb their slippery sides.

House spiders use their legs to feel their way

Drawers and cupboards

Silverfish live in cupboards, where they eat tiny specks of spilled food. Clothes moths sometimes live in drawers and wardrobes – their tiny caterpillars feed on wool.

Silverfish like starchy and sweet food, including flour and sugar

Tricks and traps

The world is a dangerous place for insects because, for lots of other animals, they are a food source. Fortunately, insects have many ways of hiding and of fighting back. Wherever you are, it's easy to spot insects that survive thanks to some clever tricks and traps. Some of the most common insect tricksters are click beetles and small sap-suckers called spittlebugs. Spittlebugs blow bubbles to make a sticky froth to hide in. If you see a frothy mass on a plant, wipe the foam away with a finger. You will find a soft-bodied bug inside.

This young spittlebug has been revealed by wiping away its froth

Spittlebug froth is sometimes known as cuckoo spit, although it is not made by birds

Hiding in foam

Spittlebugs suck sap from grasses and other soft-stemmed plants. Adult spittlebugs can quickly hop away from danger, but young ones can only crawl. A shield of frothy bubbles helps to keep them out of harm's way. The best time to look for spittlebug froth is in spring and early summer.

WHERE TO LOOK

- Spittlebugs – on plants in gardens and grassy places
- Ant lions – on the ground in warm places with loose, sandy soil
- Click beetles – on plants in gardens, grassy places, and fields
- Bombardier beetles – on the ground among stones or fallen leaves

Insect artillery

Ant lion grubs dig pits in sandy soil and then lurk inside them. If another insect walks by, the ant lion flicks sand at it to make it fall into the pit. If you find an ant lion pit, try tapping a blade of grass on the edge. The ant lion will flick sand at it, mistaking it for prey.

Ant lion grubs have camouflaged bodies and extra-large jaws for gripping their prey

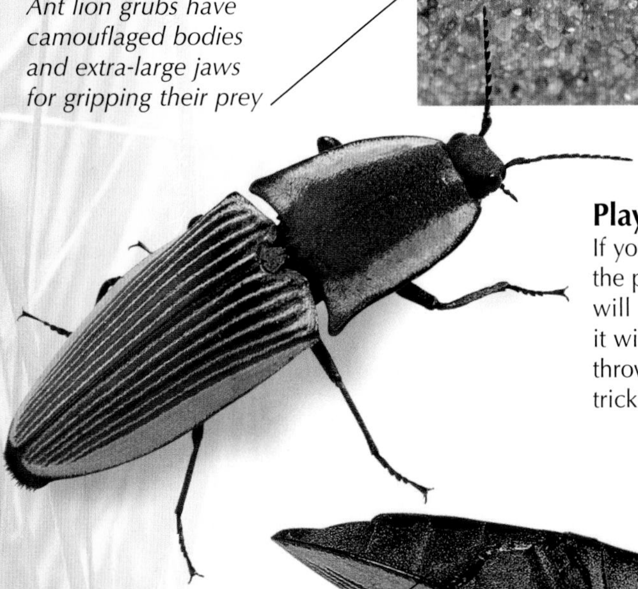

Playing dead

If you find a click beetle, try putting it in the palm of your hand. At first, the beetle will pretend to be dead. A few seconds later, it will click a hinge behind its head, which throws it into the air. Click beetles use this trick to escape from their enemies.

When it pretends to be dead, a click beetle folds up its legs against its body

CHEMICAL WEAPONRY

The bombardier beetle is a famous expert in self-defence. If it feels threatened by another animal, it releases poisonous chemicals into a chamber inside its abdomen. The chemicals explode, spraying a jet of hot gas out of its body and towards its attacker. The beetle can produce up to 50 explosions in a row, giving it a chance to run away.

Model of a bombardier beetle

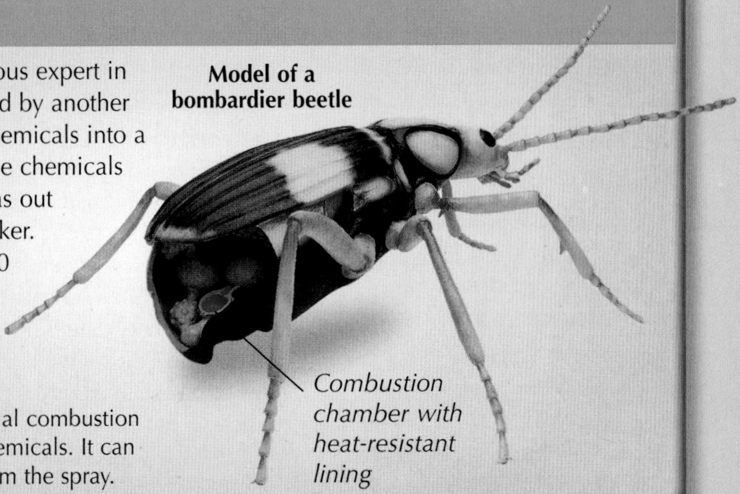

Combustion chamber with heat-resistant lining

Explosive defence ▶
The bombardier beetle has a special combustion chamber for mixing poisonous chemicals. It can swivel the tip of its abdomen to aim the spray.

After dark

Lots of bugs are on the move after dark, when humans are asleep. Some bugs fly through the night air, but many more crawl and scuttle over the ground. By making a simple pitfall trap, it is easy to catch these nocturnal creepy-crawlies. Then you can return to the trap during the day to examine your catch.

WHAT YOU WILL NEED

- Trowel
- Plastic cup or jam jar
- Food for baiting (cheese, fruit, or meat)
- Four small stones, corks, or marbles
- Tile or plywood about 10 cm (4 in) square
- Magnifying glass

IMPORTANT

Don't go outside after dark without an adult, and remember to release the insects you catch when you have finished studying them.

1 Dig a hole in soft ground and bury the cup exactly up to its rim. Place a piece of bait inside the cup.

2 Put the stones on the ground around the cup and place the tile over the top to make a rainproof roof.

3 Leave the trap overnight and examine your catch in the morning. You can dig up the cup and take it indoors for a closer look. Vary the bait to see if it attracts different bugs.

BEETLES ON THE PROWL

Night patrol ▲
Ground beetles hunt caterpillars and other garden pests.

Many beetles are nocturnal hunters that feed on the ground. They are ideally built for this kind of life, with sturdy legs and hard forewings that fit over their back like a case to protect their delicate hindwings. Ground beetles are often black. This camouflages them in the darkness, providing some protection from predators.

LIGHTING UP

Unlike most nocturnal insects, fireflies and glow-worms are easy to find because they light up after dark. These insects make light inside their bodies and use it to attract a mate. Glow-worms light up on the ground, but fireflies light up on trees or bushes, or while they are on the wing. If you disturb one of these insects, its light will often dim or go out. But if you stay nearby and keep still, it will slowly come back on.

◀ **Glowing in the dark**
This female glow-worm is signalling to males flying overhead. Her light comes from special organs underneath her abdomen. Unlike the males, the female does not have wings and cannot fly.

Attracted by the smell of food, beetles and other animals fall into the trap and cannot climb back out

Raising caterpillars

WHAT YOU WILL NEED

- 5 l (1 gl) plastic bottle
- Scissors
- Piece of muslin • Jam jar
- Water • Food plants
- Caterpillars
- Large, thick elastic band

If you are a keen bugwatcher, it's hard to beat the excitement of seeing caterpillars turn into adult butterflies. It's not difficult to find caterpillars, but if you want to keep them, you need to make a suitable home for them. One of the best ways is to use a large plastic bottle fitted with a fabric roof. This lets the caterpillars get the fresh air that they need.

1 **Cut off** the sloping sides and top of the bottle. Cut out a square of muslin around the bottom of the bottle, about 5 cm (2 in) bigger all round.

2 **Fill the jam jar** with water and stand the caterpillar food plants in the water. Put the jar and plants in the bottle.

3 **Carefully put** the caterpillars on the plants. Then put the muslin over the top of the bottle and use the elastic band to hold it in place.

SHEDDING SKIN

In order to grow, all bugs have to shed their outer skin every so often. Each time they do this, they leave the old, empty skin behind. Caterpillars usually drop their skins on the ground, but spiders often leave theirs hanging from their webs. People often mistake the empty skins for living spiders, but it's easy to find out which is which. Touch it gently with a pencil – a skin won't scuttle away!

A fresh start ▲
This spider has just finished shedding its skin. Its old skin is above it, held in place by strands of silk. Spiders shed their skins many times in their lives. Insects stop once they have become adult and do not grow any more.

IMPORTANT

Caterpillars are fussy eaters, so give yours the same plants that you found them on. Remember to check the water level in the jam jar every day, so the leaves do not wilt.

Changing shape

All insects change shape as they grow up. Grasshoppers change gradually each time they shed their skins. Young grasshoppers look like their parents, but without wings. Butterflies and moths change in a different way. They start life as caterpillars and change totally during a resting stage called a pupa.

◀ Egg
Most insects hatch from eggs. Butterflies glue their eggs to the leaves of plants so the caterpillars have food.

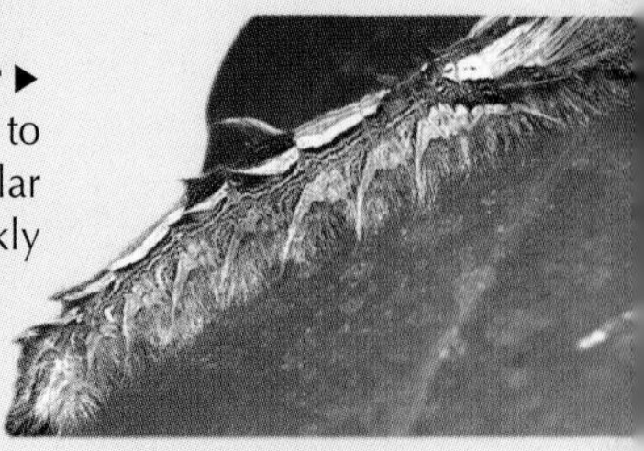

Caterpillar ▶
A caterpillar's job is to eat. As the caterpillar feeds, it grows quickly and sheds its skin several times.

Pupa ▲
The caterpillar stops feeding and turns into a pupa. Inside the pupa, its body is rebuilt.

◀ Adult
Finally, the pupa splits and an adult butterfly crawls out. It waits for its wings to harden, then flies away.

Adult hangs from pupa while its wings harden

Making a moth trap

WHAT YOU WILL NEED

- Torch with flat base
- Oblong cardboard box (at least 25 per cent higher than the torch)
- Egg boxes
- Stapler
- Glue stick
- Scissors

Ask an adult to help you cut the box because this can be difficult.

Moths cannot resist bright lights, which is why they often come to windows after dark. If you make a moth trap, you can collect moths overnight and examine them during the day. When you open up your trap, you'll be able to see the beautiful camouflaged patterns that many moths use to hide. Moths are completely harmless insects – they cannot sting or bite. Once you have admired them, let them fly away.

1 Open all the flaps of the box. Carefully cut off the top flaps on the shortest sides, leaving the two long ones. Keep the flaps you have cut off to use later.

2 Take one of the flaps that you have cut off and cut it into four narrow strips. Staple these to the top of the box, as shown, so they make a valley with a narrow slit about 2 cm (3/4 in) wide.

3 Put the box on one end. Remove the tops from the egg boxes and glue the bottoms to the inside of the box at each end. Moths will rest on these, once they have flown into the box.

LURED BY LIGHT

No one knows for certain why moths are attracted to light. One theory is that they fly off course, mistaking artificial light for moonlight. Lights attract lots of other insects as well, which means they create great places to go bug-watching.

Light meal ▲
This gecko is lurking near a light, where it will find moths to eat.

MOTHS INDOORS

On summer nights, moths often fly indoors but usually find their way back out. Some moths stay inside all their lives. Clothes moths lay their eggs on anything made of wool. Their caterpillars feed on the wool fibres and leave lots of tell-tale holes. Adult clothes moths are small, with dusty golden wings. When in danger, they often scuttle into dark corners.

Well wrapped up ▶
These are the caterpillars of the case-bearing clothes moth. Each caterpillar lives inside a portable case, which it makes from silk and short strands of chopped-up wool.

4 **The trap** is now ready. To use it, put it outside after dark. Turn on the torch, stand it on end, and carefully place the trap over it. Leave the trap for 1–2 hours, then gradually lift up the box to look at the moths inside.

IMPORTANT

Always ask an adult to come with you to set up the trap after dark. Choose a dry night and put the trap well away from any other bright lights.

Feeding at flowers

People like flowers because they look pretty, but insects like them because they contain food. The food is nectar – a sugary liquid that is packed with energy. In return for the supply of nectar, insects spread pollen from flower to flower, helping plants to make their seeds. Flowers are specially shaped to fit particular insect visitors. If you watch bees, butterflies, and hoverflies, you can see which kinds of flowers they visit and which ones they avoid.

Only bees can open a toadflax's petals to reach inside
Basket containing pollen that the bee has collected
The nectar lies at the bottom of the spur

WHERE TO LOOK

- **Bees – on brooms, snapdragons, toadflaxes, and roses**
- **Butterflies – on buddleia (butterfly bush), thistles, and valerian**
- **Hoverflies – on hogweed, elder, and yarrow**

Bees

This bumblebee has landed on a toadflax flower and is reaching inside to feed. A bumblebee's tongue is very long and can suck up the nectar in the flower's pointed spur, or nectar tube. As well as drinking nectar, bees also eat pollen. They scrape it off their bodies and press it into special baskets on their legs. When their pollen baskets are full, they fly back to their nest.

The butterfly pushes its tongue into each tiny flower
The scent of the flowers attracts butterflies from far away

Butterflies
Butterflies have an extra-long tongue, but their large wings stop them from clambering into flowers. Instead, their preferred flowers are shaped like narrow tubes and have nectar at the bottom. Butterflies love sweet smells, like that of the buddleia – or butterfly bush – which is one of their favourite plants.

IMPORTANT

It is safe to use your magnifying glass to watch bees as they feed, but don't get too close or touch them in case you get stung.

Hoverflies
Hoverflies have short tongues, so they cannot reach into deep flowers. Instead, the flowers they visit are often flat. Unlike bees and butterflies, hoverflies are attracted by strong-smelling flowers, often those that are not so nice to a human nose.

OPENING TIMES

Some flowers stay open 24 hours a day, but many open up only when their insect visitors are about. In the early morning, look out for flowers that are gradually opening as the air warms up. These flowers stay closed all night but open during the day when bees are on the wing. Some flowers work the other way around. They open up in the evening and stay open all night. These late openers are pollinated by moths, and many give off a sweet scent to help moths track them down.

◀ **Night shift**
Evening primrose flowers open at night. Their pale colour makes them easy for moths to spot in the dark.

WHAT YOU WILL NEED

- 20 pieces of bamboo cane, about 1 cm (½ in) in diameter and 15 cm (6 in) long
- Strong tape
- Modelling clay
- Plant pot

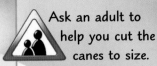

Ask an adult to help you cut the canes to size.

Bee homes

Honeybees live together in hives, but many other garden bees live alone. They lay their eggs in mini-nests and then leave their grubs to grow up on their own. Some of these bees tunnel into wood, but mason bees often nest in hollow plant stems. Solitary bees pollinate many garden plants, so it is worth encouraging them to breed. You can help mason bees set up home with a flowerpot and some bamboo canes.

LEAFCUTTER BEES

Precision cut ▲
This leafcutter bee is using its sharp jaws to slice a piece out of a rose leaf. When it has finished, it will carry the piece of leaf back to its nest.

In summer, look closely at rose plants and see if you can spot any semi-circular holes in their leaves. These holes are made by leafcutter bees – small insects that nest in hollow stems. Unlike mason bees, leafcutters do not line their nests with mud. Instead, they make small parcels from leaves – rose leaves are by far their favourite kind. Each parcel contains a single egg and a supply of pollen for the developing grub to feed on when it emerges.

1 **Stand the pieces** of cane on end to make a bundle. Then bind them together with the tape. Press the canes into a lump of modelling clay to seal one end.

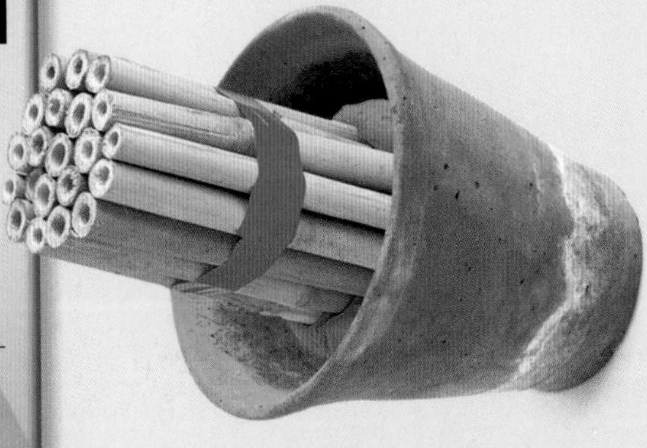

2 **Put the canes** into the plant pot, with the open ends facing outwards. Use some more modelling clay to wedge the bundle tightly inside the pot.

CARPENTER BEES

Most solitary bees are small, so they are easy to overlook. Carpenter bees are different because some of them are more than 2.5 cm (1 in) long. These impressive insects have furry bodies, their wings are often black, and they make a deep buzzing sound when they fly. Most carpenter bees make nests by chewing tunnels in dead wood. The female pats pollen into loaf shapes, lays an egg on each one, and then seals it up.

Big buzzer ▶
Carpenter bees live in warm parts of the world. This great carpenter bee is the largest kind of bee in Australia.

3 **Leave the pot** in a sunny, dry spot. In the spring, mason bees will line the canes with mud and then lay their eggs.

Insect architects

Insects are some of the finest builders in the animal world. Unlike human builders, they do not have to learn how to carry out their work. Instead, their instincts tell them what plan to follow, and what materials to use. Bees often make their nests from wax, but other insects use wood fibres, leaves, or clay. If you look carefully, you may be able to spot insects collecting building materials before heading back to their nests.

The centre of the nest contains small cells, where the queen lays her eggs

ANT NESTS

Wood ants ▲
These ants make nests from pine needles and twigs. One nest can contain thousands of ants.

Ants are among the world's most successful insects. They live in forests, grasslands, and towns and cities. Some ants make nests from piles of leaves, but most nest under fallen logs or underground. If you accidentally disturb an ants' nest, watch how the ants quickly carry their grubs away to safety.

Crunch time
If you see a wasp sitting still on a wooden post or fence, creep up to it and listen carefully. Often, you will be able to hear the sound of its jaws crunching up the wood. The colour of a wasps' nest depends on the kind of wood they collect.

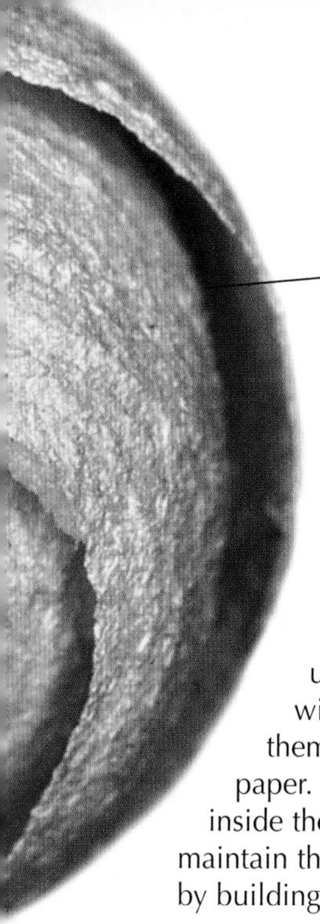

The thin paper walls of the nest look like a series of overlapping shells

Paper homes

Common wasps build their nests from fibres of dead wood. They chew up the fibres, mix them with spit, and then spread them out to make a kind of paper. The queen lays her eggs inside the nest. Worker wasps maintain the nest and enlarge it by building extra walls.

Wasps scrape and chew at the wood, mixing the fibres with their saliva

TERMITE NESTS

Cool homes ▲
Compass termites make flat-sided nests that stay cool when the sun is overhead.

Termites build the biggest nests in the insect world. Some make their nests from wood fibres, but the most impressive nests are made of clay. The clay is soft when the termites build the nest, but it turns hard as it bakes in the sun.

IMPORTANT

Wasps and ants defend their nests fiercely, so keep your distance if you see one – or you will risk getting stung or bitten.

On the trail

Ants are hard-working insects, and they scout far and wide in search of food. If one ant discovers something tasty, others soon arrive to help take the food back to the nest. Ants have very bad eyesight but a keen sense of smell. Wherever they walk, they leave a trail of scent so they never get lost. If you give ants some food, you can see how quickly they sniff it out, spread the news, and carry it back down the trail to their nest.

WHAT YOU WILL NEED

- Crumbs (bread, biscuits, cereals, crisps etc.)
- Magnifying glass
- Small stick or stone
- Watch

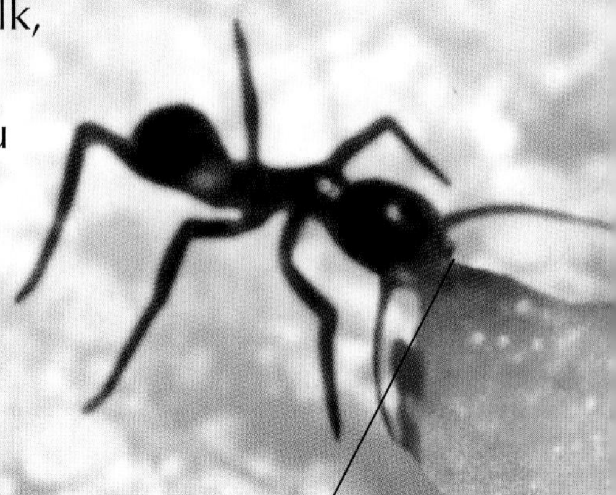

Worker ants grip the food in their jaws

1. **Look for a trail** of ants in your backyard or garden. When you find one, put some crumbs nearby. Next, put a small stick or stone 1 m (3 1/4 ft) back down the trail. When the ants find the food, check the time on your watch.

2. **Stand well back** from the ants and watch them as they carry the food away. When they get past the marker, check the time again. From this, you can tell how long it takes them to travel 1 m (3 1/4 ft) carrying their load.

MEETING AND GREETING

If you watch ants on a trail, you will notice that they often touch each other with their antennae when they meet. They do this as an identity check, and also to swap news about food. Every ant has a smell, which it gets from its nest. If an ant meets another ant with the same smell, it knows that it is a friend and is not from a different nest. Ants also smell of the food they collect, so other ants can tell what they have found.

Getting together ▶
These two red ants are touching each other's antennae. They use their antennae to smell each other as well as to test any food that they find.

FLYING ANTS

In warm weather, watch out for flying ants swarming in the air. These winged ants grow up in the safety of the nest, where they are looked after by worker ants. When the weather is right, the workers let them out so they can fly off to start nests of their own. If you see flying ants taking off, look for birds swooping in to enjoy this feast of flying food.

Airborne ▶
These winged ants have crawled up a plant and are taking off. The males die soon after mating. The females shed their wings after they land, and then look for somewhere to make a nest.

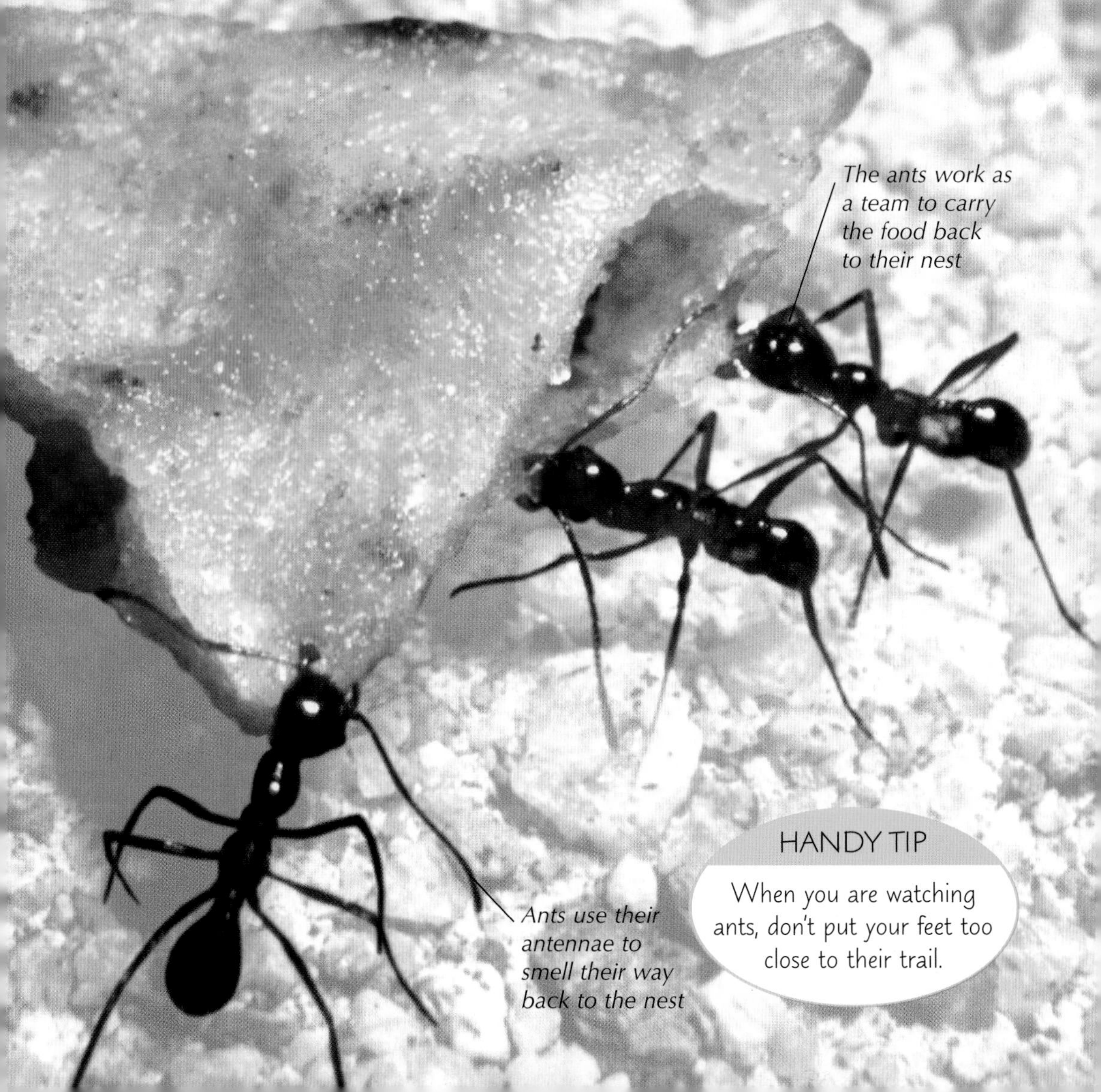

The ants work as a team to carry the food back to their nest
Ants use their antennae to smell their way back to the nest

HANDY TIP

When you are watching ants, don't put your feet too close to their trail.

Friends and enemies

Aphids, or greenfly, are among the fastest-breeding bugs on Earth. They live by sucking sap from plants and are easy to find because they cannot run away. Aphids have lots of enemies, but they are not as helpless as they seem. They are protected by ants, which work like a team of security guards. If you find some aphids, take a closer look. You will often see ants scurrying around them and even over their backs. In return for protection, the ants receive drops of sugary honeydew.

Teaming up
This ant is collecting drops of honeydew from an aphid. Aphids produce honeydew as they feed, and ants collect it and take it to their nests. If any other insects come near the aphids, the ants attack them and chase them away.

The ant touches the aphids with its antennae to make them release honeydew

Aphids have sharp mouthparts so they can pierce plant stems to suck the sap

WHERE TO LOOK

The best time to find aphids is in spring and early summer. They feed near the tips of stems and on the undersides of leaves. These are some of their favourite garden plants:

- Beans
- Fruit trees
- Potatoes
- Roses

Booming families

Most insects breed by laying eggs, but aphids often give birth to live young. This female is producing a baby while she feeds. In spring and summer, female aphids often have several babies a day. A few weeks later, they are surrounded by many fast-growing young. Unlike most insects, aphids can breed without mating.

Aphid eaters

Ladybirds and their grubs are very useful garden insects because they help to keep aphids under control. Other aphid enemies include lacewings and tiny parasitic wasps that lay their eggs inside aphids' bodies. These predators and parasites are not put off by the aphids' security guards.

HONEYDEW

Aphids suck up several times their own weight of sap every day. Once they have digested it, lots of sugar and water is left behind. Aphids get rid of this sugary liquid by producing droplets of honeydew. If you stand under a tree that is full of aphids, you may feel a honeydew mist landing on your face. Honeydew leaves shiny smudges on leaves and sticky blotches on parked cars.

Hungry helpers ▲
If honeydew collects on leaves, it encourages the growth of a mould that is harmful to aphids. Hungry ants prevent this from happening.

Growing a home

Some insect grubs have a clever way of keeping out of sight – they release chemicals that make plants grow them a home. These homes are called galls and they often look like small buttons or fruit. The grubs live inside the galls and use their juicy flesh as food. When the grubs have grown up, they crawl out and fly away. You can find galls on all sorts of plants, including trees, bushes, and garden weeds. If you collect some galls, you can open them up to see if any grubs are still inside.

WHAT YOU WILL NEED

- Selection of galls from various plants
- Sharp knife
- Chopping board
- Magnifying glass

Ask an adult to help you cut open the galls. Some are hard and must be opened carefully.

1 Search for galls on leaves and on the tips of stems and small twigs. Pick the leaf or twig carefully. Oak trees are great places to start looking because many kinds of gall insects live on them.

2 Look at the gall to see if you can spot a hole. If there is one, it means that the gall grub has already grown up and flown away. If you cannot see a hole, cut open the gall and you may find a gall grub inside.

Cherry galls develop on the underside of oak leaves

The gall's spongy flesh hides the grub and gives it something to eat

The grub lives in the middle of the gall and feeds on it as it grows up

PLANT PROTECTION

In warm parts of the world, some ants spend all their lives in trees. The ants make their nest in hollow galls, and the tree gives them all the food they need. In return, the ants work like armed guards. If an animal tries to eat the tree's leaves, the ants pour out of their nest. They bite and sting the intruder until it gives up and goes away.

Whistling thorn ▲
This African tree has hollow galls at the base of its thorns. Ants set up home inside them, nibbling a hole to make an entrance. When the wind blows, the galls sometimes make a whistling sound.

Attack from outside

Gall bugs are safe from birds but not from other insects. If you look at galls while they are still on plants, you may sometimes spot flies or wasps laying their eggs inside. Fly grubs eat the gall itself, but wasp grubs are parasites – they feed on the grub that made the gall.

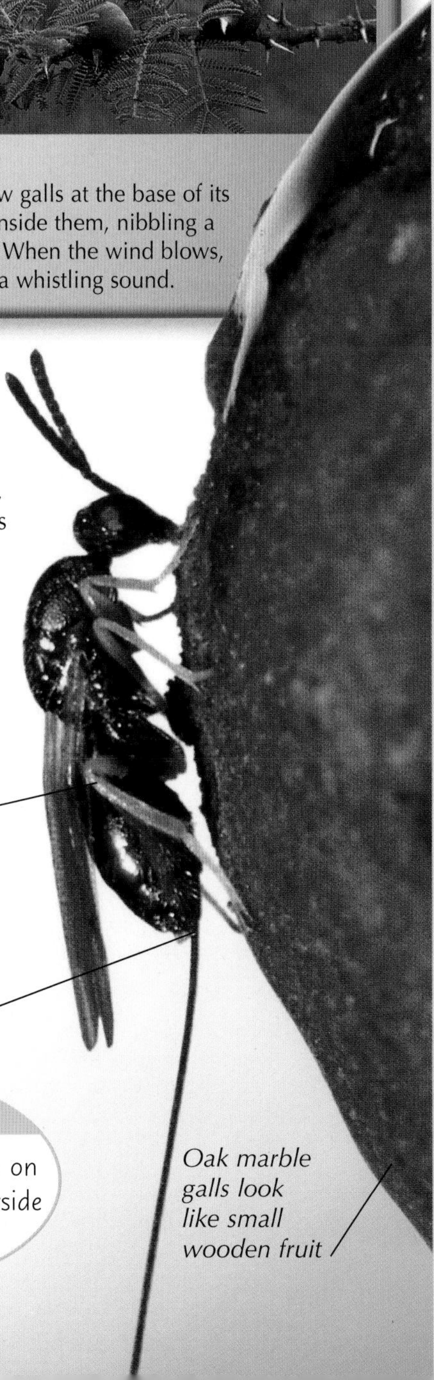

This parasitic wasp lays its eggs in oak marble galls
The wasp bores into the gall with its ovipositor (egg-laying tube)
Oak marble galls look like small wooden fruit

HANDY TIP

In autumn, look for galls on bare twigs and the underside of fallen leaves.

Gall types

Gall bugs are fussy about where they live. Each kind lives on just one kind of plant and always makes the same kind of gall. Some galls are soft and do not last for long. Others turn hard and woody as the summer wears on. These hard galls are ideal for collecting and keeping.

Spangle galls ▶
These soft galls grow in clusters on the underside of oak leaves. Each one looks like a small button fastened by a tiny stalk. The wasps that make these galls are just 3 mm (0.1 in) long.

Knopper galls ▶
Instead of growing on leaves, knopper galls grow on acorns. They are easy to spot because they are large and knobbly, and they stay on the tree for a long time.

Bedeguar galls ▲
These galls grow on wild roses. The outside of the galls is soft and furry but the inside is hard, like wood. Each gall contains lots of grubs.

Mines and galleries

For young insects, or larvae, one of the safest places to live is inside leaves and wood. Here, they can munch their way through their food with little danger of being spotted and eaten. It is not easy to find the larvae themselves, but you can look out for the tell-tale signs that they leave behind. Leaf-eaters often make wiggly mines, while bark beetles dig out tunnels called galleries in dead and dying trees.

The caterpillar left the leaf here

This apple leaf has been mined by the caterpillar of a small moth

Leaf miners
Leaf miners are tiny larvae that live between the top and bottom surfaces of leaves. As they feed, they move through the leaf, leaving a track called a mine. The mine gets wider as the larva grows, and stops where the larva climbs out to turn into an adult insect.

LOOKING AT LEAF MINES

Leaf miners attack many different plants, but brambles and fruit trees are their particular favourites. If you look at these plants in summer and early autumn, the mines are often easy to spot. To get an even better view, collect some leaves with mines and fasten them to the inside of a window with some sticky tape. The mines are hollow, so they will appear paler than the rest of the leaf. Look carefully at the thickest end of the mine to see if the caterpillar is still inside.

◀ Leaf mines on show
If you make a leaf mine collection, you will be able to see differences in the way the mines are made. Some miners wander all over a leaf. Others stick to one area and chew out a single block.

The mine starts where an adult moth lays an egg

Leaf miner larva

This leaf miner is chewing its way through an oak leaf. As it feeds, it leaves a trail of droppings in the middle of the mine. The commonest kinds of leaf miners are moth caterpillars, but they also include the larvae of beetles and flies.

BARK RUBBING

Beetle galleries have lots of interesting patterns because bark beetle larvae dig in different ways. Some galleries have tunnels in parallel lines, while others spread out through the wood like stars. You can record different types by making rubbings with a wax crayon. Find a gallery and brush away any dust or loose wood. Tape a sheet of white paper on top of it, then rub the crayon gently over the paper.

▲ **Making a rubbing**
To make really good rubbings, use a thick crayon and do not press too hard.

Tree galleries

Bark beetle larvae feed on wood, chewing tunnels, or galleries, beneath a tree's bark. To find their galleries, look at dead trees and large pieces of fallen bark. Most galleries are made up of lots of separate tunnels spreading out like slender fingers. Each tunnel is made by a single larva.

Freshwater insects

Ponds and streams are great places to watch insects. Pond skaters skim across the surface, while all kinds of bugs and creepy-crawlies swim beneath it. Some of these insects are full-time water animals, but many leave the water when they have grown up. Freshwater insects are easy to catch with a net, but you can watch many of them with no equipment at all. Just wait quietly by the water's edge and watch them come to the surface to breathe.

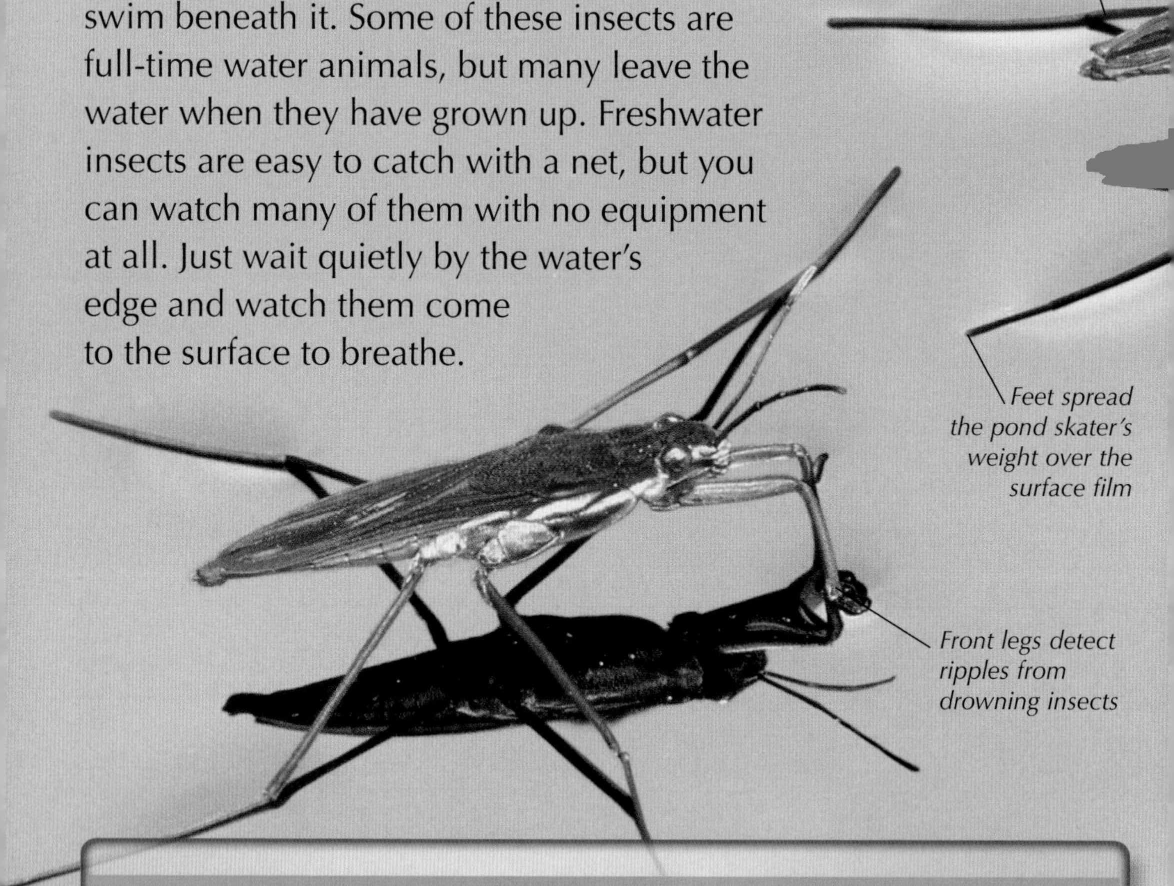
Back legs work like rudders, steering the pond skater from behind
Feet spread the pond skater's weight over the surface film
Front legs detect ripples from drowning insects

TESTING SURFACE TENSION

To find out why pond skaters don't sink, try this simple experiment. Fill a bowl with water and wait until the surface is completely still. Next, pick up a small paper clip with a pair of tweezers and gently lower it on to the water. The paper clip is light, so it will sit on the water's surface film. Pond skaters float in exactly the same way.

◂ **Floating paper clips**
Surface tension gives water a filmy surface. It can hold up light objects, such as a paper clip, but anything heavy breaks through it and sinks.

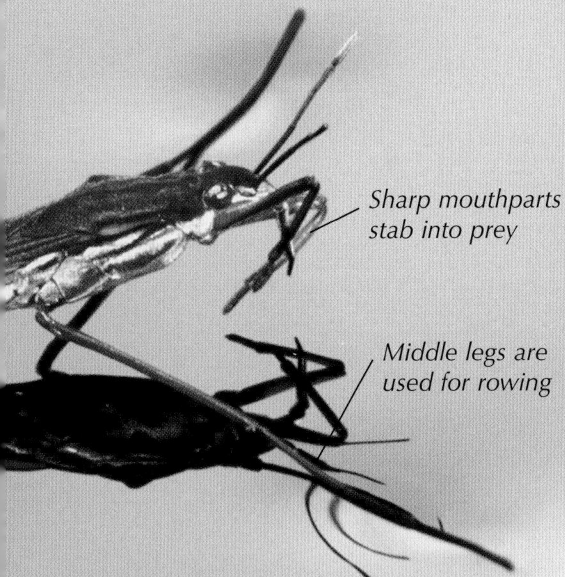
Sharp mouthparts stab into prey
Middle legs are used for rowing

Skating on the surface

Pond skaters are carnivorous bugs that literally walk on water. They have water-repellent feet and they skate on the surface film, which keeps them high and dry. Pond skaters pounce on other insects that have crash-landed, stabbing them with their jaws.

Leaving the water

After two years underwater, this young damselfly has climbed out to start adult life. It sheds its skin for a final time and then unfolds it wings so that it can fly away. To see this amazing transformation, visit a pond on a still summer morning. This is when most damselflies and dragonflies emerge.

UP AND AWAY

Water boatmen underwater ▲

Most underwater insects have wings and some are powerful fliers. Water boatmen, like the two shown here, often fly from pond to pond when the weather is warm. To see this for yourself, use a net to catch one and then put it on the ground. Be careful not to touch it because it may bite. If it cannot scuttle back into the water, it will wait until it is dry and then suddenly take to the air and fly away.

Coming up for air

Old watertanks and cattle troughs are good places for seeing how freshwater insects breathe. Mosquito larvae use tiny snorkels. They will dive down when they see you approach, but come back up in a few minutes.

Spiders

Many people don't like spiders – especially ones that have long, hairy legs. But spiders are fascinating animals and they help us a lot by keeping bugs under control. Unlike insects, spiders always live by hunting, and insects make up most of their prey. Some spiders stalk their victims, but many ambush them or trap them in silken webs. Next time you see a spider, take a closer look. Lots of spidery eyes will be looking back at you.

IMPORTANT

Some spiders have a dangerous bite or tiny hairs that get into your skin. To be safe, never pick up a spider with bare hands.

Spider basics

This male house spider has just caught a fly. Like all spiders, it has eight legs and a pair of poisonous fangs. Its mouth is tiny, so instead of chewing its food, it has to suck it up. House spiders have four pairs of eyes. They find their prey by sight and also by touch.

Four pairs of eyes give the spider an all-round view
Body is made of two parts – the head and the cephalothorax
Fangs stab into the prey to inject venom
Once the fly is dead, the spider squirts digestive juices into it to make it edible

HIDDEN SPIDERS

Spiders are easy to spot when they scuttle across the ground. But lots of spiders take care not to be seen. If you look carefully at bark and among leaves, you will often find spiders that are beautifully camouflaged. The world's biggest spiders hide in burrows and come out to feed at night.

Into the open ▼
At sunset, this tarantula comes out of its home in a tree hole to hunt.

Long legs covered with sensitive hairs that detect tiny vibrations from other animals
Spiders' legs end in small pads or claws

Spider parade

There are more than 40,000 kinds of spiders in the world, and they come in many shapes and sizes. Look out for these common kinds – they often live in gardens, backyards or indoors.

Crab spider ▶
These colourful spiders lurk among flowers and catch insects as they land to feed. Although they are only about 2 cm (3/4 in) long, their venom is powerful enough to kill bumblebees and butterflies.

◀ Jumping spider
Jumping spiders have large front eyes. They hunt by day, watching for tiny animals and leaping on them. They often have stripy bodies and short legs.

Orb-web spider ▶
These common spiders catch flying insects in their circular webs. The largest orb-web spiders live in warm parts of the world and make webs of more than 1 m (3 3/4 ft) across.

◀ Grass spider
Grass spiders have long bodies and four pairs of small, forward-facing eyes. If they are threatened, they often stretch out along a twig or a grassblade to hide.

Spiders without webs

All spiders make silk, but only some of them use webs to catch food. Many other kinds hunt by lurking in flowers or by searching out their prey. These roaming hunters include spiders that get stuck in baths, as well as huge tropical tarantulas that feed on lizards and even birds. Some of these spiders are true wanderers, but most build themselves a lair. When they have finished hunting, they go home and hide.

SPIDERS IN THE BATH

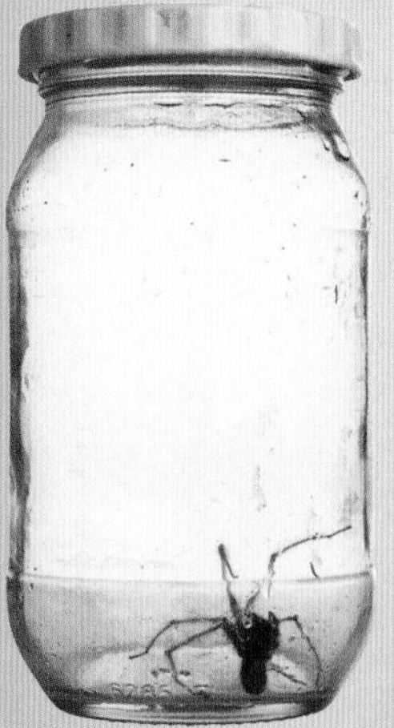

◄ Spider rescue
If you find a spider trapped in the bath, don't wash it away. Instead, use a jam jar and a piece of card to catch it and put it outside. Put the jar over the spider, then slide the card underneath. Turn the jar upright, then take away the card and replace it with the jam jar's lid.

Bathrooms are great places for spotting spiders, which often seem to lurk in baths and basins, giving people a nasty shock. But how do they get there, and why? Despite what you may have heard, spiders definitely don't come up the plug-hole. They fall in while they are looking for food or for a mate. Once they are in, they are trapped because their feet cannot get a grip on a bath's shiny sides.

Spider's bright colour may be easy for a human to spot, but it is not so easy for an insect to see

Lurking in flowers

If you see a bee or a butterfly that seems stuck to a flower, take a closer look. It's very likely that it has been caught by a crab spider. Crab spiders lurk in flowers with their front legs held out like a crab's claws. If an insect lands, the spider snaps shut its legs to grab its prey.

Ground hunters

Many spiders hunt on the ground. This wolf spider is a daytime hunter, and it uses speed to catch its prey. It runs over the soil and up small plants, catching anything that comes its way.

A tarantula's feet are covered with short hairs, which give the spider a good sense of touch

Hunting at night

The world's biggest spiders are tarantulas. They are ground-based hunters, although they sometimes climb trees. Unlike wolf spiders, they creep about after dark, using their legs to feel for food.

Downward-pointing fangs pin the spider's prey to the ground when it attacks

LOOK HERE!

Jumping spiders are small, perky creatures, which often walk over fences and walls. They have good eyesight, and they jump like tiny acrobats, landing on their prey. If you find a jumping spider on a wall or paving stone, hold an upright pencil a few centimetres away. Move the pencil in a circle around the spider. The spider will turn around to watch the pencil moving and may even look up to glance at you.

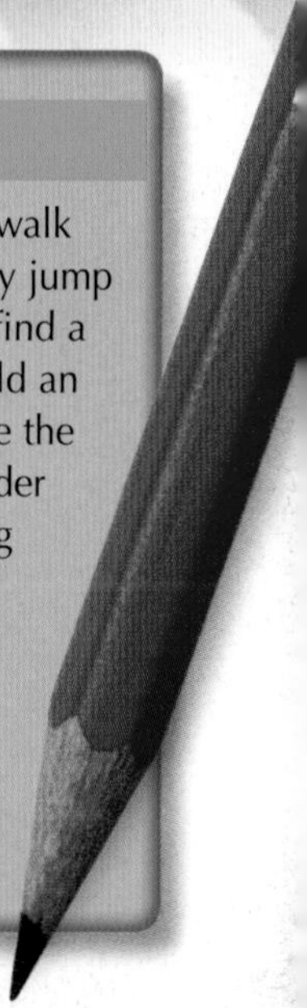

◀ Double take
Unlike other spiders, jumping spiders are not afraid of people. Using their big front eyes, they will have a good look at anything you put in their way.

Earthworms

Apart from insects, earthworms are some of the most important animals in the world. By burrowing through the soil, they mix it up and help plants to grow. Earthworms look soft and squishy, but they are very good at tunnelling through the soil. To find out how they do it, all you have to do is pick one up and hold it in your closed-up hand. The worm will squeeze its way between your fingers, just as it squeezes through soil tunnels underground.

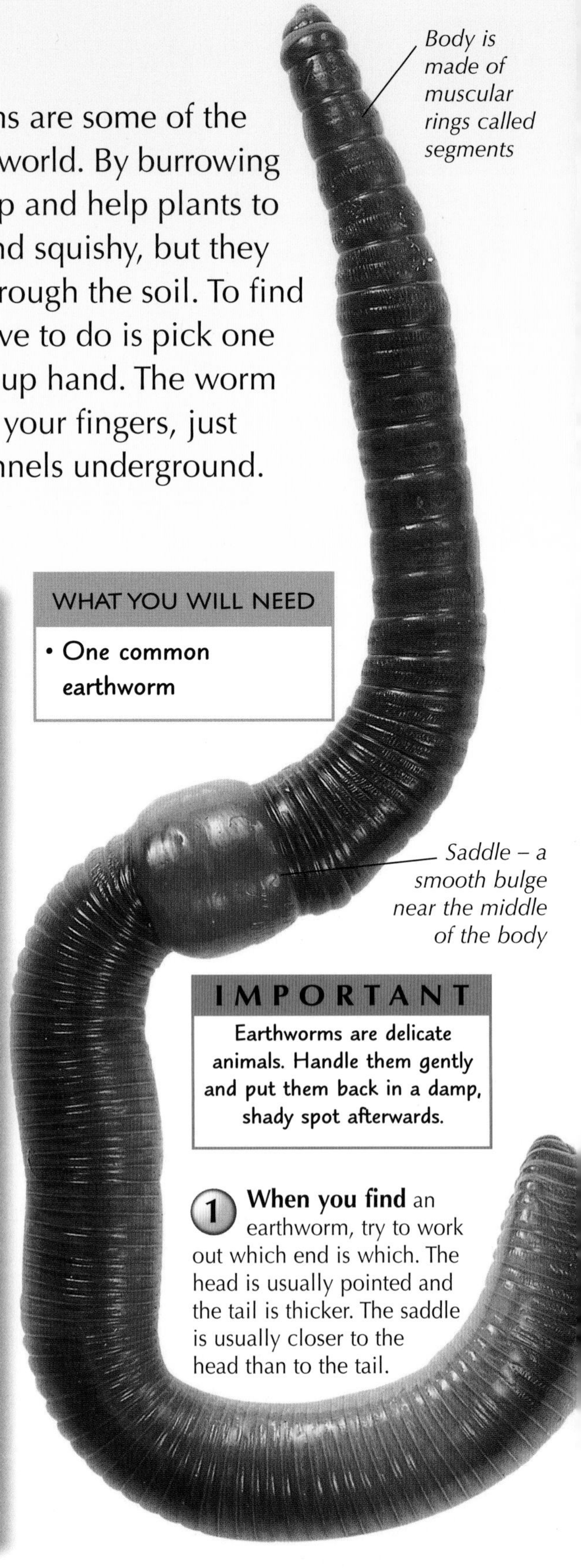

Body is made of muscular rings called segments

Saddle – a smooth bulge near the middle of the body

AMOROUS EARTHWORMS

Earthworms spend almost all their lives underground. The one time they stay on the surface is in late spring and early summer, when they are searching for a mate. They usually come out on warm, damp nights. If you want to see them, take a torch covered with a piece of red plastic, because worms react less to red light. Tread carefully, because they can sense vibrations and quickly disappear underground.

Earthworm embrace ▲
When earthworms mate, they lie side by side and cover themselves in sticky mucus.

WHAT YOU WILL NEED

- **One common earthworm**

IMPORTANT

Earthworms are delicate animals. Handle them gently and put them back in a damp, shady spot afterwards.

1 **When you find** an earthworm, try to work out which end is which. The head is usually pointed and the tail is thicker. The saddle is usually closer to the head than to the tail.

EMERGENCY ESCAPE

When earthworms are on or near the surface, they are at risk from hungry birds. To avoid being eaten, they have to be alert. They do not have true eyes, so they cannot see danger. Instead, they rely on their sense of touch. An earthworm's skin is full of sensitive nerves. If a bird touches a worm's tail, the worm immediately contracts its body. With luck, it gets underground before the bird can pull it out.

Earthworm breakfast ▲ This thrush has caught an earthworm and is about to swallow its meal. Birds find earthworms partly by sight, and also by listening for the faint sounds they make as they tunnel through the soil.

2 **Pick up the worm** and hold it gently by its tail. Its head will move around and its body will start to lengthen as it tries to reach the ground.

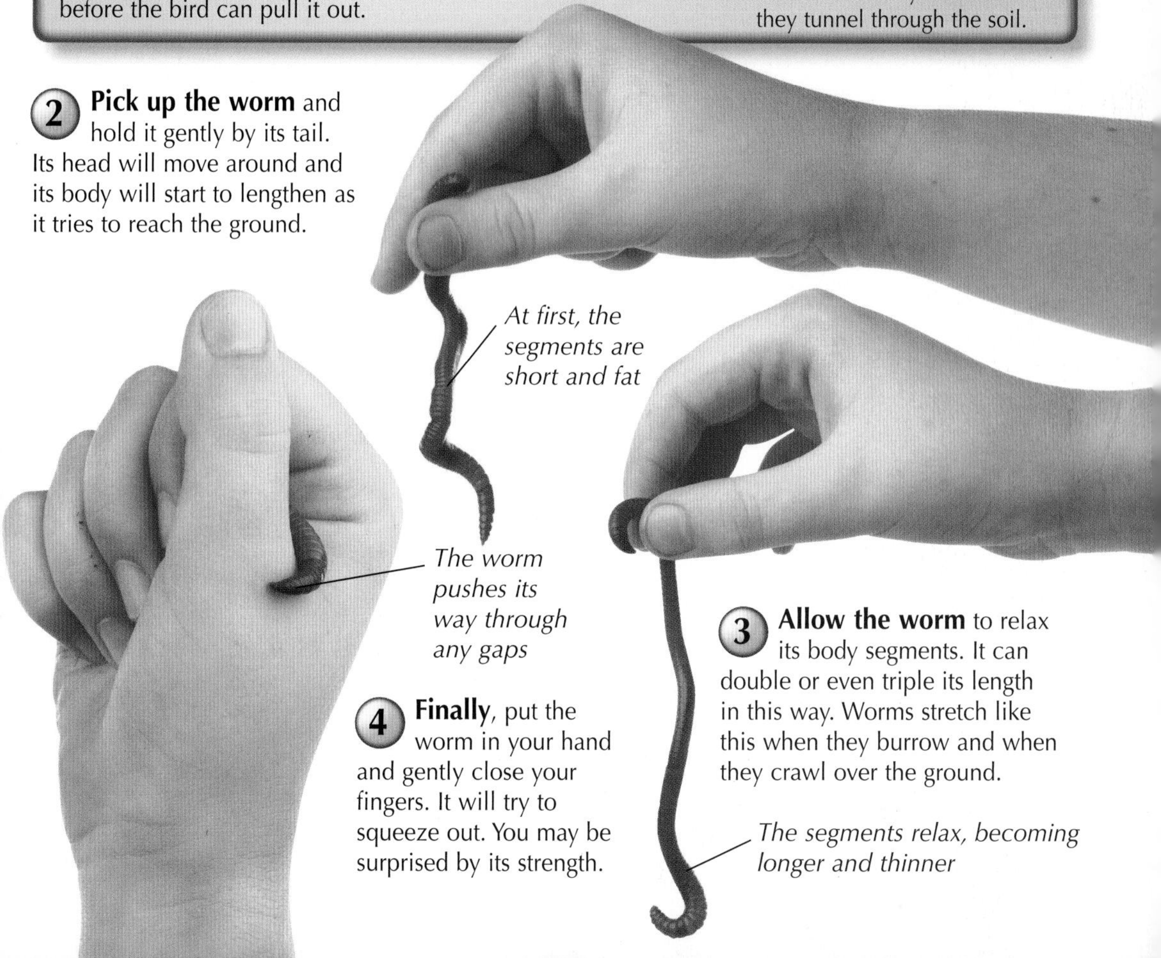

At first, the segments are short and fat
The worm pushes its way through any gaps
The segments relax, becoming longer and thinner

3 **Allow the worm** to relax its body segments. It can double or even triple its length in this way. Worms stretch like this when they burrow and when they crawl over the ground.

4 **Finally**, put the worm in your hand and gently close your fingers. It will try to squeeze out. You may be surprised by its strength.

Bug classification There are at least a million species of insects in the world, together with lots of other kinds of bugs. Scientists classify them into different groups based on key features that they share.

INSECT	NAME OF GROUP	SPECIES TOTAL	KEY FEATURES	EXAMPLES
 **Ground beetle**	BEETLES **Coleoptera**	370,000	Beetles have hardened forewings that fit over their hindwings like a case. They live on land and in freshwater in most parts of the world, and eat all kinds of food.	Stag beetle Burying beetle Ladybird
 **Dragonfly**	DRAGONFLIES AND DAMSELFLIES **Odonata**	5,500	These large-eyed insects have long bodies and two pairs of filmy wings. As adults, they hunt other insects while on the wing.	Emperor dragonfly Green darner Azure damselfly
 **Housefly**	FLIES **Diptera**	122,000	Flies are the only flying insects with a single pair of wings. Most adult flies feed on liquids, but some eat pollen from flowers.	House fly Crane fly
 **Cicada**	BUGS **Hemiptera**	82,000	True bugs feed on plants or animals, using their sharp mouthparts to pierce their food. They have two pairs of wings.	Cicada Giant water bug Pond skater
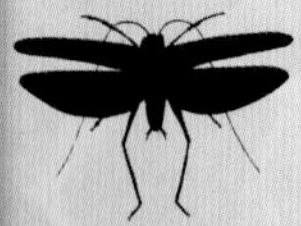 **Cricket**	CRICKETS AND GRASSHOPPERS **Orthoptera**	20,000	These stout-bodied insects have powerful hindlegs and are good at jumping. Most also have two pairs of wings, but some have tiny wings and cannot fly.	Speckled bushcricket Desert locust
 **Cockroach**	COCKROACHES **Blattodea**	4,000	Cockroaches are large, flat-bodied insects that sometimes feed indoors. They have powerful legs and can run away from danger.	American cockroach Madagascan hissing cockroach
 **Butterfly**	BUTTERFLIES AND MOTHS **Lepidoptera**	165,000	These insects are covered with tiny scales. The adults feed on nectar and other sugary liquids, and coil up their tongues when not in use.	Monarch butterfly Hawkmoth
 **Wasp**	BEES, WASPS, AND ANTS **Hymenoptera**	108,000	All these insects have slender waists, and many of them also have a sting. Most have two pairs of wings joined by tiny hooks, but worker ants are wingless.	Honeybee Bumblebee Common wasp

On the left, you can find out about some of the most important groups of insects. For other bugs and creepy-crawlies, look below. The species totals show the number that have been identified so far.

INSECT	NAME OF GROUP	SPECIES TOTAL	KEY FEATURES	EXAMPLES
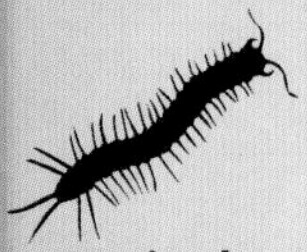 **Centipede**	CENTIPEDES **Chilopoda**	3,000	Centipedes are long, flat-bodied animals with lots of legs. They are fast-moving hunters, and attack their prey with their poisonous claws.	Giant centipede
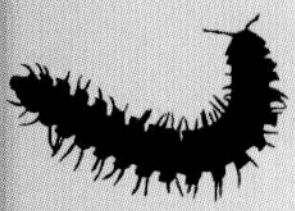 **Millipede**	MILLIPEDES **Diplopoda**	8,000	Millipedes resemble centipedes, but they have four legs on each segment of their bodies instead of two. They feed on plant remains.	Giant millipede
 **Woodlouse**	CRUSTACEANS **Crustacea**	40,000	Crustaceans have hard body cases and several pairs of legs. Most of them live in water, but some kinds live in damp places on land.	Woodlouse
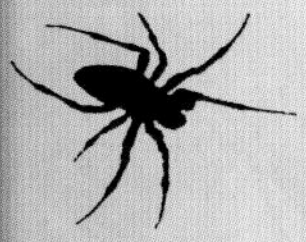 **Spider**	SPIDERS **Araneae**	40,000	Spiders are eight-legged predators with venomous fangs and several pairs of eyes. Many kinds make silk webs to catch their prey.	Garden orb-web spider Tarantula
 **Harvestman**	HARVESTMEN **Opiliones**	5,000	Harvestmen look similar to spiders, but have slender legs and oval bodies without a waist. Unlike spiders, they never make webs.	Harvestman
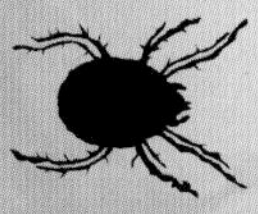 **Mite**	TICKS AND MITES **Acari**	30,000	These eight-legged animals feed on a wide variety of food. Ticks suck blood, but mites attack both plants and animals.	Sheep tick House dust mite
 **Scorpion**	SCORPIONS **Scorpiones**	1,400	Scorpions are flat-bodied animals with four pairs of legs, two pincers, and a tail that has a venomous sting.	Imperial scorpion
 **Pseudo-scorpion**	PSEUDO-SCORPIONS **Pseudoscorpiones**	33,000	These tiny scorpion-like animals often live in leaf litter. Unlike true scorpions, they do not have a sting.	Pseudo-scorpion

Star gazer

Stargazing

Have you ever looked at the night sky and been amazed by all the stars? If so, this section is for you. Stargazing is the world's oldest hobby, and anyone can try it. It's not just about learning constellations: you can see galaxies and shooting stars, find planets in the night sky, and watch an eclipse.

Where and when

The best time to stargaze is on a dark, clear night when there's no Moon. Winter nights are longer than those in the summer, but you can stargaze all year round. What's more, you'll see different things at different times of the year. You'll see more if you travel out of town, as city lights create a hazy glow called light pollution, which blocks out all but the brightest stars. If you stargaze from home, turn out the lights in your house and stand in the darkest spot in the garden. Better still, visit the countryside or go on a camping holiday.

Night vision

It takes about 20 minutes for your eyes to adjust to darkness. So, if you're patient and stay in the dark, you'll see more and more stars. Don't look at bright light when your eyes have adjusted, because you'll spoil your night vision. Some people use a red torch for reading star charts and books because red light doesn't interfere with your night vision. Another technique is to close one eye when you're using a torch, so the other remains as sensitive as possible.

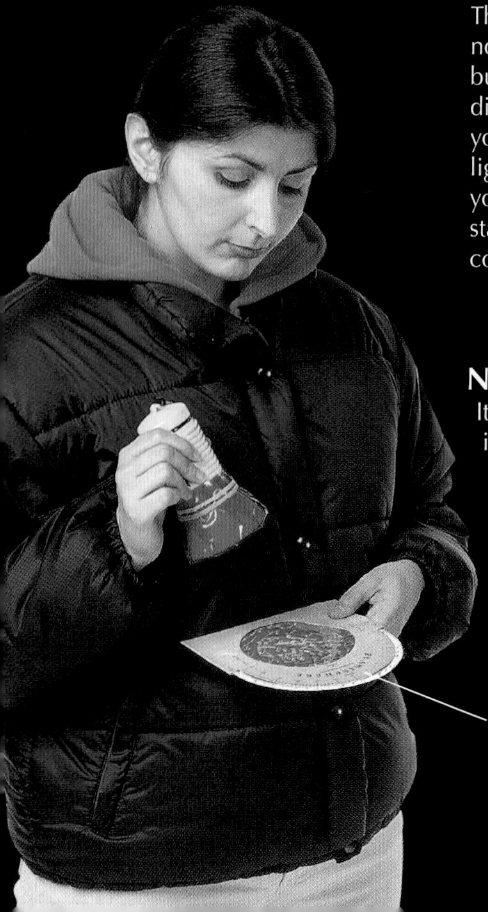

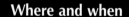

A planisphere (star chart) shows which stars are visible at different times and dates

USING THE INTERNET

The Internet is another exciting way to look at space. You can use it to see pictures taken by the world's best telescopes, or by spacecraft and rovers that are exploring the planets. Online planetarium websites can show you exactly which stars and planets are visible from where you live at any time. Astronomy news websites will give you information on forthcoming events to watch out for, such as meteor showers, eclipses, or passing comets.

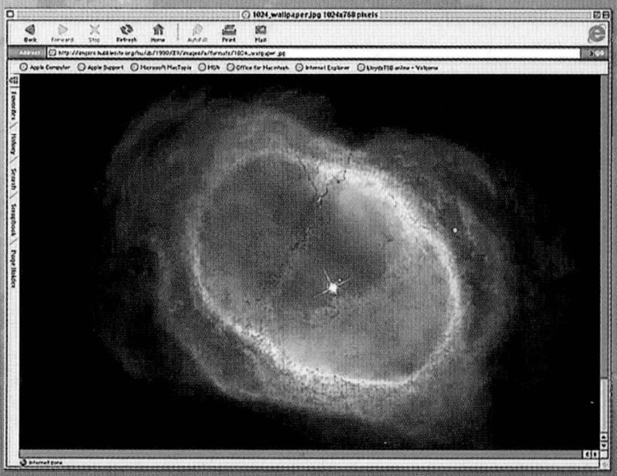

Planetary nebula ▲
The latest pictures from the Hubble Telescope can be seen on the Internet. This one shows the glowing shell of gas around a dying star.

Useful gear

The only essential equipment for stargazing is warm clothing, as stargazers spend a lot of time standing or sitting still. A star chart or astronomy book are useful if you want to find particular stars. To read them, you'll need a torch. A red torch is best, as it will not affect your night vision. To make one, cover the end with a sheet of clear red plastic film. A compass, watch, notebook, and pen are also useful. Binoculars will help you to see small or faint objects much more clearly. Only expensive telescopes are significantly better than binoculars.

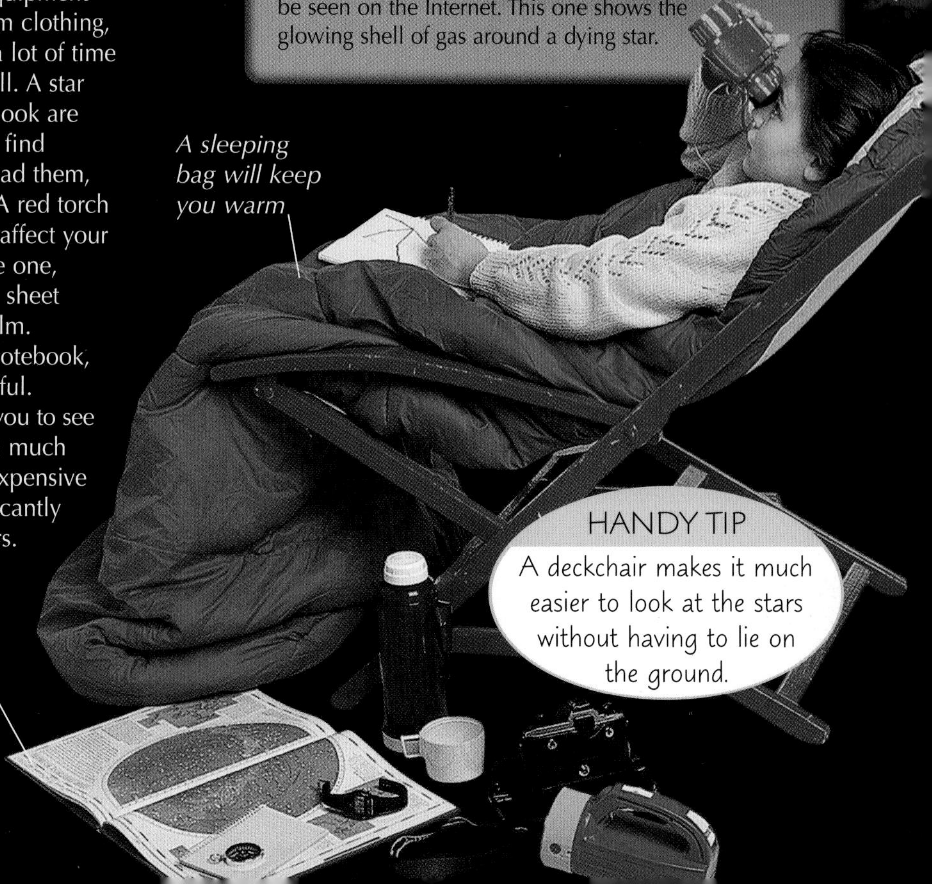
A sleeping bag will keep you warm
Keep books and papers off the ground, which may become wet with dew

HANDY TIP
A deckchair makes it much easier to look at the stars without having to lie on the ground.

The sky at night

The night sky can be very bewildering. There are thousands of stars, apparently sprinkled at random. To make matters worse, they are constantly moving around the sky. To help us make sense of the stars, we group them in patterns called constellations. To help us make sense of their movement, we imagine them being fixed to a giant moving globe that surrounds Earth.

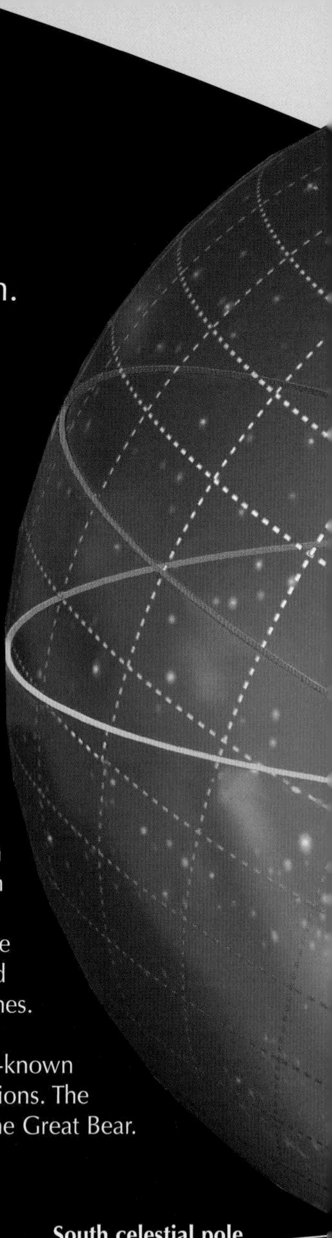
South celestial pole

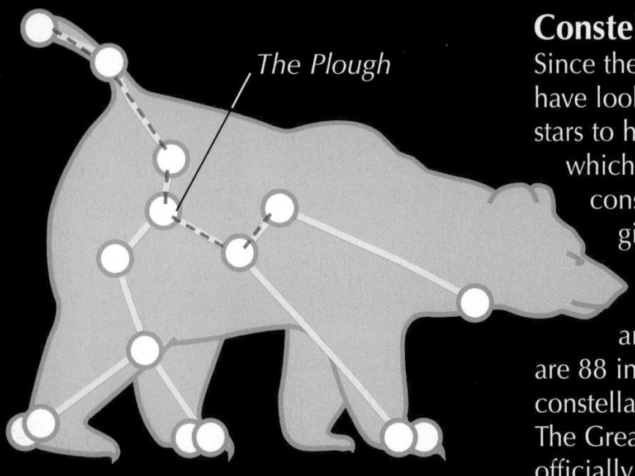
The Plough

URSA MAJOR

Constellations

Since the earliest times, people have looked for patterns in the stars to help them remember which star is which. Many constellations were later given names from Roman and Greek myths, such as Orion (the Hunter) and Aries (the Ram). There are 88 internationally recognized constellations, all with Latin names. The Great Bear, for instance, is officially Ursa Major. Some well-known groups of stars are not constellations. The Plough, for example, is part of the Great Bear.

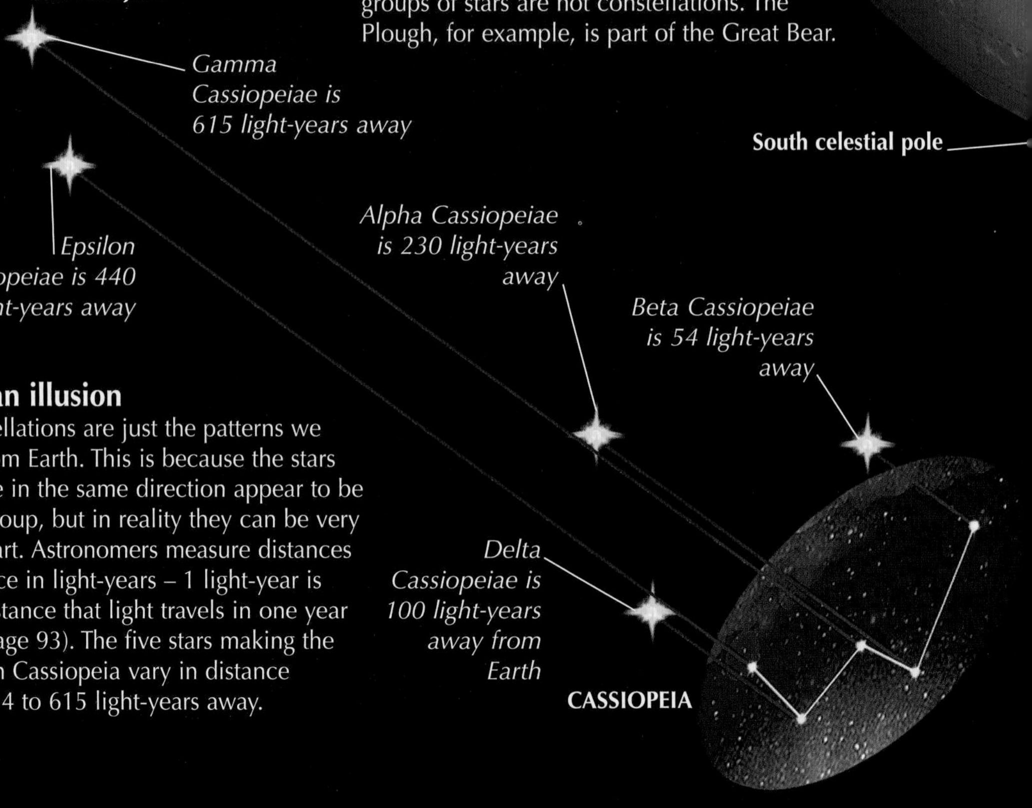
Gamma Cassiopeiae is 615 light-years away
Epsilon Cassiopeiae is 440 light-years away
Alpha Cassiopeiae is 230 light-years away
Beta Cassiopeiae is 54 light-years away
Delta Cassiopeiae is 100 light-years away from Earth

CASSIOPEIA

Just an illusion

Constellations are just the patterns we see from Earth. This is because the stars that lie in the same direction appear to be in a group, but in reality they can be very far apart. Astronomers measure distances in space in light-years – 1 light-year is the distance that light travels in one year (see page 93). The five stars making the "W" in Cassiopeia vary in distance from 54 to 615 light-years away.

The celestial sphere

Stars move across the sky during the night much as the Sun does during the day. They move as though they were fixed points on a gigantic, rotating ball that surrounds the Earth. This ball doesn't really exist, but astronomers find it a useful concept and call it the celestial sphere. The points of the sphere directly over Earth's North and South Poles, where the stars hardly move, are called celestial poles. Halfway between them is the celestial equator. Every star has a fixed position on the celestial sphere and never shifts from that spot. In contrast, planets move against the starry background.

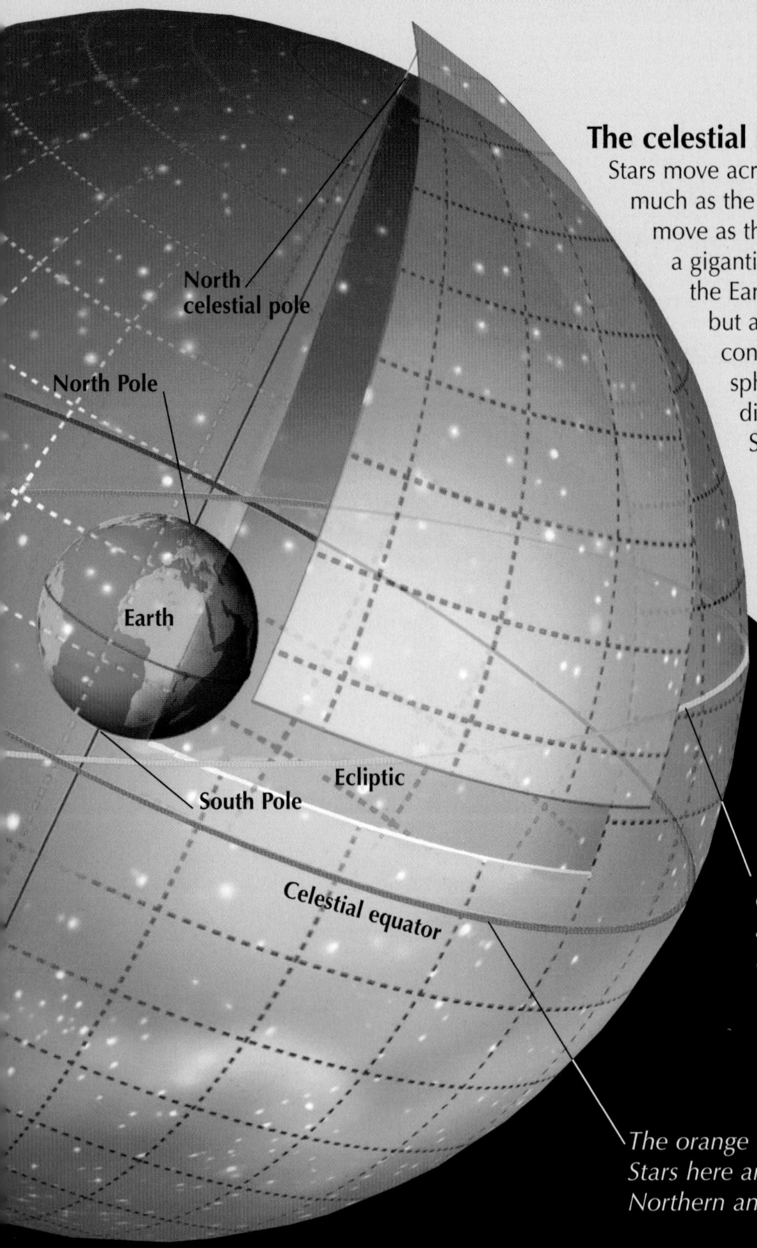

The yellow line – the ecliptic – is the Sun's apparent path across the celestial sphere

The orange line is the celestial equator. Stars here are visible in both the Northern and the Southern Hemispheres

MEASURING DISTANCE

Astronomers measure distances across the celestial sphere in degrees (°). The whole sphere covers 360°, but at night you can see only half the sphere (180°). You don't have to be a professional astronomer to measure distances; you can use your hand. Hold your hand at arm's length and use the guides shown on the right; these work no matter what age you are.

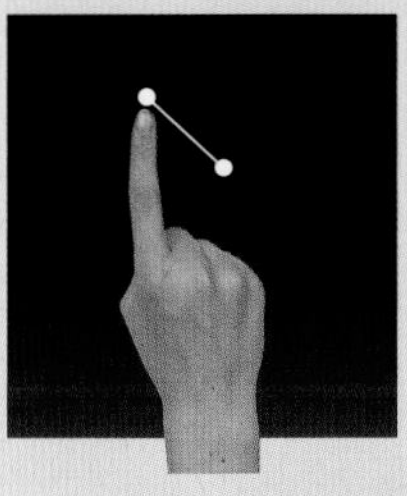

A finger's width
One finger is about 1° (twice the width of a full Moon).

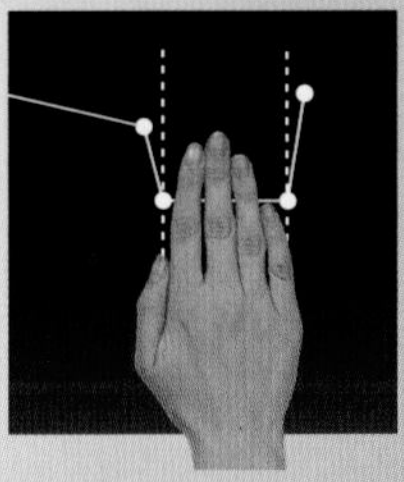

Half handspan
A closed hand at arm's length is about 10° across.

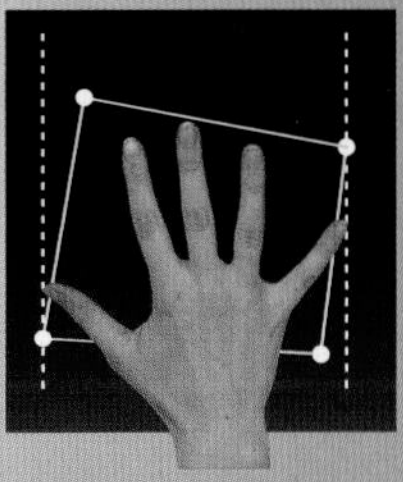

Whole handspan
An open hand with fingers fully splayed is about 22°.

Our place in space

For centuries, people thought that planet Earth was the centre of the universe, with all the planets and stars revolving around us. With the invention of the telescope, astronomers started to realize that things were, in fact, quite different. Earth, as it turned out, is a small and insignificant planet orbiting just one of countless quadrillions of stars scattered across the vast cosmos.

Warmth from the Sun causes activity in the atmosphere, which affects the climate on Earth

Planet Earth and its star

Our planet is the only place in the universe known to support life. Earth is just the right distance from the Sun for water to be able to exist in all its forms: liquid water, solid ice, and water vapour. Water is essential for life. It covers two-thirds of the surface of Earth, and fills the sky with cloud. Our Sun is an average star. Its source of power is buried deep in the central core, where nuclear fusion reactions transform matter into energy. The Sun contains nearly all the matter in the solar system. It has tremendously powerful gravity, which keeps the planets trapped in orbit around it.

The planets

The Sun and planets make up the family of bodies that we call the solar system. There are eight major planets orbiting the Sun, many with their own moons. The inner planets, including Earth, are made of rock and metal. Most of the outer planets are giant globes of hydrogen and helium, left over from the formation of the Sun. Between the outer and inner planets is a ring of rocky space debris, called the asteroid belt.

EXPLORING THE COSMOS

Distances in space are too big for the human mind to imagine. Astronomers measure them in light-years – 1 light-year is the distance that light (the fastest thing in the universe) travels in one year, or 10 million million km (6 million million miles). The light we see from stars left them many years ago, and so we are looking back in time. With the world's most powerful telescopes, astronomers can see almost 14 billion light-years across space.

Scanning the skies ▲
An amateur astronomer tries out the telescope at Kitt Peak Observatory, USA. The observatory's domed roof opens to reveal the Milky Way.

The universe

Beyond the planets lies interstellar space, the darkness between the stars. If you travelled for long enough – about 500,000 years at the speed of an airliner – you would reach the Sun's nearest neighbouring star, called Proxima Centauri. It is one of about 200 billion stars that make up our local galaxy, the Milky Way. Every star that you can see in the night sky belongs to this galaxy. Beyond the Milky Way are mind-bogglingly vast stretches of emptiness, and beyond these are yet more galaxies. There are probably hundreds of billions of galaxies stretching into the distance in all directions, but we will never know the exact number because we can only see a fraction of them. The galaxies and all the emptiness of space make up the universe.

Seeing sunspots

The Sun is incredibly bright and you should never look at it directly. But you can create a safe image of it with binoculars and a screen made from card. You can use this technique to watch planets pass in front of the Sun (transits) and to search for sunspots.

Anchor the binoculars and card securely with books

WHAT YOU WILL NEED

- 2 large pieces of card
- Binoculars
- Scissors
- Paper
- Sticky tape
- Pencil or pen

Don't look directly at the Sun and NEVER look at it through a telescope, binoculars, or even via a mirror.

WHAT ARE SUNSPOTS?

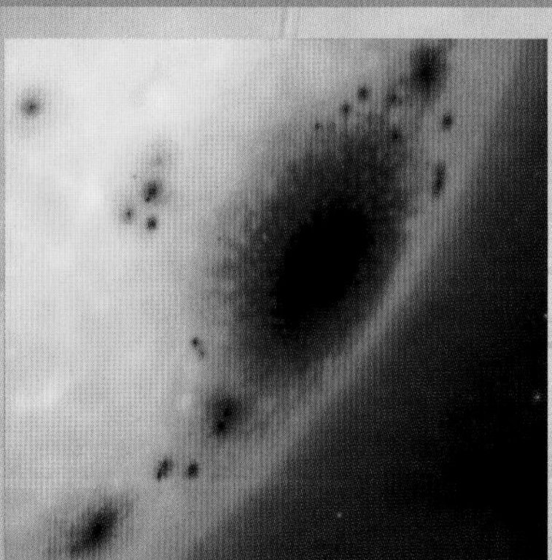

Sunspots are slightly darker, cooler patches on the Sun's surface. They might look small on the image made by your binoculars, but they are big enough to swallow Earth. By tracking sunspots over a period of time, astronomers discovered that the Sun doesn't rotate as a solid object. The poles take 35 days to rotate once, but the equator takes only 25 days.

◀ **Sunspots on the Sun's surface**

GREAT BALL OF FIRE?

The Sun isn't really a ball of fire but a gigantic globe of superhot hydrogen gas. Its power comes from its sheer weight. It contains 99.9 per cent of all the matter in the solar system, and this huge mass crushes the core and forces atoms together in nuclear fusion reactions. The energy escapes as heat, light, radiation, and violent eruptions from the surface.

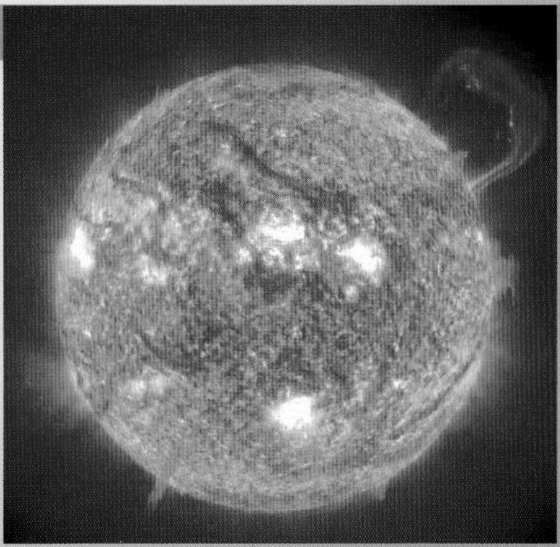

Sun storm ▶
A loop of superhot gas erupts from the Sun. Storms like this are most frequent during a solar maximum – a period every 11 years when sunspot numbers reach a peak.

Sun's rays
Angle the screen so that it's facing the binoculars

1 **Make a shield** to hold the binoculars using some card and scissors. To allow sunlight through one lens only, cover the other lens with card or a lens cap. Prop the shield with the binoculars on a chair so they face the Sun directly and secure them.

2 **Place the other piece** of card in the shadow of the binoculars, about 1 m (3 ft) away, to act as a screen. Tilt the binoculars until an image of the Sun appears on the screen. Sharpen the image by focusing the binoculars.

3 **Look for dark sunspots** in the image. Tape some paper on to the screen and trace the Sun and any sunspots. Repeat the next day and look for the same sunspots – they will have shifted as the Sun turns.

What's the time?

Earth turns around once every 24 hours, and this is why the Sun appears to cross the sky and vanish over the horizon, creating our day and night. Earth's rotation is so regular that you can use the Sun to tell the time. The best way to do this is to build a sundial, a device that was first used about 6,000 years ago.

WHAT YOU WILL NEED

- Pencil
- Block of wood
- Ruler
- Protractor
- Permanent marker pen
- Atlas
- Small piece of thin wood
- Plasticine/modelling clay
- Craft glue
- Compass

Ask an adult to help you construct the solid base.

Use a compass to ensure your sundial faces in the right direction

Solid wooden base

Setting up your sundial

Take the sundial outside and place it on a flat surface. Point the pencil north if you live in the Northern Hemisphere or south if you live in the Southern Hemisphere. If your country adjusts clocks according to the season, the time may be an hour or more out.

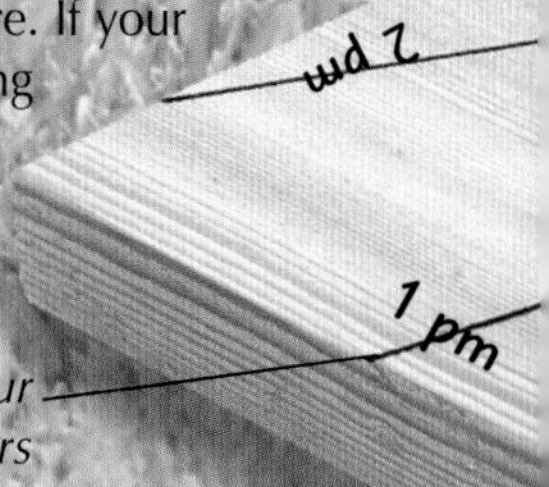

Hour markers

1 Draw a straight line across the board 2.5–5 cm (1–2 in) from one end and mark its centre with a dot. Use the protractor to draw rays 15° apart from this point; draw these rays in pencil first in case you make any mistakes. When you've finished, use the permanent marker pen to draw over the pencil lines and write the times as shown (above right). If your base is circular, start from the centre of the board and draw rays all around, as on a clock face.

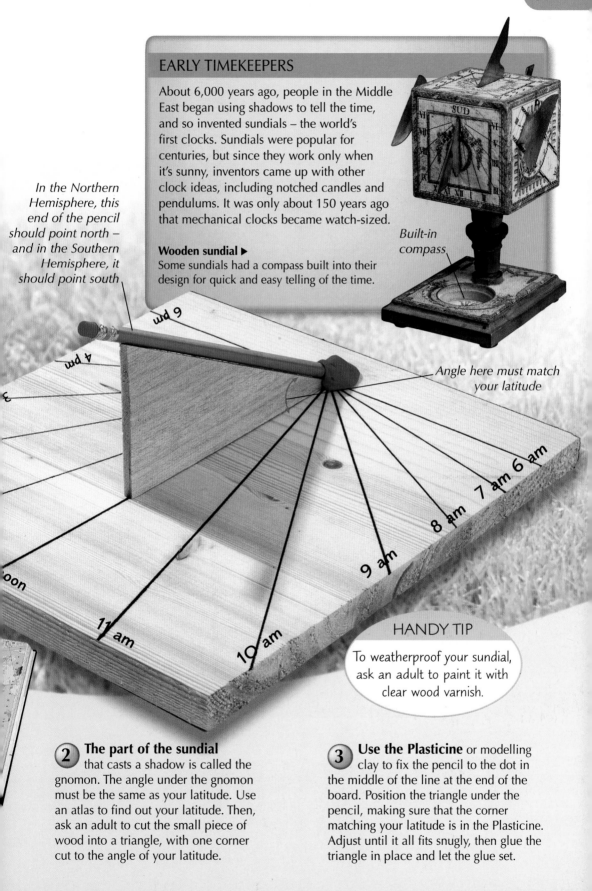

EARLY TIMEKEEPERS

About 6,000 years ago, people in the Middle East began using shadows to tell the time, and so invented sundials – the world's first clocks. Sundials were popular for centuries, but since they work only when it's sunny, inventors came up with other clock ideas, including notched candles and pendulums. It was only about 150 years ago that mechanical clocks became watch-sized.

Wooden sundial ▶
Some sundials had a compass built into their design for quick and easy telling of the time.

In the Northern Hemisphere, this end of the pencil should point north – and in the Southern Hemisphere, it should point south

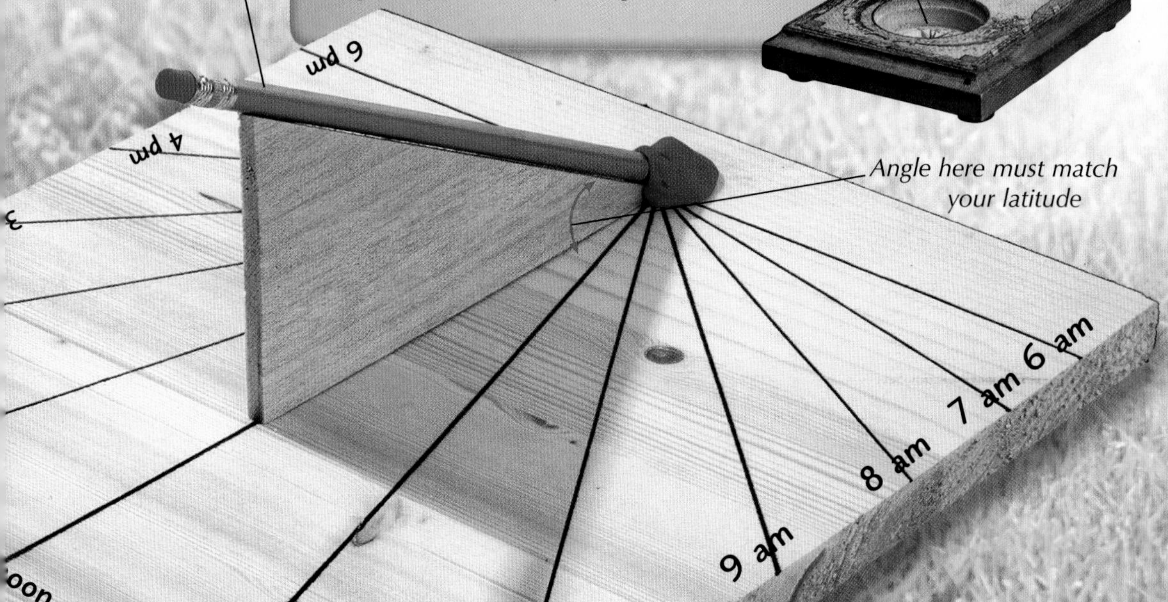

HANDY TIP

To weatherproof your sundial, ask an adult to paint it with clear wood varnish.

2 The part of the sundial that casts a shadow is called the gnomon. The angle under the gnomon must be the same as your latitude. Use an atlas to find out your latitude. Then, ask an adult to cut the small piece of wood into a triangle, with one corner cut to the angle of your latitude.

3 Use the Plasticine or modelling clay to fix the pencil to the dot in the middle of the line at the end of the board. Position the triangle under the pencil, making sure that the corner matching your latitude is in the Plasticine. Adjust until it all fits snugly, then glue the triangle in place and let the glue set.

Lunar landscape

The Moon is the closest heavenly body to Earth and the easiest to see. Even with the naked eye you can see the dark lunar "seas" and brighter highlands, but with binoculars or a telescope you can also see a wealth of craters, mountains, and other features.

SCARFACE

The Moon's highlands are covered with craters made by meteorite collisions, but the darker seas have few craters. Astronomers think most of the craters formed early in the Moon's history. Earth was battered by meteorites at the same time, but our craters have since been worn away by weather and geological forces. After the bombardment ended, molten lava oozed from the Moon's interior and spread across the lowlands, wiping out some craters and forming the lunar seas, or maria.

A large lunar crater with central hills

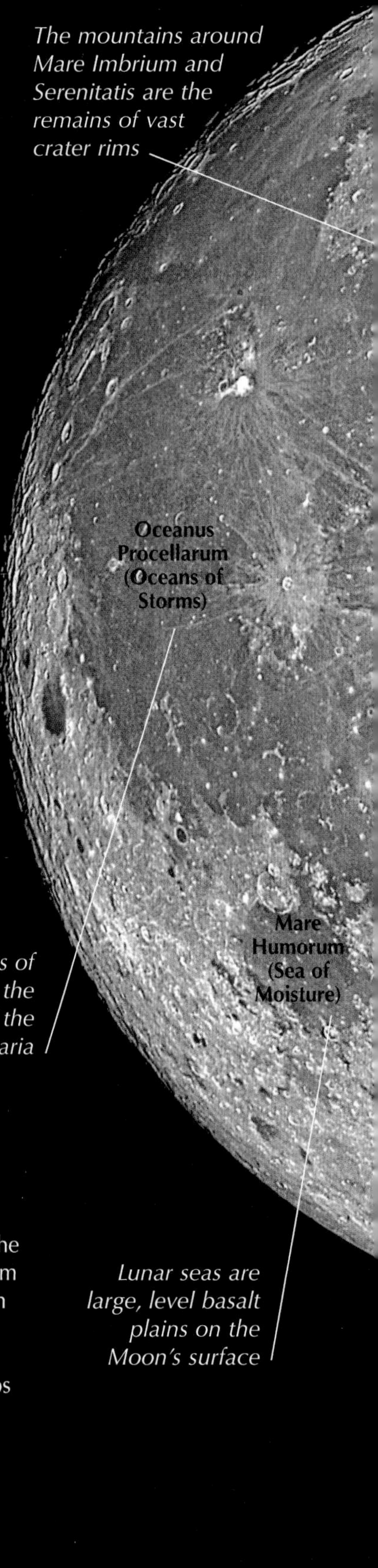
The mountains around Mare Imbrium and Serenitatis are the remains of vast crater rims
Oceanus Procellarum (Oceans of Storms)
The Oceans of Storms is the largest of the Moon's maria
Mare Humorum (Sea of Moisture)
Lunar seas are large, level basalt plains on the Moon's surface

When to observe the Moon

The full Moon is not the best time to view the Moon. All other times are better because the Sun's sideways illumination casts shadows from lunar mountains and crater rims, making them stand out more. The Moon's features are most clear at the terminator – the border between the lit and the unlit area. The terminator sweeps across the Moon over the course of a month (see pages 100–101), making different features stand out at different times.

MAKING CRATERS

The Moon has been pounded by so many meteorites that many of the craters overlap or formed on top of older craters. You can create a similar effect with a tray of sand and "meteorites" of varying sizes, such as balls and marbles. Flatten the sand, then drop the meteorites from overhead.

Home-made craters

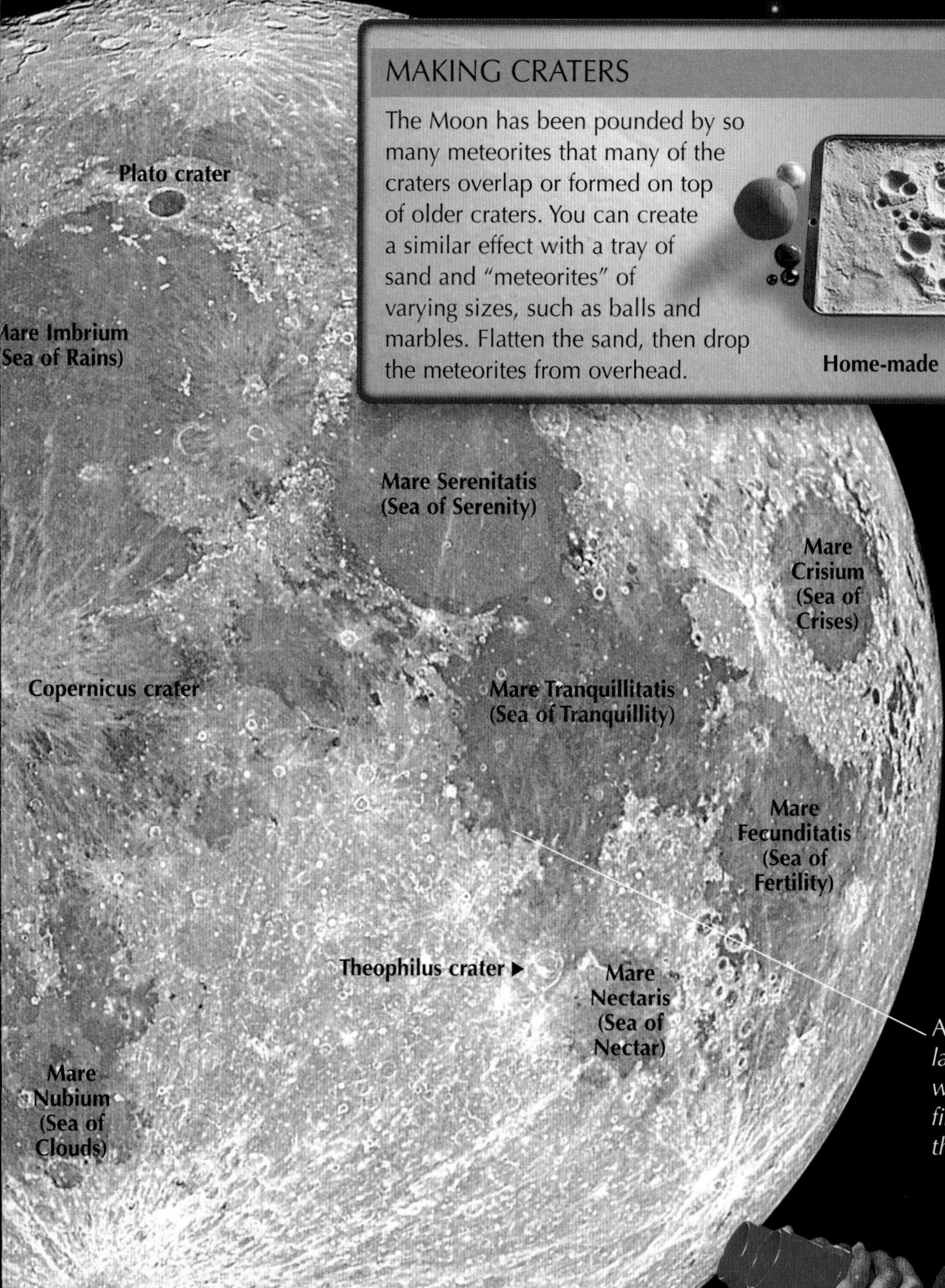

The bright rays around Tycho are vast streaks of debris thrown out by the meteorite impact that formed the crater. These are best seen at full Moon

A lunar calendar

Unlike the Sun, the Moon doesn't make light of its own. Instead, we see the Moon in the sky only when it reflects light from the Sun – it acts like an enormous mirror. As the Moon travels around Earth on its monthly orbit, we see it at different angles relative to the Sun. It changes from a thin crescent to a full disk, passing through a series of stages called phases. If you watch the Moon every day for a month, you can record the whole cycle of phases.

WHAT YOU WILL NEED

- Pen
- Sheet of white paper
- Compasses
- Sheet of black paper
- Scissors
- Glue
- Aluminium foil
- Binoculars

1 **Draw a chart** with 29 squares, made of four rows of seven squares and one extra square (see right). Cut out 29 circles from the black paper and stick one in each square.

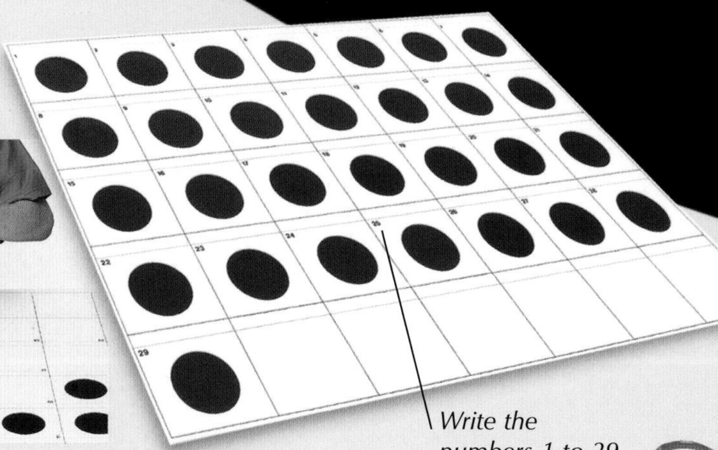

Write the numbers 1 to 29 in the squares

2 **Wait for a clear night** when you can see the Moon. Binoculars might help you check the Moon's shape, but they aren't essential. Cut out its shape to match in aluminium foil and glue it on to the first black circle of the chart.

3 **Do the same** every day for a month. To find out when the Moon rises and sets each day, look in a newspaper or search on the Internet. Some nights will be cloudy, so leave those blank.

THE PHASES OF THE MOON

At new Moon, the Moon is between the Earth and the Sun. It crosses the sky during daylight hours, but we don't see it because it's hidden by the Sun's glare, and only its far side is sunlit. Over the next days, the Moon moves away from the Sun in the sky and sunlight spills around its edge, forming a crescent that is easiest to see after sunset. When half the Moon's face is lit, it is a quarter of the way through its orbit (first quarter), and at this stage is visible from noon to midnight. As the sunlit area grows (waxes), we see the Moon more at night. When it is halfway through its orbit, it is opposite the Sun and fully lit in the night sky – then, we see it as a full Moon.

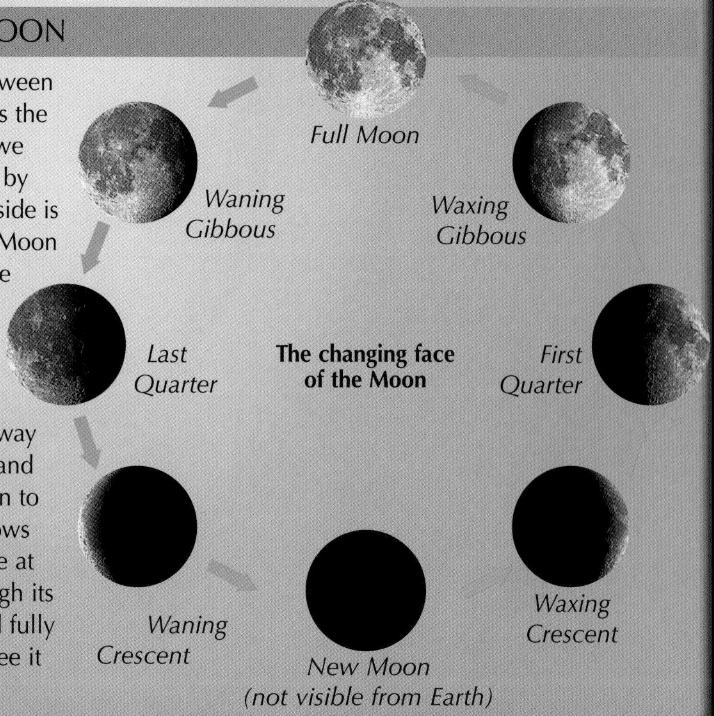

The changing face of the Moon

Moon detective

If you have binoculars, take a close look at the Moon each day. You'll see different features as the month progresses, and the angle of sunlight striking the Moon changes. The best place to look is near the terminator – the dividing line between the areas of shadow and light.

Finding Venus

The lone bright star that often appears in the evening as the Sun goes down is not a star at all, but the planet Venus. Venus is the nearest planet to Earth, and the brightest object in the night sky after the Moon. Sunlight reflected from its dense clouds can make Venus 15 times brighter than the brightest star.

EARTH'S UGLY SISTER

Of all the planets, Venus is most like Earth. It's about the same size, has a similar composition, and has a cloudy atmosphere. But, unlike Earth, Venus is a roasting, waterless desert, far too hot for life – the surface temperature is 482°C (900°F). One reason for the extreme heat on Venus is that it's nearer to the Sun. Another reason is that its dense atmosphere is full of carbon dioxide gas, which traps heat by the greenhouse effect.

◀ **Through the clouds** Clouds cover Venus, but radar cameras can see through. This image reveals volcanoes, twisting valleys, and ancient lava flows.

1 **Go outside** on a clear evening just after sunset and look west, towards the sunset. Alternatively, go out just before dawn and look east. If you can see a single, very bright "star" that doesn't twinkle, it's probably Venus. Venus is always close to the Sun, so as the sky darkens and the Sun sinks deeper beyond the horizon, Venus will set, too.

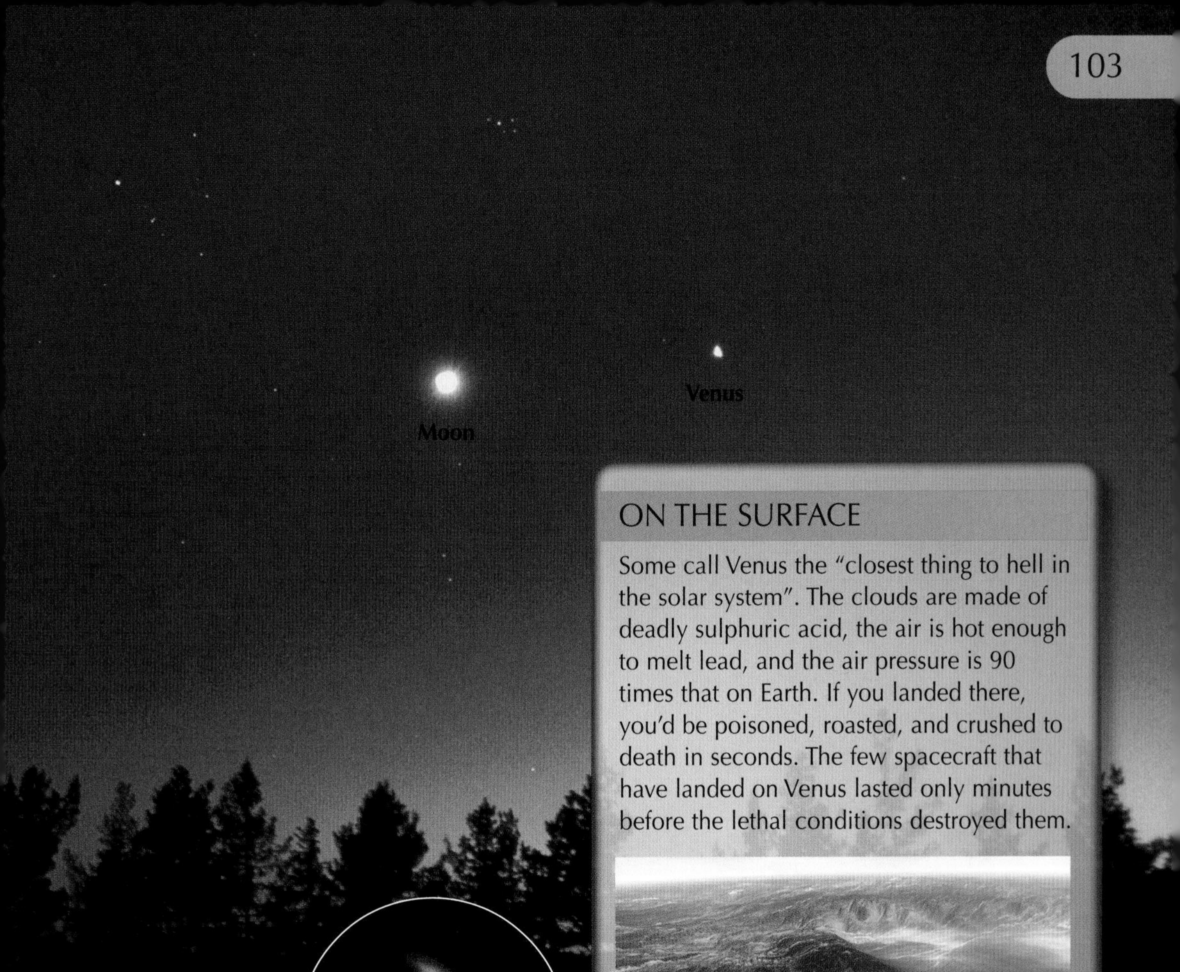

ON THE SURFACE

Some call Venus the "closest thing to hell in the solar system". The clouds are made of deadly sulphuric acid, the air is hot enough to melt lead, and the air pressure is 90 times that on Earth. If you landed there, you'd be poisoned, roasted, and crushed to death in seconds. The few spacecraft that have landed on Venus lasted only minutes before the lethal conditions destroyed them.

Venusian mountains ▲
Scientists used radar data to create this 3-D view across the highlands of Venus. Some of the mountains might be volcanoes.

2 Look at Venus with binoculars. You won't see any surface details because the planet is covered with thick cloud. But sometimes you can see a crescent shape formed by the pattern of sunlight and shade on the planet (just as the Moon sometimes forms a crescent). Venus looks biggest when it's a crescent, and smallest when it's full because of the way we see it during its orbit.

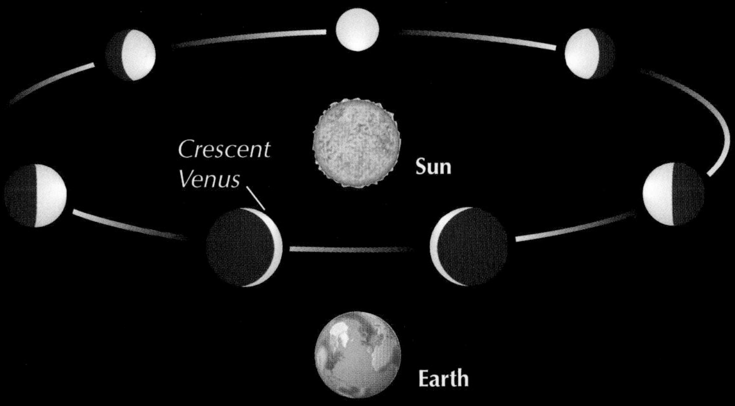

Going through phases

Venus's appearance changes as it orbits the Sun. As it approaches its closest point to Earth, we see a large crescent Venus. As it reaches its furthest point from Earth, we see a small disk. Halfway between these points we see a semicircle, and when Venus lines up exactly with the Sun, we don't see it at all because it is lost in the Sun's glare.

Why is Mars red?

The Greeks named the planet Mars after a god of war because its colour reminded them of blood. The colour is easy to see with the naked eye when Mars passes close to Earth, though it's more of an orangey-brown than a red. The cause, as you can find out for yourself, is a very familiar substance: rust, or iron oxide.

WHAT YOU WILL NEED

- Sand
- Tray
- Rubber gloves
- Scissors
- Wire wool
- Jug of salty water (1 teaspoon of salt to 2 or 3 cupfuls of water)

In 1997, the Sojourner *rover landed on Mars and studied chemicals in the rocks*
Iron oxide in the dust on Mars gives the planet its colour

SIGNS OF WATER?

Three billion years ago, water may have flowed on Mars. There may have been shallow oceans, a thick atmosphere, and life. Today, Mars is a bitterly cold desert, with air so thin that liquid water would vaporize in seconds. Even so, there is tantalizing evidence that water still exists, perhaps in a frozen form deep underground or trapped in Mars's polar ice caps. Space probes have photographed freshly eroded gullies on Mars, in places like Newton Basin. Perhaps such features formed when underground ice reserves thawed and seeped to the surface.

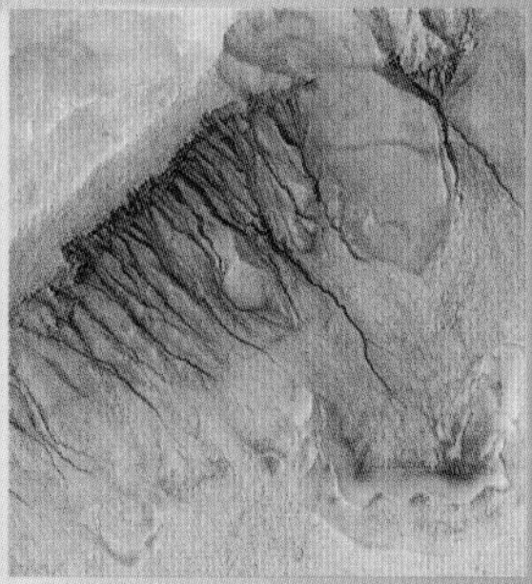

Newton Basin

1 Place a layer of sand on the bottom of a tray. Put the rubber gloves on and use the scissors to snip wire wool into small bits across the sand. Try to pull the bits apart to stop the wire wool clumping and to help spread it out through the sand. While wearing the gloves, mix it well into the sand with your hands.

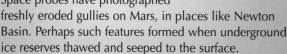

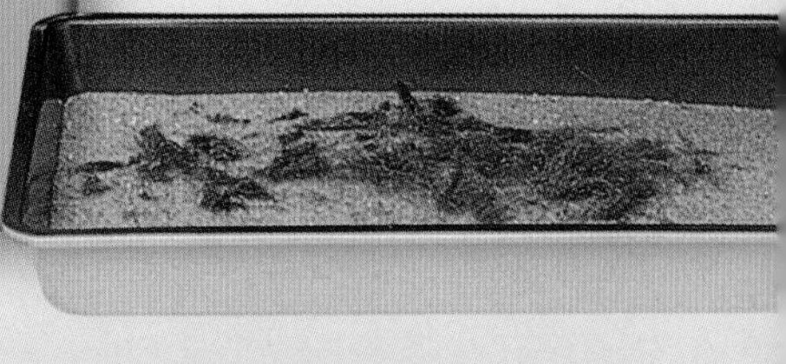

THE RED PLANET

Scientists are not sure how the iron oxide on Mars formed. On Earth, rust forms when iron reacts with the oxygen in air, a process that is much faster when water is present. But Mars has no liquid water on the surface and its air is almost oxygen-free. Some experts think the iron oxide formed long ago when iron in Martian rocks reacted with water in ancient rivers and seas. Another theory is that the iron built up from tiny meteorites raining on to the surface.

Martian weather ▸
The Hubble Telescope took this picture of Mars. It shows an ice cap at its south pole, swirling clouds of ice in the north, and a dust storm in the southeast.

HANDY TIP

Stir the sand around each day to create an even colour.

2 **Pour the salty water** on the sand to wet it but without covering it completely. Leave the tray where it won't be disturbed for a few days.

3 **Check the tray** daily and add water if it dries out. The sand will slowly turn rusty red – like Martian soil.

Jupiter and its moons

Jupiter is one of the brightest planets you can see from Earth. Through good binoculars you can see its rounded shape and its four largest moons. With a telescope, you can even see its stripes.

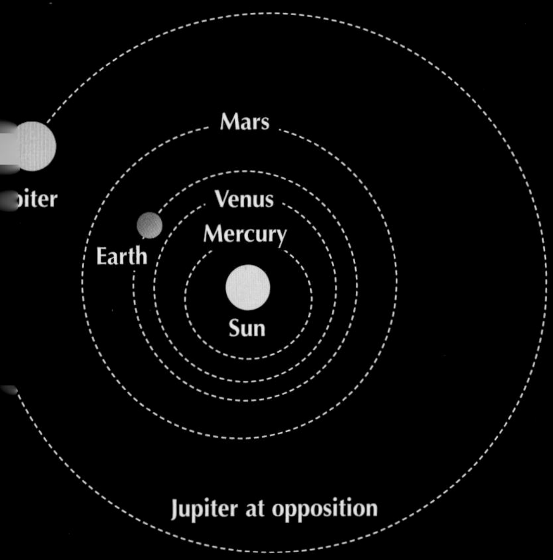

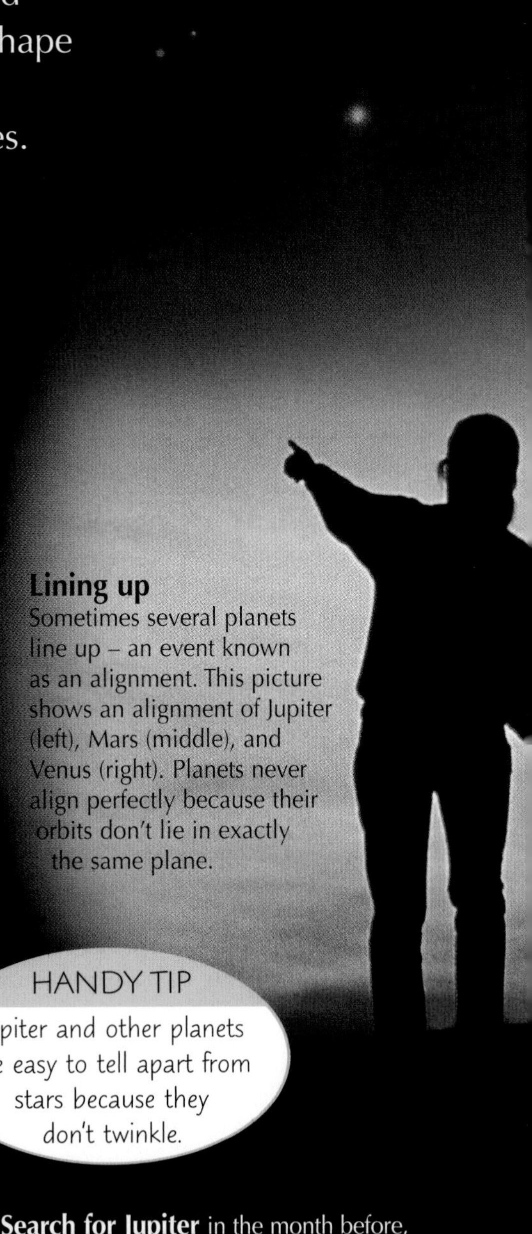

Lining up
Sometimes several planets line up – an event known as an alignment. This picture shows an alignment of Jupiter (left), Mars (middle), and Venus (right). Planets never align perfectly because their orbits don't lie in exactly the same plane.

1 **Find out** when Jupiter is at opposition – that is, when Jupiter's orbit brings it closest to Earth and on exactly the opposite side of Earth from the Sun, making Jupiter visible all night. You can see Jupiter easily for weeks before, and after, opposition. In the period after opposition, Jupiter is high in the evening sky, so it's easy to see without staying up late.

Dates when Jupiter is at opposition	Constellation it appears in
21 September 2010	Pisces
29 October 2011	Aries
3 December 2012	Taurus
5 January 2014	Gemini
6 February 2015	Cancer
8 March 2016	Leo
7 April 2017	Virgo
9 May 2018	Libra
10 June 2019	Ophiuchus

HANDY TIP
Jupiter and other planets are easy to tell apart from stars because they don't twinkle.

2 **Search for Jupiter** in the month before, or after, opposition. Go out on a clear night and use a compass to face south if you live in the Northern Hemisphere, or north if you live in the Southern Hemisphere. Using a planisphere, locate the constellation listed in the table on the left, then look in that constellation for an unusually bright and yellowish "star" that doesn't twinkle – that's Jupiter.

WHAT YOU WILL NEED

- Compass
- Planisphere
- Binoculars

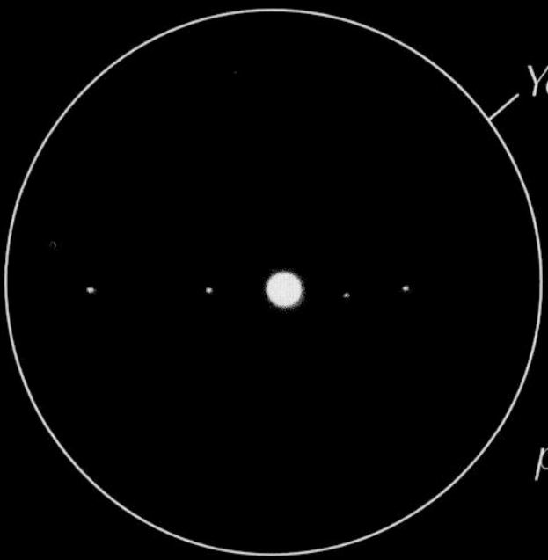

You can see the four largest moons via binoculars as pinpricks of light. Look again on a different night to see how their patterns change

3 **Look at Jupiter** with binoculars. Rest your elbows on a firm surface to steady your view. Can you see Jupiter's four largest moons? If any are missing, they may be in front of, or behind, Jupiter.

FOUR OF A KIND

At least 60 moons orbit Jupiter, trapped in the massive planet's powerful gravity. Many are captured asteroids, but several are so big that we'd call them planets if they orbited the Sun. The four largest are called the Galilean moons, after the Italian astronomer Galileo. Their order from Jupiter is Io, Europa, Ganymede, then Callisto, and the closer they are to Jupiter, the more active they are. Below they are shown in order of size, smallest first.

Europa ▶
Sheets of ice cover this moon, but there may be an ocean of liquid water deep beneath. Some scientists think primitive life forms might live in this hidden ocean.

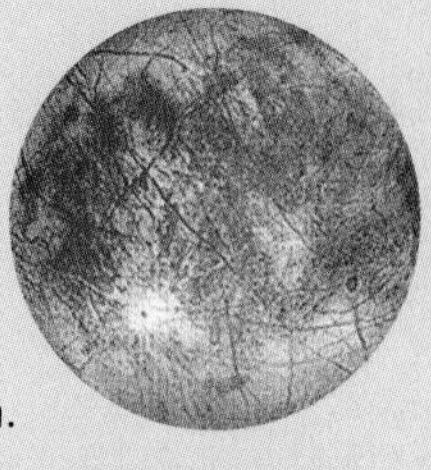

Io ▶
The most volcanically active object in the solar system, Io has more than 100 volcanoes spewing sulphur and gas far out into space. The volcanic activity leads to changes in Io's surface colour.

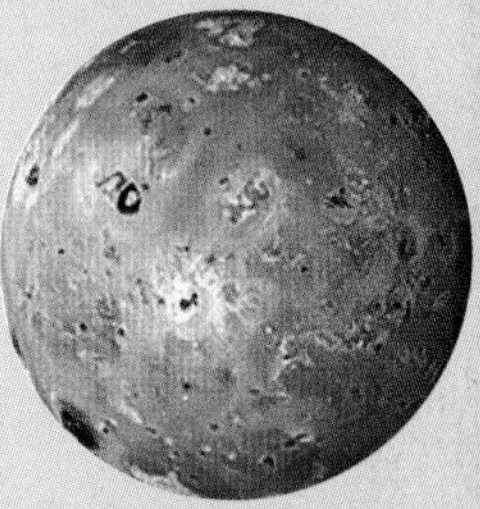

Callisto ▶
Billions of years ago, meteorites rained down on this moon and peppered its surface with craters. Since then, Callisto seems to have barely changed. Like Europa, this moon may have a subsurface ocean, but the evidence for this is uncertain.

Ganymede ▶
The largest Galilean moon is Ganymede. This world is a mixture of rock and ice, with white scars where swirling forces inside the moon have cracked the surface. Ganymede has mountains, valleys, and solidified lava flows.

Stormy weather

Gigantic Jupiter is the largest planet of all – more than twice the weight of all the other planets combined. It is a colossal ball of liquid covered with swirling gases. Its ferocious winds and storms stir the gases into colourful stripes and whirlpools. You can create a very similar effect with milk and food colouring.

WHAT YOU WILL NEED

- Large bowl
- Full-fat milk
- Teaspoon
- Red and yellow food colouring
- Washing-up liquid

Spots and stripes

In Jupiter's freezing upper atmosphere, the gases have condensed into stripy clouds coloured by a cocktail of chemicals. Spots and ovals are storms. Jupiter's Great Red Spot is a hurricane twice the size of Earth that has been raging for 300 years.

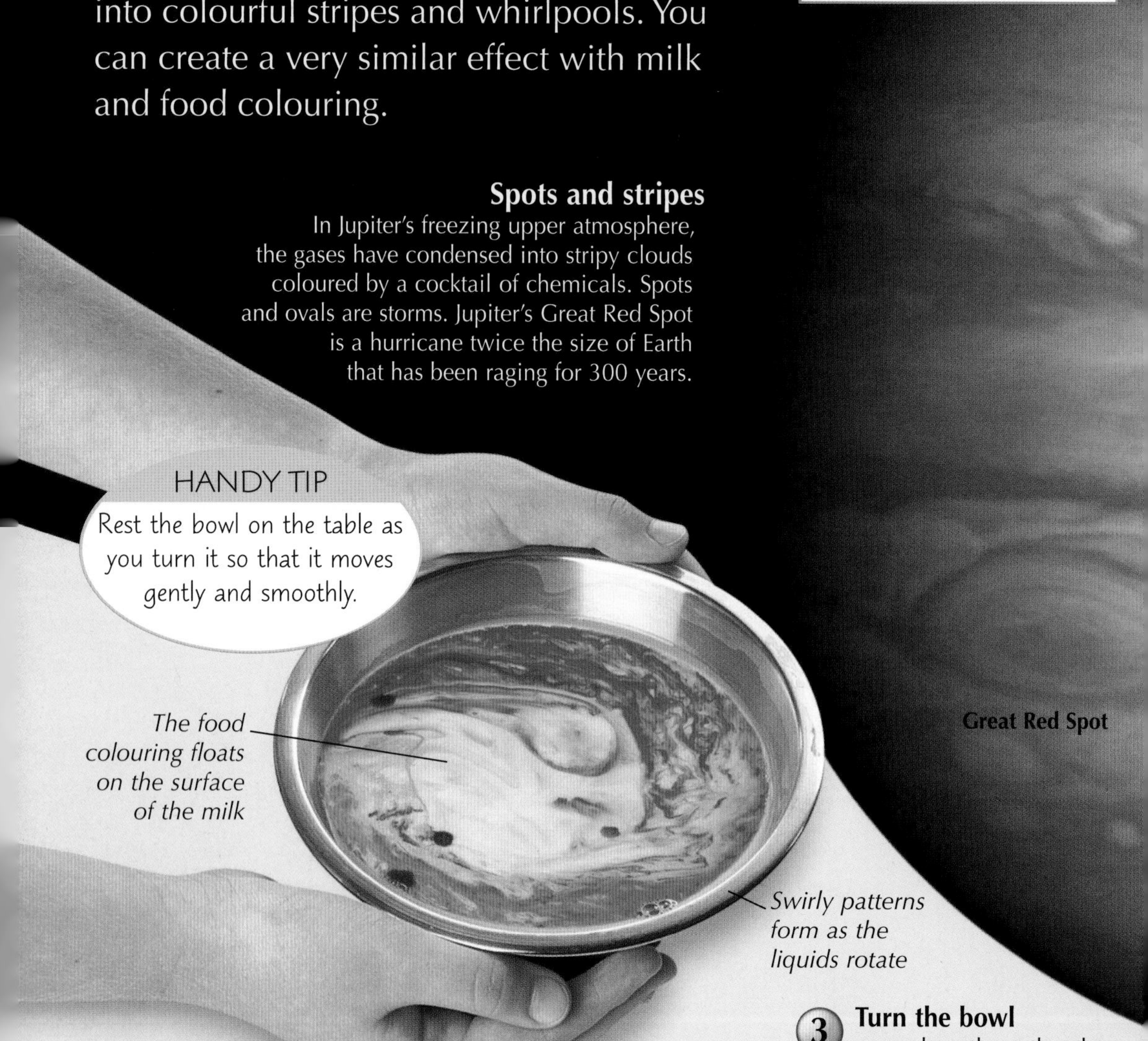
Great Red Spot
The food colouring floats on the surface of the milk
Swirly patterns form as the liquids rotate

HANDY TIP

Rest the bowl on the table as you turn it so that it moves gently and smoothly.

1 Carefully pour half a mug of full-fat milk into a large mixing bowl. Pour it down the side of the bowl so it doesn't splash and form bubbles on the surface. Let it stand for a minute until the milk is still.

2 With great care, use a teaspoon to add a big drop of each food colouring to the surface of the milk. Do this by touching the milk gently with the spoon, and don't stir.

3 Turn the bowl around gently so that the milk and food colouring start to swirl, like the coloured clouds in Jupiter's storms. It takes some practice to get a really good storm. Experiment with different amounts of food colouring, and take care not to swirl the bowl too quickly.

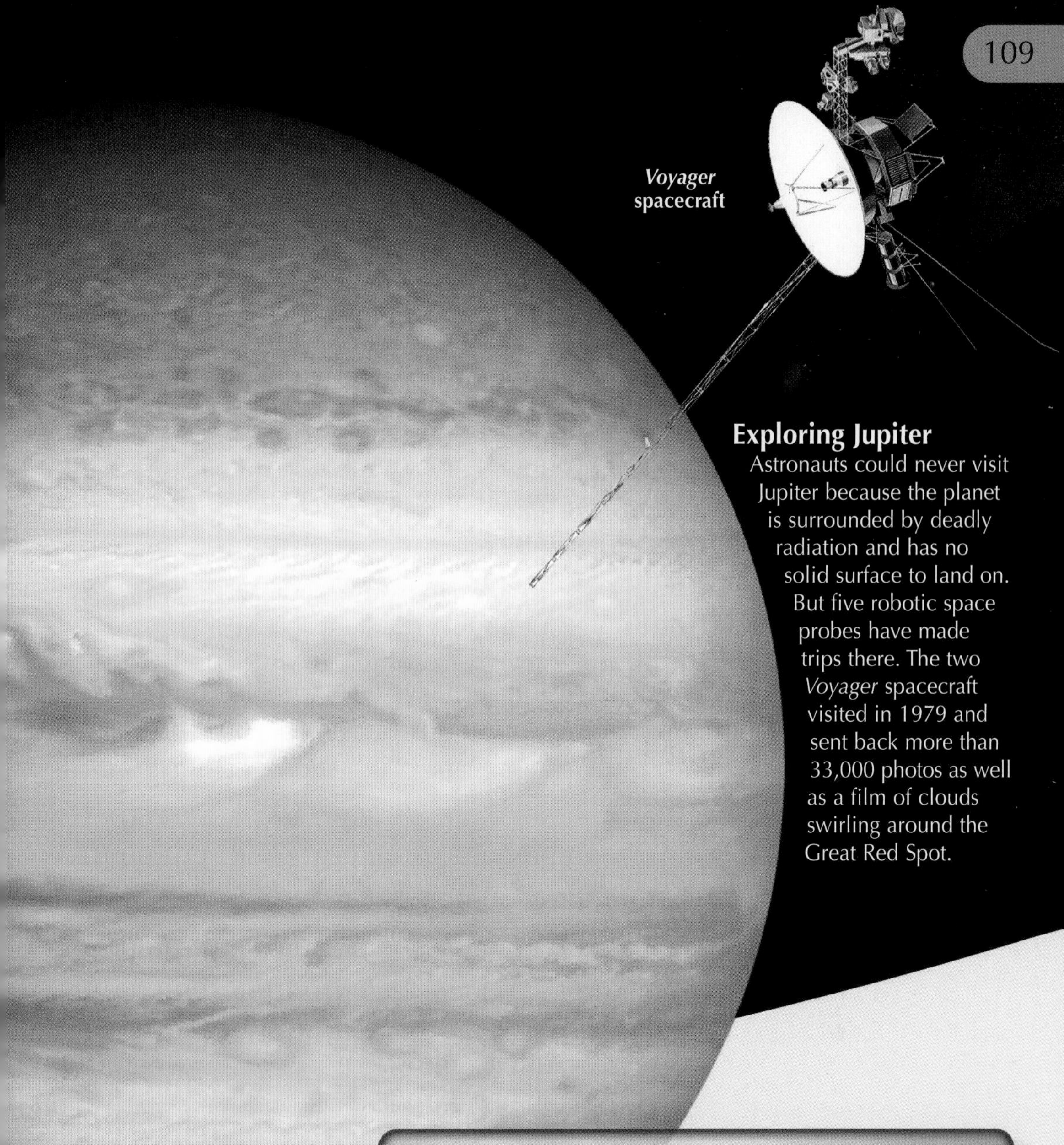

Exploring Jupiter

Astronauts could never visit Jupiter because the planet is surrounded by deadly radiation and has no solid surface to land on. But five robotic space probes have made trips there. The two *Voyager* spacecraft visited in 1979 and sent back more than 33,000 photos as well as a film of clouds swirling around the Great Red Spot.

SUICIDE PROBE

In 1995, a coffee-table-sized package parachuted into Jupiter's clouds to study the planet's stormy weather. The *Galileo* probe hit Jupiter at 185,000 kph (115,000 mph) but soon slowed down in the thick air. Its canopy opened, and the probe spent nearly an hour measuring the wind and analysing chemicals before heat destroyed it.

◂ **The *Galileo* probe**

4 **To kick up** a really violent storm, add a single drop of washing-up liquid. This will disperse the colours quickly by helping the food colouring dissolve.

Shooting stars

When specks of rock debris hit Earth's atmosphere and burn up, they make streaks of light called shooting stars. You can see shooting stars every clear night, but they are more common at certain times of year when they fall in meteor showers. Most shooting stars are caused by debris the size of sand, but occasional apple-sized rocks produce fantastic fireballs with long tails.

1 **Choose a clear, moonless night** and a dark location far from city lights to see the most shooting stars. It's best to watch after midnight, when Earth's night-side faces incoming space debris head-on, producing faster and brighter shooting stars. You should see a shooting star about every 15 minutes or so.

2 **Take a folding camping chair** and make sure you're comfortable. The two biggest challenges for a shooting-star spotter are cold and patience. To keep you occupied, use a constellation guide and try to identify as many constellations as possible. To keep you warm while you're waiting, wear lots of clothes and take a sleeping bag.

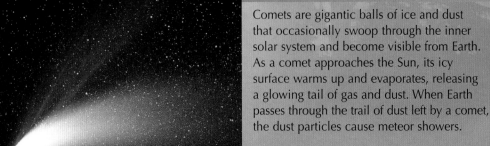

SPECTACULAR COMETS

Comets are gigantic balls of ice and dust that occasionally swoop through the inner solar system and become visible from Earth. As a comet approaches the Sun, its icy surface warms up and evaporates, releasing a glowing tail of gas and dust. When Earth passes through the trail of dust left by a comet, the dust particles cause meteor showers.

◄ **A comet's tails**
Comet Hale-Bopp passed Earth in 1997 with a blue and a white tail. The tails of a comet point away from the Sun, whichever way it flies.

WHAT YOU WILL NEED

- Folding chair or recliner
- Warm clothes
- Sleeping bag
- Notebook
- Pen

Never go out alone at night – ask an adult to come.

METEOR SHOWERS

A shower of meteors

During a meteor shower you might see dozens of shooting stars an hour. On rare occasions, the rate goes up to thousands an hour – a meteor storm. Meteor showers happen at the same time each year, when Earth's orbit crosses the dust trail of a comet. The paths of the meteors are in fact parallel, but appear to radiate out from a single point because of their position and distance from Earth.

Warm clothes are essential when you're watching shooting stars, even in summer

HANDY TIP

A fully reclining lounger makes it even more comfortable to skywatch for long periods.

3 **During a meteor shower**, shooting stars all appear to come from the same point in the sky – the radiant. Most meteor showers are named after the constellation in which the radiant is located. Make a note of the size and colour of each shooting star.

2 FIND THE NORTH OR SOUTH CELESTIAL POLE AND LEARN TO USE THE STARS AS A COMPASS

Compass stars

Stars appear to rotate around the night sky because Earth is spinning round. But there are two points that never move – the north and south celestial poles. These are always at the same points in the sky, due north and due south. Once you know how to find a celestial pole, you can use it as a compass to find your way.

Star trails

If you take a long-exposure photograph of the night sky, the stars' movement across it will create circles of light called star trails. As well as showing the apparent movement of stars (actually caused by Earth's rotation), star trails reveal the stars' different colours. The central star in this picture is Polaris (the Pole Star), which is about 1° away from the true celestial pole, so it makes a short but bright streak.

FIND THE NORTH CELESTIAL POLE

If you live in the Northern Hemisphere, you can see the north celestial pole, but not the southern one. Finding the north celestial pole is fairly easy because there's a star that almost exactly marks the spot – the Pole Star, Polaris.

1 **To find Polaris**, first locate the Plough – one of the brightest groups of stars to see. It's always visible in the Northern Hemisphere (if you live at latitude 40° or more), though it's much lower in the night sky in autumn than in spring, when it's overhead at midnight.

2 **Draw an imaginary line** from the Plough between the last two stars – the Pointers – and extend it five times the distance between the stars to take you to Polaris. Measuring three hand-widths from the Pointers will also take you to Polaris. If you face Polaris (due north), you can work out all directions.

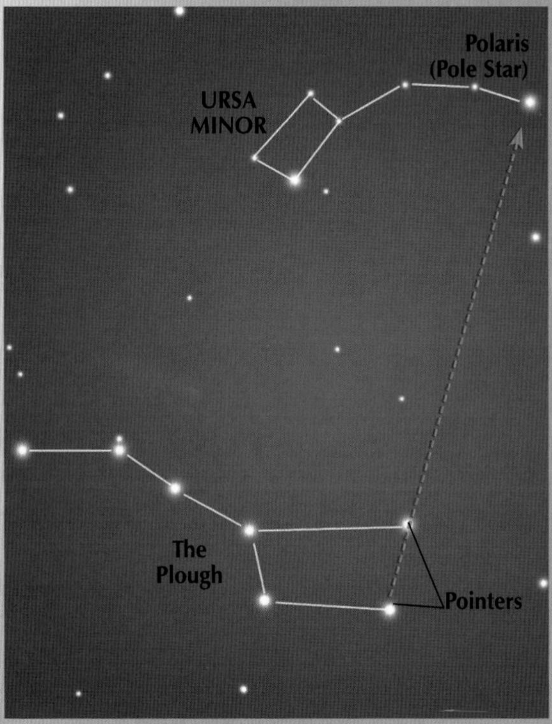

FIND THE SOUTH CELESTIAL POLE

For people who live in the Southern Hemisphere, the south celestial pole is always above the horizon at the same point, due south. However, it's trickier to find than the north celestial pole because there are no stars in it – it's just a blank area of sky.

1 **First**, locate the Southern Cross – a distinctive constellation in the southern sky. Like the Plough, the Southern Cross is visible throughout the year because it's quite close to the pole. The easiest way to find it is to look for two exceptionally bright stars nearby, called the Southern Pointers, which point to the Southern Cross.

2 **Draw an imaginary line** from the base of the Southern Cross (the star Acrux). Extend it by about five times the height of the cross, or three hand-widths, to take you to the south celestial pole. You could also imagine a straight line at right angles to the Pointers. The pole lies where this line intersects the line from the cross.

Northern star-hopping

If you live in the Northern Hemisphere, you can use the Plough and Polaris (the Pole Star) as stepping stones to find other stars. Try finding some of the constellations near Polaris, which are in the sky all year round. You will need a clear, dark night to see them all, as some are faint.

1 **First**, find the Plough and locate the Pointers – the last two stars in the Plough. Draw an imaginary line **(a)** from the Pointers and extend it to the Pole Star, Polaris. Polaris is part of the faint constellation Ursa Minor, which you can see only on clear, dark nights.

2 **Extend the line** a little way past Polaris to find the faint constellation Cepheus, which looks like a lopsided house. If you have binoculars, sweep the area around the base of the "house". You'll see a very red star – the Garnet Star. This is the reddest star visible to the naked eye and the largest star yet discovered.

3 **Draw a new line (b)** to Polaris from the third star in the Plough's handle, and then onwards to a bright constellation that looks like a flattened letter W. This is Cassiopeia.

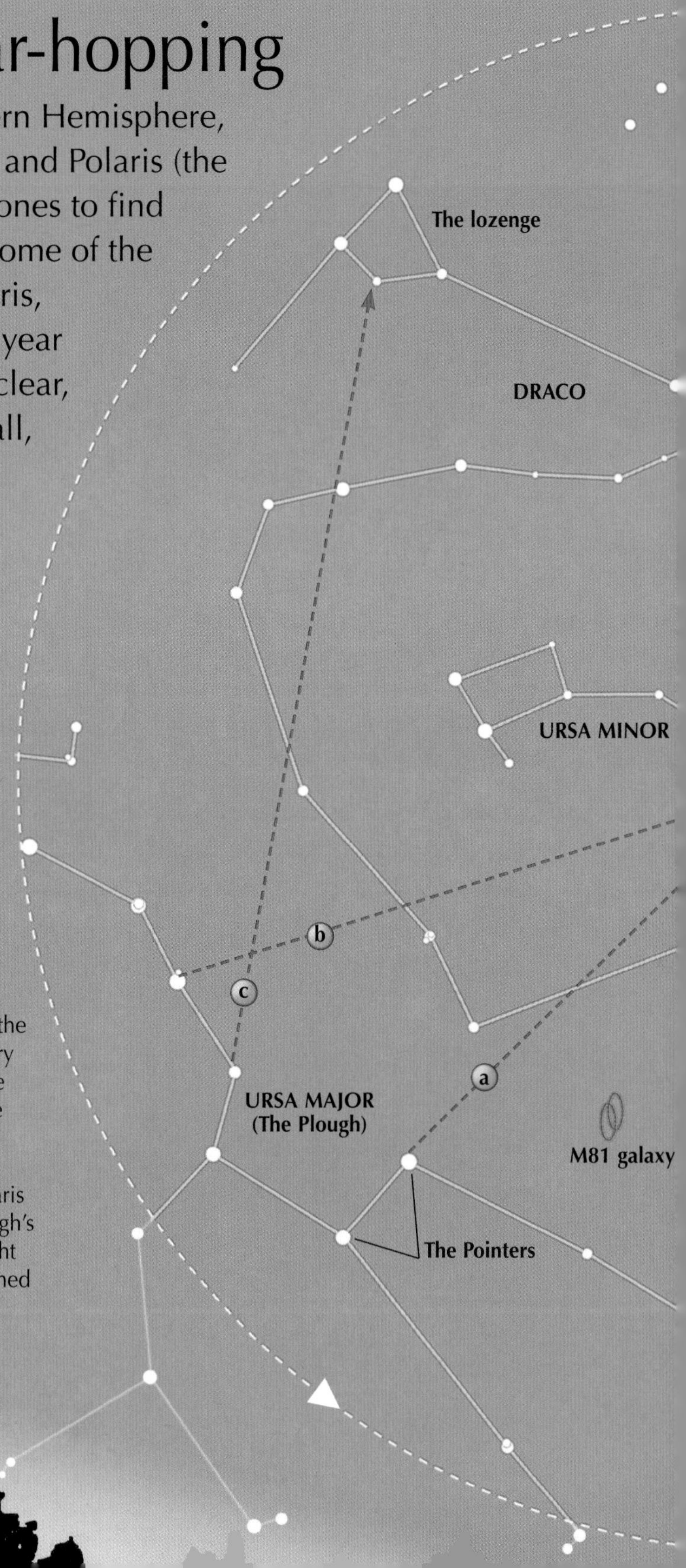

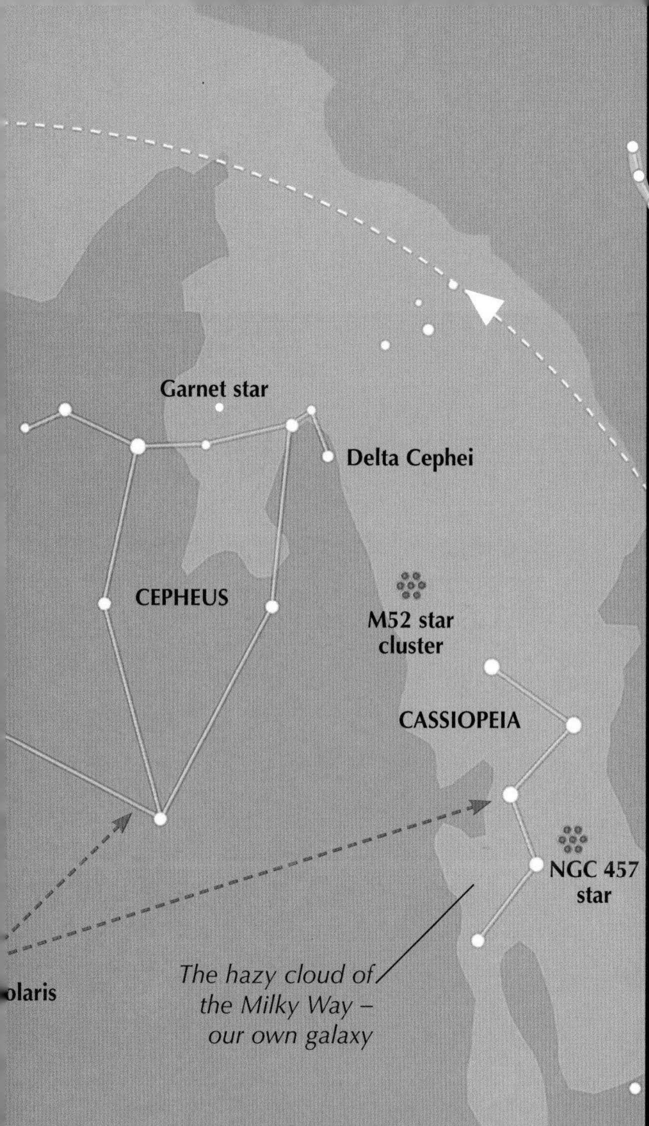

4 **The next constellation** is faint and tricky to see, so look for it only if the sky is very dark. Draw a line **(c)** starting from the fourth star in the Plough's handle (as shown) to a long, winding constellation called Draco. Four stars make up the dragon's head – a pattern of stars called the lozenge.

5 **Use some binoculars** to try to find a galaxy. Return to the area around the Plough and look for a pair of tiny fuzzy patches (shown here by two brown ovals). These are galaxies. The brighter one is a beautiful spiral galaxy called M81.

POLAR CONSTELLATIONS

◄ Ursa Minor
Also known as the Little Bear, this faint constellation looks like a miniature version of the Plough. Its brightest star is Polaris, which has been used for centuries as an aid to navigation. Sailors used to call Polaris Stella Maris, which means "star of the sea".

Ursa Major ►
The seven stars of the Plough make up the tail and rump of the Great Bear, or Ursa Major as it's officially known. One of its most interesting stars is the second star along the handle of the Plough. If you look closely and have sharp eyes, you will see it's actually a double star.

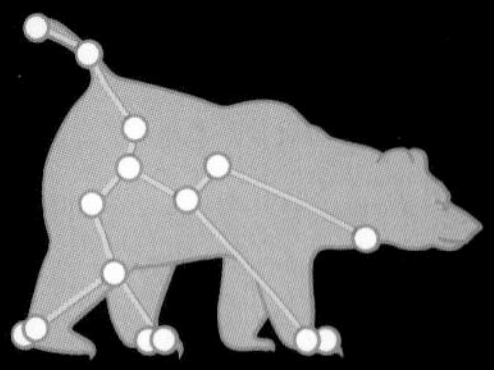

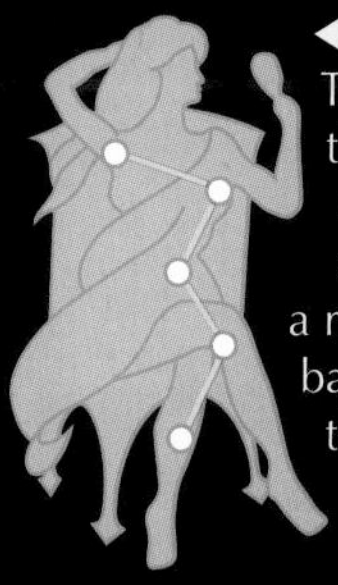

◄ Cassiopeia
The ancient Greeks named this constellation after a vain queen, and pictured her on a throne, admiring herself in a mirror. Cassiopeia lies in the band of the Milky Way. Sweep this area with binoculars to see if you can see several star clusters around it.

Cepheus ►
In Greek mythology, Cepheus was married to Cassiopeia. An interesting star in this constellation is Delta Cephei, which is a variable star. Variable stars pulse in size and brightness. Delta Cephei has a five-day cycle so you can watch it change with binoculars over successive nights.

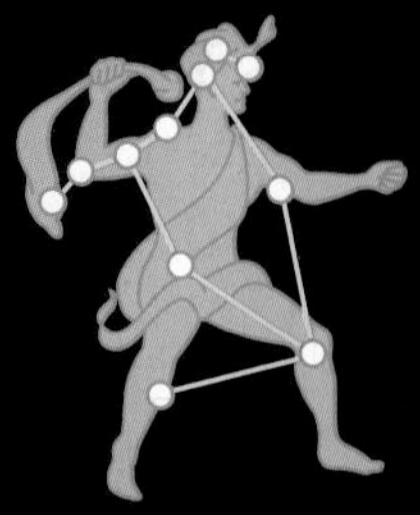

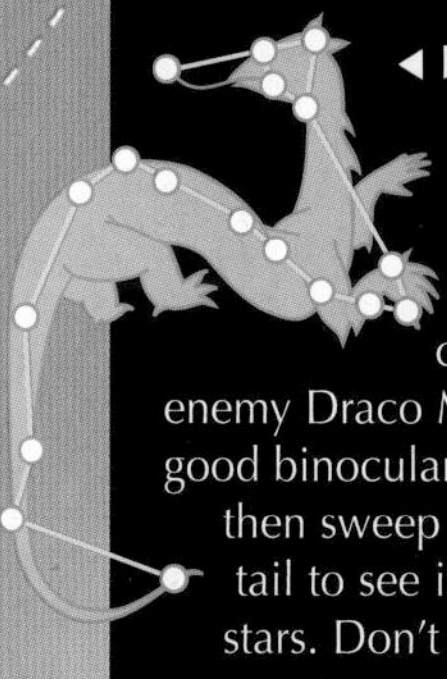

◄ Draco
Draco means "dragon" – an apt name for a constellation that snakes across the night sky. The name was also chosen for Harry Potter's arch enemy Draco Malfoy. If you've got some good binoculars and a clear, dark night, then sweep the area along the dragon's tail to see if you can find any double stars. Don't worry if you can't make any out, as many stars in Draco are quite faint.

Southern star-hopping

Stargazers who live in the Southern Hemisphere don't have the advantage of a pole star to help them hop around the night sky. But, they can see far more bright stars in the polar region, as well as colourful nebulas, galaxies, and star-packed parts of our own galaxy – the Milky Way. Crux and the Southern Pointers are the starting points for a hop around the southern sky.

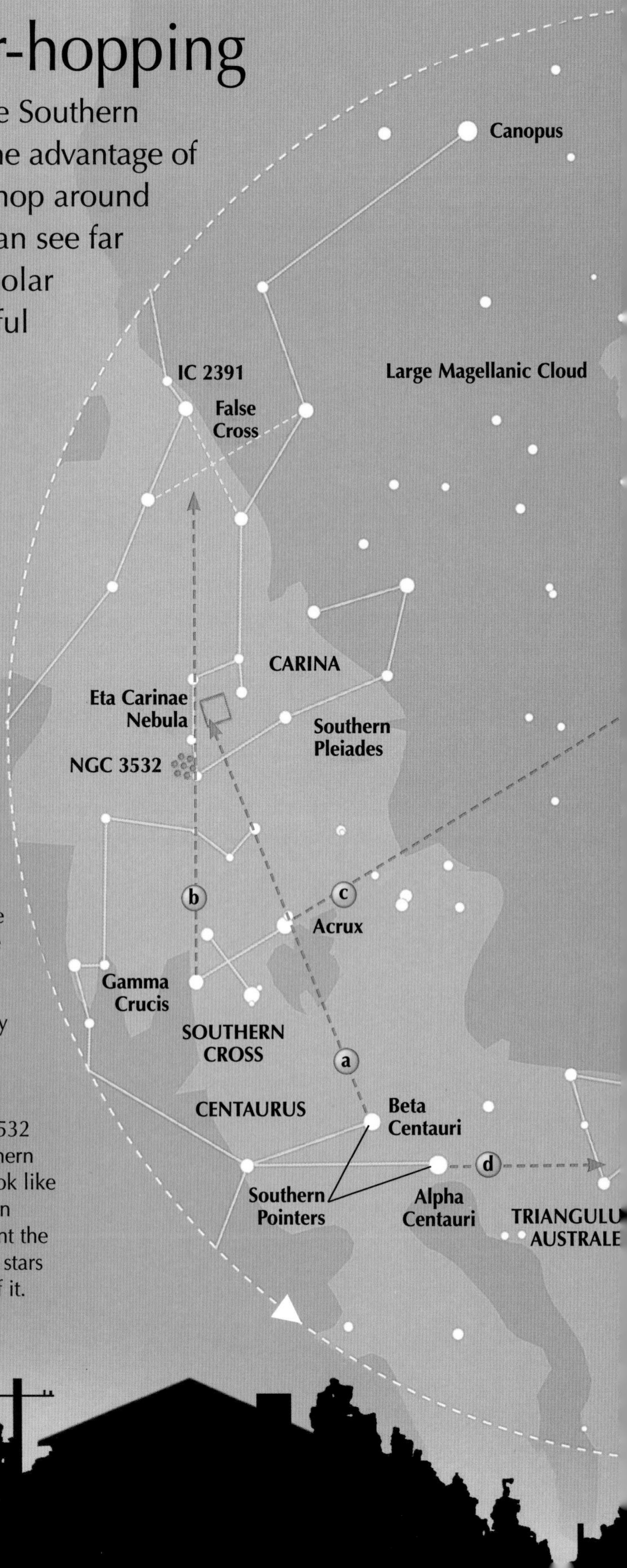

1 **First**, locate the Southern Cross and Southern Pointers (Alpha and Beta Centauri). Draw a line **(a)** from Beta Centauri through the bottom of the Southern Cross and extend it by the same distance again. You'll reach a red cloud in the constellation Carina – the Eta Carinae Nebula (shown as a red square). Take a closer look at this fabulous sight with binoculars. Deep inside is a massive star (Eta Carinae) that is likely to explode in the distant future.

2 **Close to the nebula** are two beautiful star clusters – NGC 3532 (shown as orange dots) and the Southern Pleiades. Through binoculars they look like sparkling jewels. Look at the Southern Pleiades without binoculars and count the stars. You'll find you can count more stars when you look slightly to one side of it.

3 **Now, draw a line (b)** from the top of the Southern Cross, past the Eta Carinae nebula, and onwards by the same distance again. This takes you to what looks like another cross – the false cross, which often confuses stargazers. Just beyond it is star cluster IC 2391 that's worthy of closer inspection with binoculars.

4 **Draw the next line (c)**, continuing the long bar of the Southern Cross straight out across the empty part of the sky to a small, fuzzy cloud – the Small Magellanic Cloud. This cloud is a small galaxy, 200,000 light-years from Earth. Through binoculars, you can see nebulas and star clusters within it. Close by is the second-best globular cluster (a dense ball of very ancient stars) in the night sky, called 47 Tucanae.

5 **Finally**, return to the Southern Pointers and draw a line **(d)** from Alpha Centauri to discover three bright stars in a triangle shape. This is the constellation Triangulum Australe.

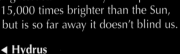

POLAR CONSTELLATIONS

Southern Cross (Crux) ▶

The Southern Cross is in the main band of the Milky Way. Near its base is a dark patch in the Milky Way – a dust cloud called the Coalsack. The foot of the Cross is the star Acrux (in fact, a double star). The top is a red giant called Gamma Crucis.

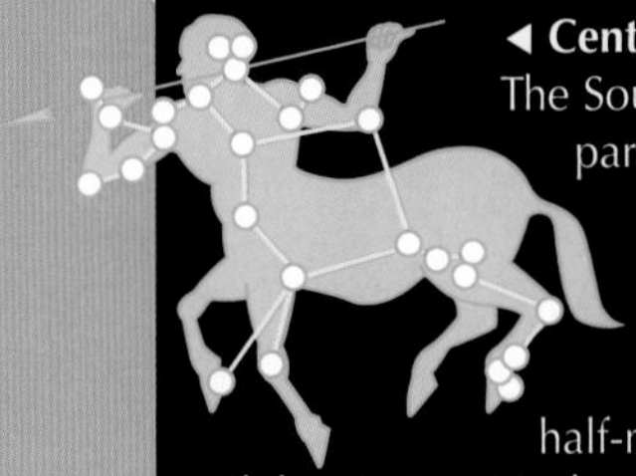

◀ Centaurus

The Southern Pointers are part of the constellation Centaurus, which is said to resemble a mythical beast called a centaur, a creature half-man and half-horse. Alpha Centauri is the third-brightest star in the sky and the nearest star that's visible to the naked eye, at only 4.4 light-years away from Earth.

Carina ▶

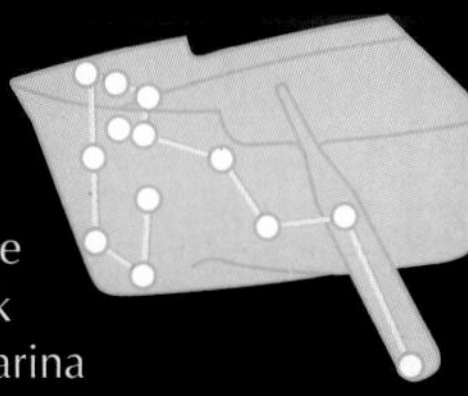

The constellation Carina contains the brightest nebula in the night sky (the Eta Carinae Nebula). From the Greek for the keel of a boat, Carina stretches across to brilliant Canopus, the second-brightest star in the sky. Canopus is 15,000 times brighter than the Sun, but is so far away it doesn't blind us.

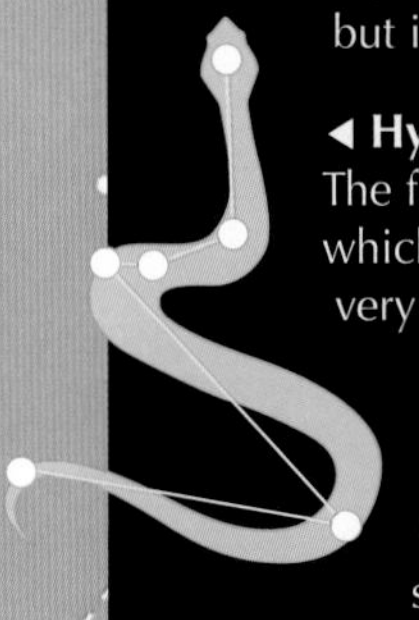

◀ Hydrus

The faint constellation Hydrus – which means "water snake" – is very close to the Small Magellanic Cloud. Like many southern constellations, Hydrus was named relatively recently by European explorers when they sailed the southern seas. With good binoculars, you can see a pair of red giant stars in the middle of Hydrus.

Triangulum Australe ▶

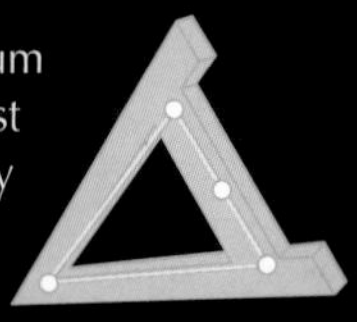

The three bright stars of Triangulum Australe stand out strongly against the hazy background of the Milky Way, in which this constellation lies. Triangulum Australe – or Southern Triangle – was named by European explorers in the sixteenth century. Sweep the area around it with binoculars to see if you can find the star cluster NGC 6025.

A star is born

New stars are born inside vast gas clouds called nebulas, that lie between the stars. One of the most spectacular nebulas you can see is the Orion Nebula, which is visible from the Northern and the Southern Hemispheres.

1 **The best time to see** the Orion Nebula, which is in the constellation of Orion, is from December to February, when it's high in the night sky. If you live in the Northern Hemisphere, look south. If you live in the Southern Hemisphere, look north.

2 **When you've spotted** the distinctive shape of Orion, look for the three stars that make up Orion's "belt". Hanging from the belt is Orion's "sword", in the middle of which is the Orion Nebula. You can see the nebula with the naked eye, but binoculars will reveal more detail. Deep inside this cloud, new stars are forming. Photographs of the Orion Nebula reveal glorious colours. Unfortunately, you can't see these colours with the naked eye or binoculars.

3 **Look again at the star** in the centre of the Orion Nebula. With the naked eye you can see one star, but with binoculars you might see two. In fact, there's a group of at least four newly formed stars called the Trapezium, named after their shape, right in the heart of the nebula. The energy emitted by these new stars is making the gas in the nebula glow.

Orion the Hunter
Orion is named after a hunter in Greek myths. Southern Hemisphere viewers see the hunter upside-down, with his feet at the top and shoulders at the bottom.

Horsehead Nebula

4 **If you had** a powerful telescope, you could search for another interesting nebula in Orion, shown in the picture above. It's called the Horsehead Nebula, because of its shape. It is actually a dark cloud of dust silhouetted against the red gas cloud behind it. The Horsehead Nebula is just below Alnitak, the left star in Orion's belt.

STARBIRTH NEBULAS

Stars form when the force of gravity makes pockets of gas in nebulas shrink. Exactly the same process gave birth to our Sun. The gas in most starbirth nebulas is too faint to see, even with binoculars. However, cameras can capture the hazy colours with breathtaking results.

North America Nebula ▶
This strange nebula in the constellation Cygnus looks like a map of North America, complete with its own Gulf of Mexico. The nebula is lit up by the newly formed stars within it.

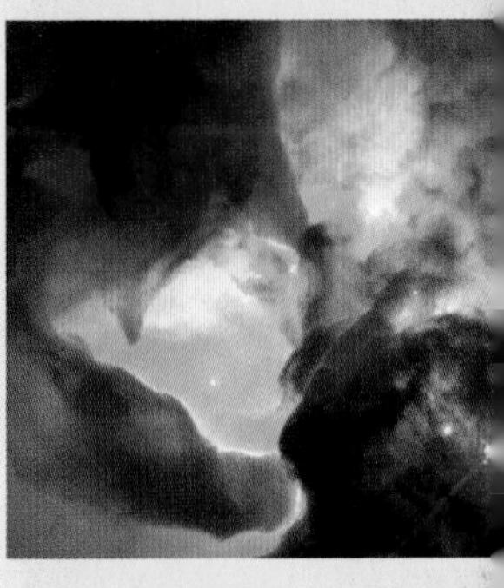

Lagoon Nebula ▶
The Lagoon Nebula is in the constellation Sagittarius and is easy to see with the naked eye or via binoculars. This close-up image from the Hubble Telescope shows twisted columns of gas and a new star.

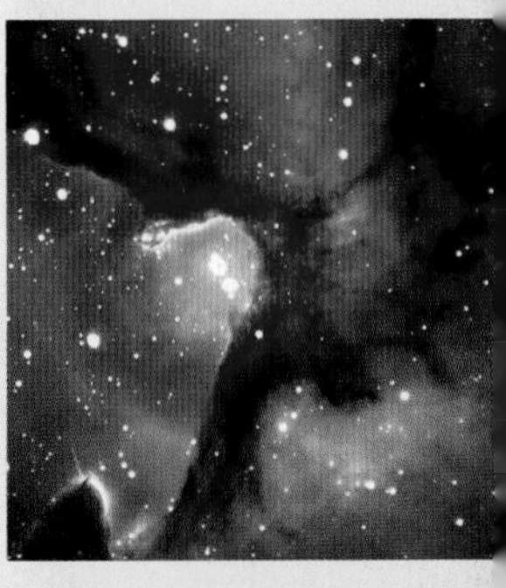

Trifid Nebula ▶
This nebula is also in Sagittarius. You can just see it with binoculars, but you need a good telescope to see any level of detail. The dark bands crossing the nebula are lanes of dust that block the light.

Columns in the Eagle Nebula ▶
These colossal pillars of hydrogen gas were also photographed by the Hubble Telescope. New stars are forming in the "fingers" of gas at the top of the biggest pillar. The fingers are bigger than our solar system.

Find the Seven Sisters

The Seven Sisters is the common name for a star cluster called the Pleiades. Oddly, nobody actually sees seven stars in the Pleiades – most people see six. Good eyesight, or binoculars, actually reveals more than seven.

When to look

If you live in the Northern Hemisphere, the best time to see the Pleiades is in autumn or winter. For southerners, the best views are in spring and summer. The cluster reaches its highest point in the sky at midnight in November. The image (right) is a highly magnified view.

WHAT YOU WILL NEED

- No equipment essential, but binoculars and a planisphere are useful

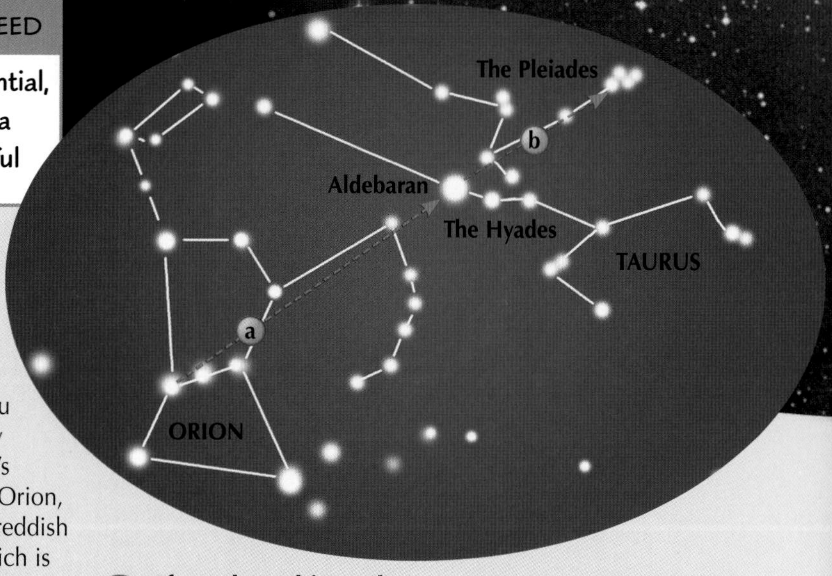

1 **First**, locate Orion and its belt. (To find out more about Orion, look on pages 118–119). In the Northern Hemisphere, you should draw an imaginary line **(a)** up through Orion's belt, past the shoulder of Orion, and onwards to a bright, reddish star called Aldebaran, which is part of the constellation Taurus. If you live in the Southern Hemisphere, where Orion is upside-down, draw the line down from his belt and then on to Aldebaran.

2 **If you have binoculars,** take a close look at Aldebaran, a red giant star that varies slightly in brightness. (Find out about red giants on pages 122–123.) Next to Aldebaran, you can see an open star cluster (see box right) called the Hyades.

3 **Now, hop beyond** Aldebaran, travelling away from Orion in roughly the same direction but for a slightly shorter distance **(b)**. You'll come to the Pleiades star cluster – one of the most beautiful sights in the night sky.

The starlight from the Pleiades takes about 400 years to reach Earth

HANDY TIP

Do not look for faint objects when the Moon is full, because its light is too bright.

4 **Take a good look** at the Pleiades with the naked eye. How many stars can you count? If you have binoculars, look again. Can you count more? There are actually more than 3,000 stars in the Pleiades. At only 78 million years old, these stars are babies in astronomical terms and wouldn't have been in the night sky during the age of the dinosaurs. With a powerful telescope you can see a blue haze around the stars, which is a dust cloud through which the stars are currently passing.

STAR CLUSTERS

Double star cluster in LMC NGC 1850

Tightly packed groups of stars are called star clusters and there are two main types. Open clusters, such as the Hyades and the Pleiades, are loose groups of young, hot stars that glow with a bluish brilliance. Globular clusters, on the other hand, are dense balls of hundreds of thousands of very ancient stars. Unlike open clusters, which lie within the Milky Way galaxy, globular clusters are often above or below the galaxy's plane. One of the most spectacular is Omega Centauri in the constellation Centaurus, which is visible from the Southern Hemisphere. The most impressive globular cluster visible to northern viewers is the Hercules Cluster, in the Hercules constellation.

Going, going, gone

All stars eventually run out of energy and die. As they grow older, their surface cools down and turns red. Stars also swell in size with age, becoming red giants and red supergiants. Such stars are easy to spot, and their warm colour is obvious even to the naked eye.

If Betelgeuse blew up

Betelgeuse is a red supergiant in Orion. Astronomers think it's near the end of its life and is about to blow apart in a colossal explosion called a supernova. The artist's impression on the right shows what a Betelgeuse supernova might look like from Earth. For a few weeks, the star would outshine the Moon and cast shadows on Earth.

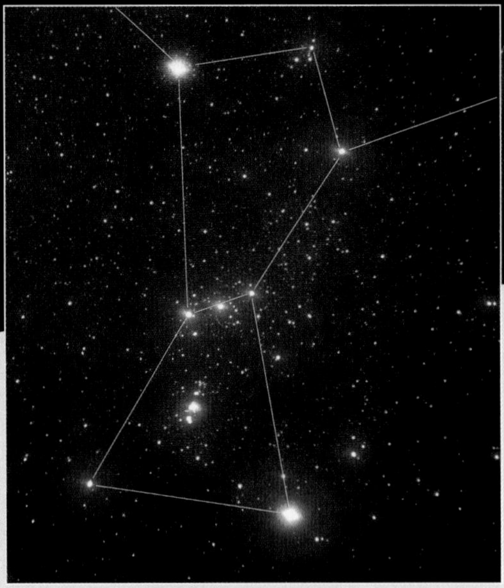

The Orion constellation

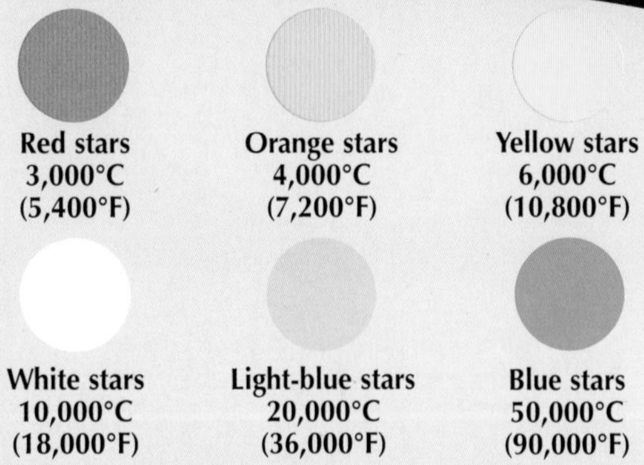

1 **One of the easiest** red supergiants to see is Betelgeuse, on the left shoulder of Orion (as we look at it). Betelgeuse is about 800 times wider than our Sun. Look at Betelgeuse with binoculars and compare its colour to the blue supergiant Rigel – the very bright star in the opposite corner of Orion (the right foot). Blue supergiants form when red supergiants lose some of their outer atmosphere. They can also explode as supernovas.

2 **You can tell** a star's surface temperature from its colour. Blue stars are hottest, red are coolest. Use the guide above to work out the temperature of these stars: Rigel, Vega (the brightest star in Lyra), Arcturus (the brightest star in Boötes), Capella (the brightest star in Auriga), Sirius (the brightest star in Canis Major), and Deneb (the brightest star in Cygnus).

WHEN STARS DIE

What happens when a star dies depends on its weight. Light stars swell into red giants and then throw off their outer layers into space, forming ghostly clouds called planetary nebulas, leaving behind a small star called a white dwarf. Massive stars swell into much bigger red supergiants. When they finally run out of enough energy to resist the awesome inward pull of their own gravity, they collapse in an instant. The collapse creates a devastating shockwave that hurls out the star's outer layers in an explosion brighter than a billion suns, called a supernova. The dense core may then survive as a neutron star. But the most massive cores continue to shrink under their gravity until they are smaller than an atom. The result is a black hole – a gravitational trap from which nothing can escape.

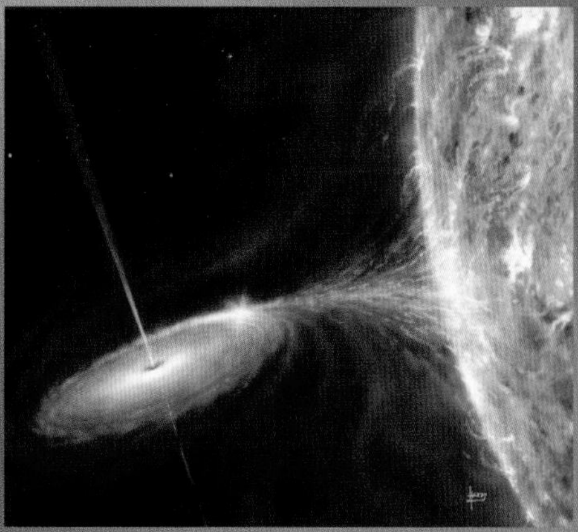

Black holes ▲
This artist's impression shows a black hole (left) sucking in a spinning cloud of matter from a neighbouring blue giant star (right).

The red supergiant Antares (far left)

Awesome Antares

If you live in the Southern Hemisphere, look for the red supergiant Antares, the brightest star in Scorpius. Antares is one of the reddest stars in the sky. It's almost as bright as Betelgeuse and about 1 million kilometres (620,000 miles) wide, making it 700 times wider than the Sun.

Our local galaxy

Almost every star you can see in the night sky belongs to the Milky Way – our local galaxy. The Milky Way is a gargantuan, spinning whirlpool of 200 billion stars, most of which are clustered in the centre, or spread along spiral arms. On dark, clear nights, you can sometimes see it stretching across the sky as a hazy band.

Distorting dust

Dust clouds in some parts of the Milky Way block out the light from the stars beyond, creating dark lanes in our view of the galaxy. In the picture above, dark clouds of dust have mixed with glowing gas clouds, creating a multicoloured spectacle.

From a distance

If you could see the Milky Way from a great distance, it might look like the spiral galaxy NGC 1232. This is because we're inside the Milky Way, so we see it side-on and can't see its spiral shape. If there were no dust clouds in the way, we might get a view like the one below. This image shows the galaxy's flat shape and central bulge, where stars are packed most densely. From side to side, the whole Milky Way measures about 1 billion billion km (600 million billion miles).

Spiral arms curve out from the heart of galaxy NGC 1232

Galaxy NGC 1232

Our solar system is in one of the spiral arms about halfway from the centre

The Milky Way viewed side-on from space

Viewing the Milky Way

To see the Milky Way in all its glory, you need a clear, moonless night, free of light pollution. Parts of the Milky Way are visible for much of the year, but to see the best areas you need to know when and where to look. Northern Hemisphere viewers should look at the constellations Cygnus and Aquila in late summer. In the Southern Hemisphere, you should look at Sagittarius and Scorpius in winter for a stunning view of the galaxy's star-packed centre.

GALAXY IN A CUP

You can make a model of the Milky Way with everyday ingredients, such as coffee and cream. Ask an adult to make a cup of black coffee for you. Stir the coffee quite quickly to make it spin, then gently lower in a spoonful of cream. The cream will form a spinning spiral. In reality, the Milky Way spins in a very different way from cream in a coffee cup. The spiral arms don't rotate as whole objects – they are simply places where stars get temporarily crowded during their journey around the galaxy, like cars passing through a traffic jam.

A home-made spiral galaxy ▸

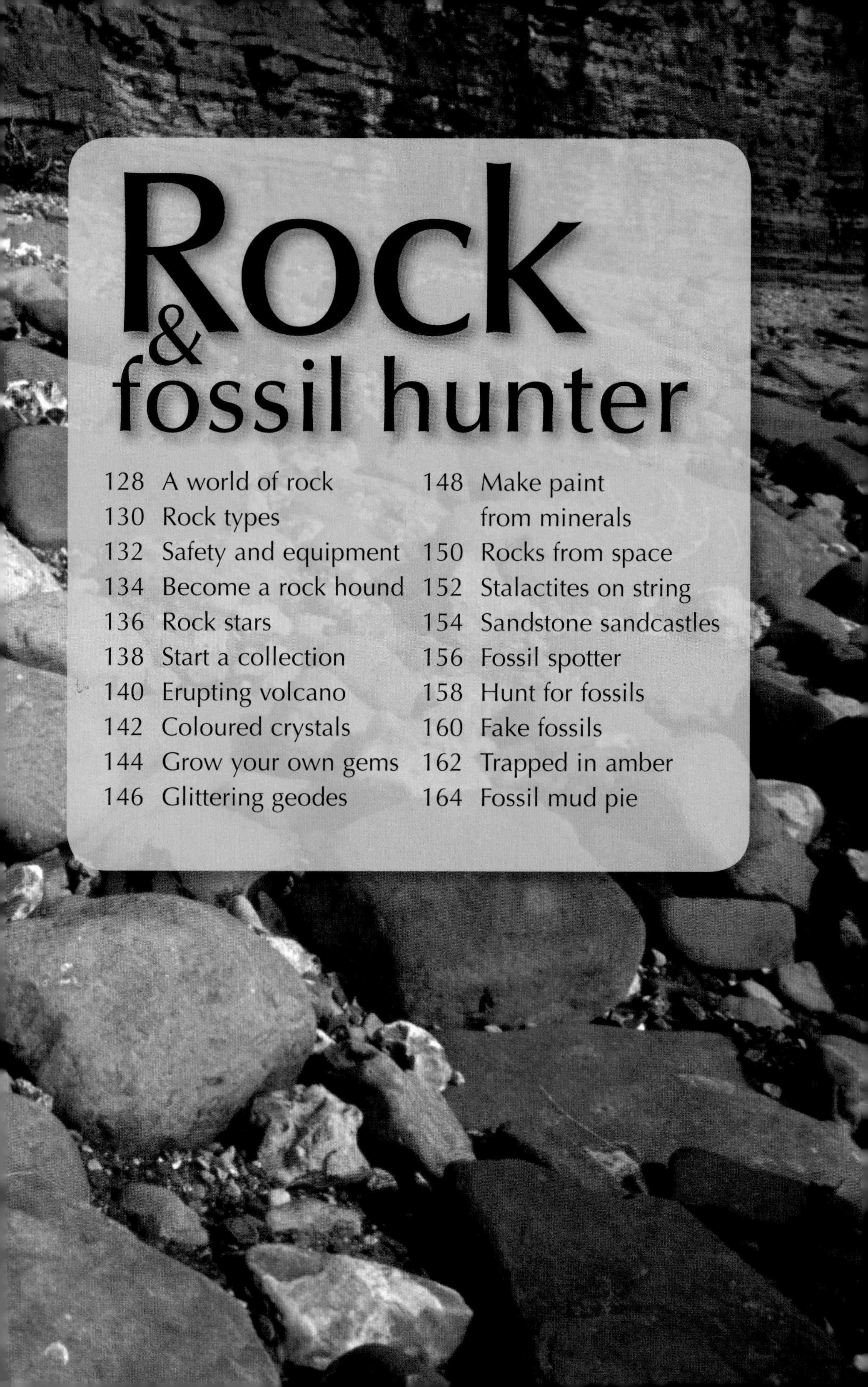

Rock & fossil hunter

A world of rock

Rock is the main ingredient in planet Earth. Nearly everything under your feet is rock. It may be buried out of sight, but it's always there. Rocks are full of surprises and secrets. They give us precious gems, gold, and vital resources like iron and glass. Written into rock is a record of Earth's fascinating history, preserved as fossils.

Giant's Causeway
At Giant's Causeway in Northern Ireland, pillars of rock run like stepping stones into the sea. They formed 60 million years ago when lava solidified into a type of rock called basalt.

This microscope view shows interlocking crystals of the minerals that make up basalt rock

THIRD ROCK FROM THE SUN

After Earth formed 4.5 billion years ago, it became hot and molten. The heaviest materials, such as iron, mostly sank to the centre, while lighter materials, such as rock-forming minerals, floated to the top. As a result, Earth now has a layered structure, like a soft-boiled egg. In the centre is a hot, partly liquid core of iron. Around the core is a deep layer of hot, softish rock (the mantle), and around that is a brittle crust of cold, hardened rock, like an eggshell.

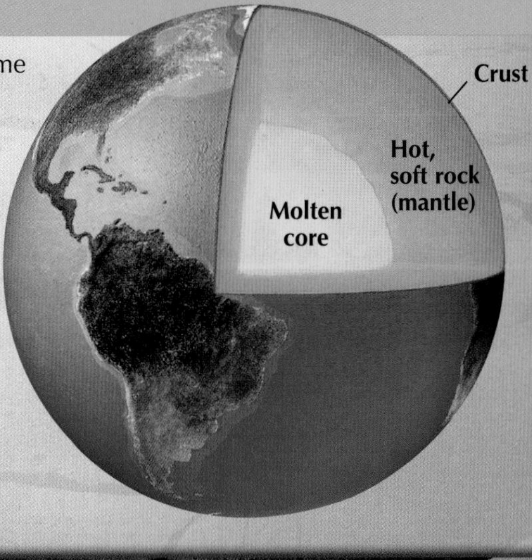

Inside Earth ▶
Planet Earth is a gigantic ball of rock and metal. Most of the metal is in the core, and most of the rock is in the outer layers.

◂ What is rock?

A typical rock is a mixture of solid chemicals called minerals, which are pressed tightly together like jigsaw pieces. If you look closely, you can sometimes see the separate minerals as grains (small crystals) in a rock. Most rocks are hard and brittle, but some crumble into powder when you rub them.

Malachite

What is a mineral? ▴

Minerals are naturally occurring solids that are inorganic (not from living things) and usually made of crystals. Ice is a mineral because it fits this definition. So are the tiny, shiny grains in sand, which consist of the mineral quartz. There are thousands of different minerals, including diamond, gold, and salt. Most rocks are made of a limited range, called the rock-forming minerals.

Tourmaline crystals

What is a crystal? ▴

A crystal is a solid chemical with a regular, geometrical shape. Crystals typically have smooth, flat faces that meet in sharp edges. They often look shiny or glassy. Their shape comes from the regular arrangement of atoms inside the crystal. In many rocks the crystals are too small to see, but they are there, nevertheless, by the thousand. In rare cases, crystals may grow as large as telegraph poles.

***Tyrannosaurus* skull**

What is a fossil? ▸

A fossil is a relic of a living thing that died thousands, or millions, of years ago. Most fossils are remains of creatures that no longer exist, such as dinosaurs. Hard parts of their bodies, like bones, were buried. Over time, minerals replaced these organic materials, turning them into rock. Some fossils are merely impressions, such as footprints.

Rock types

Scientists can classify almost all rocks into one of three main types, depending on how the rocks form. The types are known as igneous rock, sedimentary rock, and metamorphic rock. Over millions of years, each type can slowly change into one of the others in an endless process called the rock cycle.

Pink granite

Basalt

Igneous rock

About 90 per cent of the rock in Earth's crust is igneous. Igneous rock forms when molten rock cools and solidifies. When this happens underground, the molten rock (magma) solidifies slowly, giving crystals time to form. The magma becomes a hard, crystalline rock with large grains, such as granite. Igneous rock can also form on Earth's surface when lava escapes from a volcano. The lava solidifies quickly, especially if it flows into water, as in the picture below. It forms rock with no, or very tiny, visible crystals, such as basalt.

Sandstone

Sedimentary rock

Sand, mud, and even the remains of living organisms can all turn into rock. These sediments settle on the sea floor, building up in layers. Over time, deep layers are compressed by the weight of the sediment on top, and water seeping through the layers deposits minerals that glue the sediment particles together. As a result, the sediment becomes sedimentary rock. Limestone, shale, and sandstone all form this way. The layers are sometimes visible as horizontal bands called strata.

Lava flowing into the sea, Hawaii

Vermilion Cliffs, Utah, USA

The rock cycle

The rock in Earth's crust is continually being destroyed and recycled. Rock on the surface is worn down to fragments and eventually settles to become sedimentary rock. Rock underground is melted to form igneous rock, or squashed and cooked, by the heat of molten rock to form metamorphic rock. Movements in Earth's crust lift underground rock back to the surface.

Rivers wash sediment into the sea
Ice and rain eat away at mountains
Lava builds up into new mountains
Underground rock layers are crushed and folded by pressure
Sediment builds up on the sea floor
Molten rock oozes back to the surface
Heat from molten rock transforms the surrounding rock

Mylonite

Metamorphic rock

Deep underground, rock can be subjected to intense heat and pressure. These forces, while not melting the rock outright, can cause minerals to recrystallize in new forms. The result is a hard, crystalline type of rock called metamorphic rock, which frequently has wavy or stripy patterns. Metamorphic rock often forms in mountainous regions, where Earth's crust is buckling and folding under tremendous pressure. Examples include marble, slate, and mylonite.

THE MOVING CRUST

Although it looks rock solid, Earth's crust is moving. The crust is glued to the mantle below, and the mantle churns slowly about like very thick treacle. As a result, the crust has broken into huge fragments called plates. In some places, molten rock seeps up between the fragments and pushes them apart. In other places, two plates crunch together, and the weaker plate is forced deep underground, where the rock heats up and melts. These movements keep the rock in Earth's crust moving in an endless cycle.

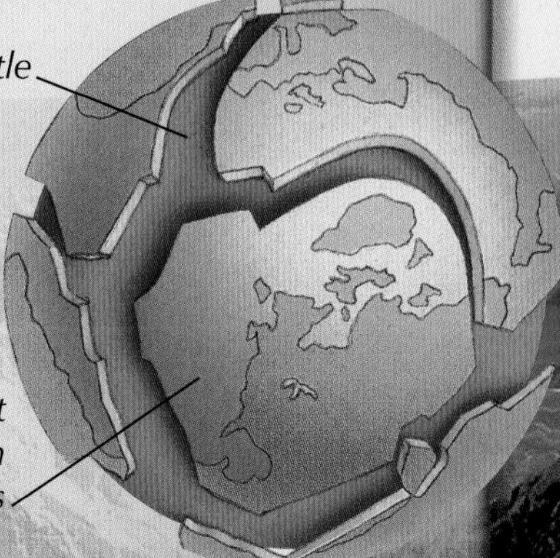
Mantle
Earth's crust is broken into plates

Mount McKinley, Alaska, USA

Safety and equipment

You don't need any special gear to start learning about rocks and fossils, but the equipment on this page may be useful. If you go hunting for rocks and fossils, take the following safety precautions: Wear highly visible clothing and make sure an adult accompanies you; don't climb cliffs or enter working quarries; avoid the base of cliffs after storms. If you visit the coast, check tide times and avoid places that are dangerous when the tide comes in.

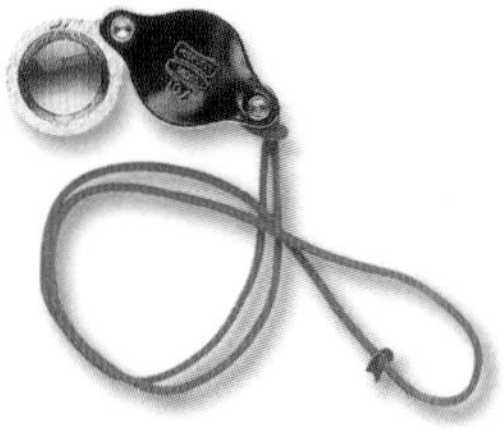

▲ Hand lens
A x10 hand lens helps expert rock collectors to identify their finds by inspecting the grain. It isn't essential for beginners.

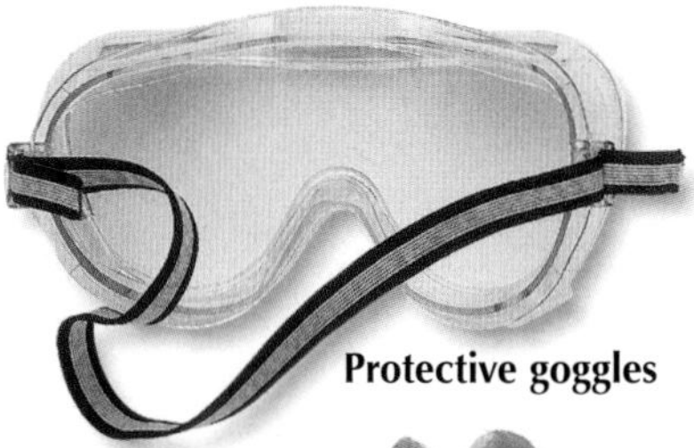

Protective goggles

◀ Boots
Wear stout boots with ankle protection when walking on rough or rocky ground. Wear waterproof boots in wet or muddy places.

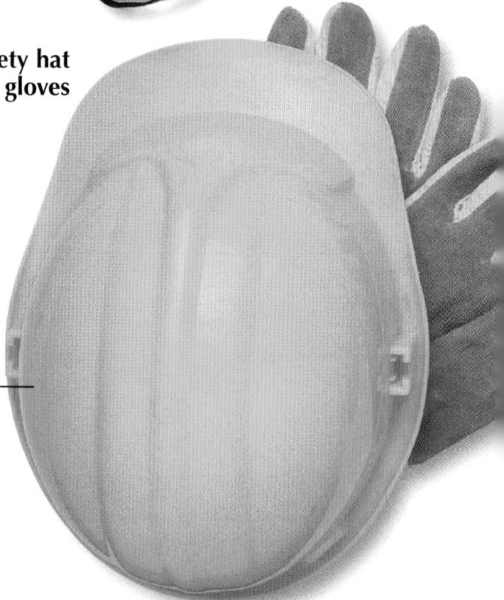

Safety hat and gloves

Brightly coloured safety hats are best

Safety equipment ▶
A hard hat is essential anywhere with a risk of rock falls, such as a quarry or cliff base. Wear strong fabric gloves for handling rough or sharp material. If you stand near someone who's using a rock hammer, wear safety goggles. Hard hats, fabric gloves, and safety goggles can all be bought from DIY stores.

Wear rubber or plastic gloves when handling chemicals

HANDLING CHEMICALS

Some activities in this section involve chemicals that must not touch your eyes, mouth, or skin. When using such chemicals, wear protective gloves and goggles. Don't touch your eyes or lips while wearing the gloves. Afterwards, throw away disposable gloves and wash your hands thoroughly. Read the manufacturer's instructions before using crystal kits, modelling resin, or plaster of Paris, and make sure you have adult supervision at all times. The symbol above appears when adult supervision is required.

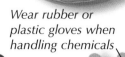

IMPORTANT

Certain parts of the countryside have protected status. Don't collect rocks or fossils in these places without permission. Wherever you look for rocks and fossils, follow the code of conduct on page 135.

Map and compass ▶
A map and compass will help you to find your site and can give you an exact reference for the location. It is very important to record the location of rock, fossil, and mineral finds for future reference.

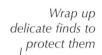

It's best to keep maps in waterproof wallets

A rock hammer is useful for breaking up large rocks

Rock hammer ▶
A rock, or geological, hammer is very useful for splitting rocks or breaking fossils away from bedrock. Only adults should use them, and a carpenter's hammer should never be used instead because the metal head may splinter. Protective goggles should always be worn by the person using the rock hammer, and by anyone nearby, because rock splinters can fly off in any direction.

◀ Penknife
A penknife is handy for prising rocks and fossils, or for scratching off dirt.

◀ Trowel
A trowel is used for carefully scraping away mud or other soft sediment. When used properly, the edge of the trowel will catch solid items, such as flints, or fossils buried in the mud.

Wrap up delicate finds to protect them

Use sample bags and containers that can be sealed

Wrapping materials ▶
Fossils can be surprisingly delicate – wrap them in newspaper, bubble wrap, or cloth. Small plastic bags or containers are useful for fiddly specimens.

▲ Notebook and pen
When you find an interesting rock or fossil, write down the location with a pen in a notebook. Do this when you make a find, not when you get home. Keep the note wrapped with the specimen.

BUYING ROCKS AND FOSSILS

Many collectors buy rocks, minerals, or fossils from shops as well as collecting them in the field. You can also pick up cheap rocks and fossils at car boot sales and jumble sales, but be sure you know what you're buying as some minerals are toxic. Only buy fossils from reputable suppliers – some of the best-looking commercial fossils are fakes.

Cut and polished agates

Become a rock hound

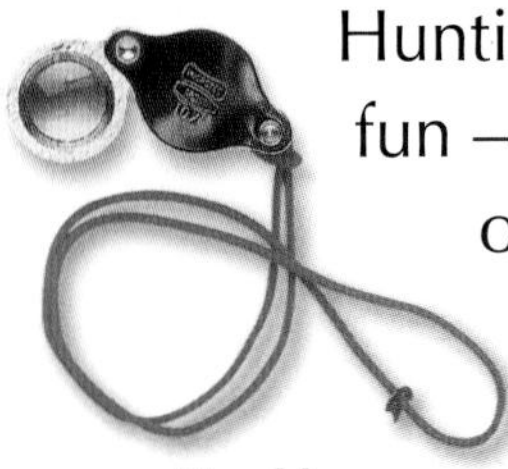

Hand lens

Hunting for rocks is enormous fun – nothing beats the excitement of discovering rare minerals or shiny crystals with your own eyes. All that you really need to become a rock hound is a pair of sharp eyes and a bit of patience. It also helps if you plan your trips in advance – if you know where to look, your hunts will be much more fruitful.

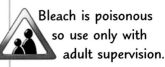

WHAT YOU WILL NEED

- Bag for collecting rocks
- Water
- Dishwashing bowl
- Scrubbing brush
- Penknife
- Bleach
- Magnifying glass

Bleach is poisonous so use only with adult supervision.

On the beach
A beach is a good place to look for interesting rocks.

IMPORTANT

To be a good rock hound, you need to follow certain safety procedures. See pages 132–133 for guidance.

1 **Walk slowly** as you look at the ground and collect as many different types of rocks as you can: hard, soft, smooth, shiny, rough, crumbly, flat, and so on. If you're with a friend, take the rainbow challenge: see who can find the most colours. Put the best small specimens in a bag. Don't worry if they're dirty – you can clean them at home.

Stromatolite

WHERE TO COLLECT ROCKS

There are two different kinds of site where interesting rocks are easy to find: outcrops and deposits. Outcrops are places like cliffs and quarries, where the bedrock that normally lies hidden below ground is exposed. Deposits are places where small, loose stones collect, such as beaches, river beds, and fields.

◄ River beds
Hard-wearing stones accumulate as gravel in rivers and streams. If you're very lucky, you might find gemstones among the gravel.

Shelly lime

Obsidian

CODE OF CONDUCT

Remember to behave sensibly when collecting rocks and minerals. Always seek permission before entering or collecting rocks from private land. A rock hammer should be used as little as possible, and only by an adult. Don't use it in protected areas, such as national parks. Wherever possible, collect from fallen rocks, rubble, or scree rather than hammering outcrops. If you open any gates, close them behind you. Don't leave litter or disturb animals, and don't collect rocks from walls or buildings.

▲ **On the hunt**
It's better to collect loose, fallen rock than hammering outcrops, but don't climb rubbly slopes like this one – they are dangerous.

2 **Clean the rocks** when you get home. Brush off loose dirt, or scrape it off with a penknife. Then wash the rocks in warm water with a little detergent. Use a scrubbing brush to remove dirt, or leave very dirty rocks to soak overnight. If a rock has a green stain caused by algae, ask an adult to soak it in water containing a dash of bleach.

3 **Leave the rocks to dry**, then inspect them with a magnifying glass. Can you see individual grains or crystals? Feel the rocks carefully to see which ones are hard or crumbly. The rocks you've collected will be very useful for the activities in this book. You can also use them to start a collection (see page 138).

Use a scrubbing brush to remove mud and grit from your rocks

Rock stars

You don't have to go to the country to see rocks – just take a stroll in town. When you know how to spot granite, sandstone, and limestone, you'll see them in buildings everywhere. Throughout history, people have used rocks to build with. Usually, they made do with local rocks, but sometimes they looked further afield. As the buildings on this page show, the rocks often tell a fascinating story.

Stonehenge ▲
The builders of Stonehenge in England used a Welsh rock called dolerite. Unless the rock had been carried to England by glaciers, the builders must have dragged each rock 250 km (155 miles).

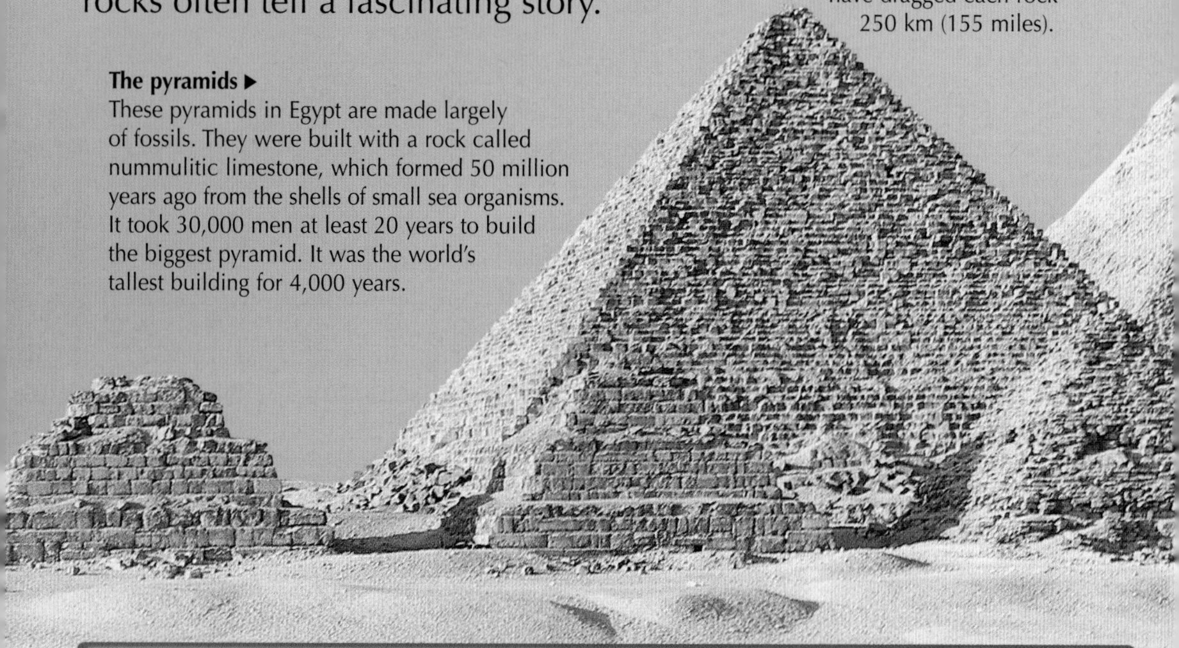

The pyramids ▶
These pyramids in Egypt are made largely of fossils. They were built with a rock called nummulitic limestone, which formed 50 million years ago from the shells of small sea organisms. It took 30,000 men at least 20 years to build the biggest pyramid. It was the world's tallest building for 4,000 years.

RECYCLED ROCK

Building materials like bricks, cement, and concrete are all recycled rock. Bricks come from clay that is shaped into blocks and cooked or dried in the sun to harden. Cement and plaster are made with minerals, such as calcite and gypsum, which are heated to drive out water and then powdered. When water is added, crystals form and make them set solid. Concrete is a mass of cement and pebbles.

Making bricks ▶
These Indian villagers are making clay bricks. Clay forms when the minerals in rocks such as granite rot and crumble. Rivers wash away the clay, which then settles as mud.

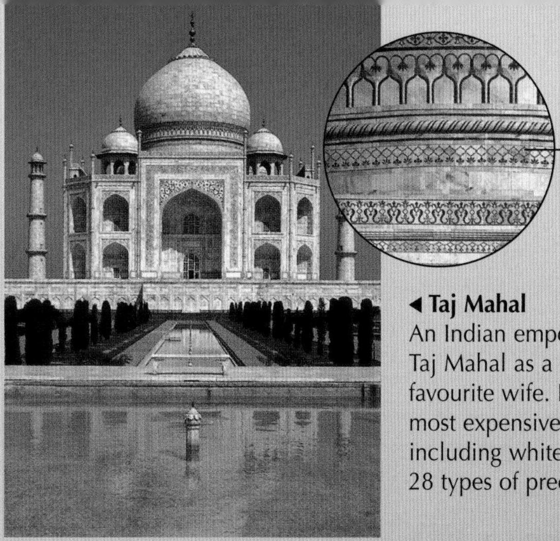

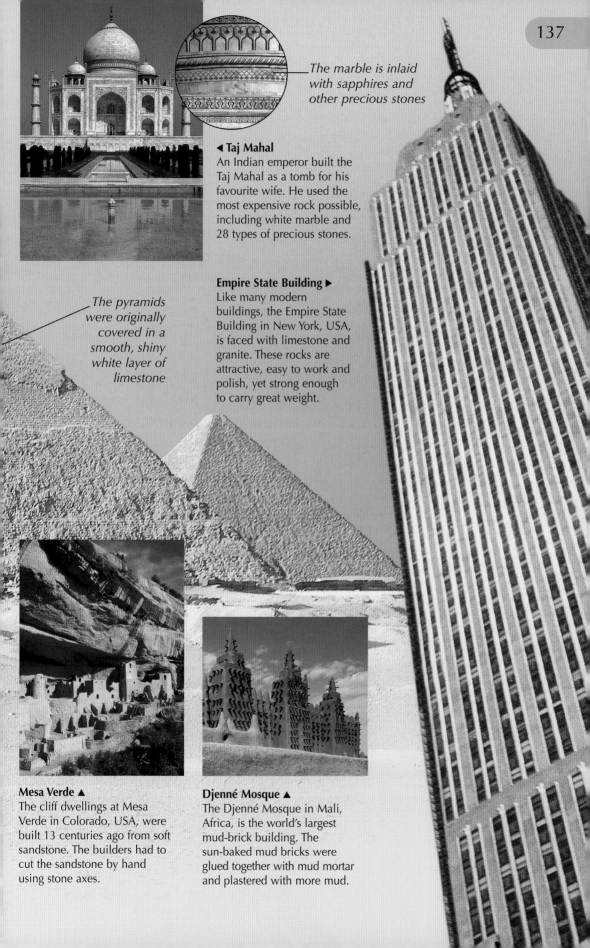

The marble is inlaid with sapphires and other precious stones

◀ Taj Mahal
An Indian emperor built the Taj Mahal as a tomb for his favourite wife. He used the most expensive rock possible, including white marble and 28 types of precious stones.

Empire State Building ▶
Like many modern buildings, the Empire State Building in New York, USA, is faced with limestone and granite. These rocks are attractive, easy to work and polish, yet strong enough to carry great weight.

The pyramids were originally covered in a smooth, shiny white layer of limestone

Mesa Verde ▲
The cliff dwellings at Mesa Verde in Colorado, USA, were built 13 centuries ago from soft sandstone. The builders had to cut the sandstone by hand using stone axes.

Djenné Mosque ▲
The Djenné Mosque in Mali, Africa, is the world's largest mud-brick building. The sun-baked mud bricks were glued together with mud mortar and plastered with more mud.

Start a collection

For most rock hounds, building a collection is the most important part of their hobby. A collection grows better and better over time, and the best specimens can be arranged to make a spectacular display. You can collect rocks, fossils, or minerals, but most people specialize in either fossils or minerals. Whatever you collect, it's important to label all your specimens and keep a careful record of everything you know about them.

WHAT YOU WILL NEED

- Your collection
- White correcting fluid or white stickers and craft glue
- Black permanent marker pen
- 2 index card files
- Card specimen trays (see right), matchbox trays, or egg boxes
- Cotton wool or tissue paper
- Magnifying glass

1 **Assemble your specimens.** Put a small dab of correcting fluid on an unimportant part of the bottom of each one and let it dry. Alternatively, use a small white sticker. Stickers will eventually drop off, so you'll need to add extra glue to prevent this happening. Use the permanent marker pen to write a reference number on each mark or sticker, starting with 1.

2 **Fill out** an index card for each specimen, writing its allocated number at the top of the card. Note the type of rock and the name of the mineral or fossil (if you know it) under the number. Also jot down where each specimen came from and any other interesting details. As you learn more about your collection, add the new information to the cards. Keep the cards in numerical order in the file.

MAKING SPECIMEN TRAYS

You can buy specimen trays from mineral shops, or make your own. Cut out a square or rectangle of card, according to the size of the specimen, and draw on the lines shown on the template below. Ask an adult to score along the lines, then cut the corners. Fold the scored lines, and tape the corners together, as shown in the pictures on the right.

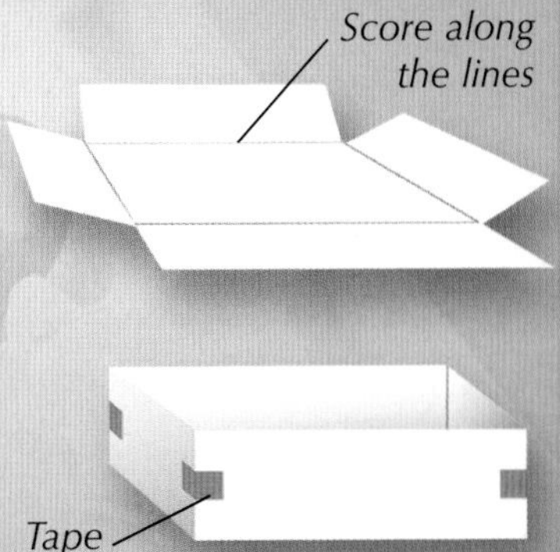
Score along the lines
Tape

Put your best specimens in a box and keep them on display in your room

Individual specimen tray template

3 **Prepare a second** index card with the name of the rock, fossil, or mineral at the top and its number under the name. Keep these cards in alphabetical order in a separate card file. You can then look up specimens both by name and by number.

4 **Place each specimen** in a small card tray (see above). Put tissue paper or cotton wool under delicate specimens. Arrange all your specimen trays in a drawer or large box to display them.

Erupting volcano

When volcanoes erupt, molten rock gushes from the ground as lava. Some volcanoes erupt gently, but others explode with a bang, blown open by a blast that can hurl millions of tonnes of rock debris into the sky. By making a home-made volcano, you can see why eruptions can be so violent.

WHAT YOU WILL NEED

- Small plastic bottle
- Water
- Measuring jug
- Tray
- Sand
- Dessertspoon
- Bicarbonate of soda
- Red food colouring
- Washing-up liquid
- Funnel (if possible)
- Vinegar

1 Rinse out a small plastic drinks bottle, then use a measuring jug to work out how much water the bottle contains. Empty the bottle and place it on a tray.

2 Pile up sand around the bottle to make a volcano shape. Be careful not to let any sand fall down the bottle neck.

3 Pour enough warm water into the jug to fill the bottle two-thirds full. Add two heaped dessertspoons of bicarbonate of soda and stir well. Add a dessertspoon each of food colouring and washing-up liquid to the jug.

Make your volcano more realistic by placing rocks, plastic trees, or models around it

IMPORTANT

This experiment can be messy, so check with an adult where you should do it. Outdoors on a flat surface, like a driveway or a path, is a good idea.

4 **Carefully pour** the liquid from the jug into the bottle, using a funnel if you have one. If you don't, pour the liquid very slowly and carefully.

VIOLENT VOLCANOES

Really violent eruptions are caused by gas bubbles, as in the home-made volcano in this activity. When molten rock is trapped underground, high pressure keeps gases dissolved inside it. But if the lava breaks through the surface, the pressure suddenly drops and the gas forms bubbles, pushing up the lava like a fizzy drink exploding from a bottle.

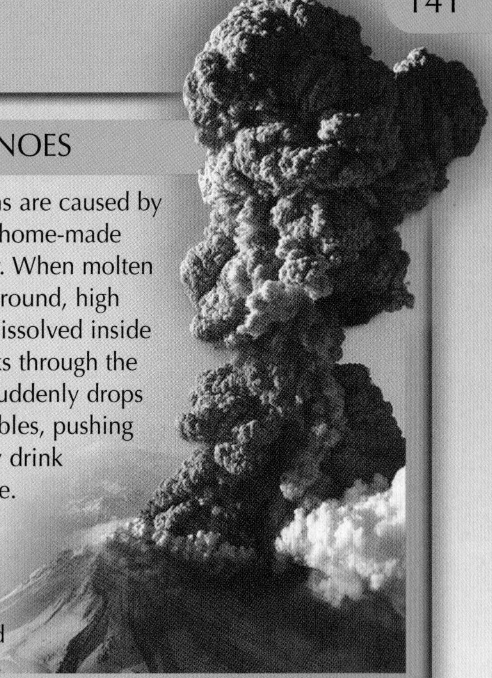

Ash cloud ▶
Mount Augustine in Alaska, USA, erupts, hurling scalding ash and rubble high into the sky.

5 **Be prepared** for the eruption, which happens very quickly. Measure 100 ml ($3\frac{1}{2}$ fl oz) of vinegar into a jug and pour it into the bottle. Jump back, keeping your eyes on the volcano.

HANDY TIP

If the sand doesn't stick to the bottle, add a little water to it.

Coloured crystals

Crystals are the building blocks of rocks. They form when minerals solidify into regular shapes with flat, often shiny faces and sharp edges. You can find out more about crystals by growing your own from some common household ingredients.

HANDY TIP

To make "amethyst" crystals, mix together blue and red food colouring.

Sugar crystals can take several weeks to grow

Salt crystals form on the bottom of the jar as well as the paper clip

1 Put 3 or 4 tablespoons of sugar in the jug and pour on about a cupful of hot water. Stir until no more sugar will dissolve. If all the sugar dissolves within 1–2 minutes, add another tablespoonful. Stir for 2 more minutes. Let the solution cool for 5 minutes.

2 Meanwhile, tie a paper clip to a piece of string and wrap the string around the middle of a pencil. Lay the pencil across the top of the jar so that the paper clip is suspended 1–2 cm (about 1 in) above the bottom of the jar.

3 Lift off the pencil. Pour sugar solution into the jar until just over three-quarters full. Add 3–4 drops of food colouring. Put the pencil back on the jar. Make a note of the colour and the substance dissolved (sugar).

4 Repeat the above steps using salt in the second jar and Epsom salts in the third. Add a different food colouring to the jars so you can tell them apart. Make a note of the colour and contents of each jar.

CHEMICAL COLOURINGS

Cross with different coloured sapphires

The colours of gems often come from chemical impurities, just as your home-grown crystals are coloured by additives. Rubies and sapphires are both varieties of the mineral corundum, which is colourless when pure. Rubies get their red from chromium, while sapphires are coloured various colours by iron and titanium.

CRYSTALS IN ROCK

Magnified granite

Many rocks contain crystals large enough to see. The grains in granite are interlocking crystals of three minerals: mica (black), quartz (grey), and feldspar (pink and white). These crystals grow large because granite forms slowly when molten rock cools underground.

Epsom salt crystals are long and spiky and grow very quickly

WHAT YOU WILL NEED

- Tablespoon
- White sugar
- Measuring jug
- Hot water
- 3 paper clips
- String
- 3 pencils
- 3 glass jars
- Food colourings
- Salt
- Epsom salts
- Gloves and goggles

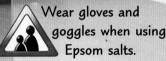

Wear gloves and goggles when using Epsom salts.

5 **Check each solution** after 30 minutes to see if crystals are forming. Leave them undisturbed for at least 2 weeks and make a daily check. Do the crystals grow at different speeds or have different shapes?

CRYSTAL SHAPES

Crystals have distinctive shapes because of the way atoms line up inside them, and the shape is a useful clue to a mineral's identity. All crystals can be placed in one of six main classes according to their symmetry.

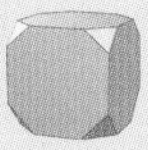

◄ **Cubic** crystals are very symmetrical, which means you keep seeing the same shape if you turn them around. Diamonds are cubic.

Pyrite

◄ **Monoclinic** crystals have much less symmetry than cubic crystals. The shape repeats only once as you turn them around.

Selenite

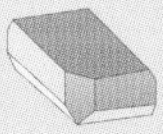

◄ **Triclinic** crystals are the least symmetrical of all the crystal shapes. They have no equal sides or angles and can look like a jumble of flat faces.

Axinite

◄ **Tetragonal** crystals typically have a rectangular shape, with equal sides and angles. They look a bit like elongated cubes.

Idocrase

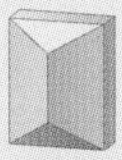

◄ **Orthorhombic** crystals are long and have tapered ends, like a rectangle with the corners chipped off. The mineral topaz forms gemstones this shape.

Barite

◄ **Hexagonal** and **trigonal** crystals have six sides. Rubies, sapphires, emeralds, and snowflakes all belong to this class.

Beryl

Grow your own gems

In rare conditions, exceptionally beautiful and hard-wearing crystals form in igneous or metamorphic rock to become gemstones. The element carbon can crystallize into a diamond, the most precious jewel of all, and the minerals corundum and beryl can form rubies, sapphires, and emeralds. Gemstones are highly prized for their beauty and rarity. You're unlikely to find any when rock hunting, so why not try making a fake?

IMPORTANT

Wear goggles to protect your eyes from splashes, and wear protective gloves when handling the alum solution. If some of the solution should splash on to your skin, wash it off immediately with lots of cold water. Do not put the alum in your mouth.

WHAT YOU WILL NEED

- Protective goggles
- Protective gloves
- Measuring jug
- Measuring scales
- Hot water
- Alum (available from toy shops in crystal-growing kits or from some grocers' as a pickling salt)
- Mixing stick
- Plate
- Tweezers
- String
- Pencil
- Glass tumbler
- Old saucepan

Ask an adult to supervise the use of alum and to help you heat the alum solution.

ARE DIAMONDS FOREVER?

Diamonds are famous for the way they sparkle. A cut diamond reflects more light than other gems and splits the light into colours, giving the diamond its "fire". They are also famous for being the hardest substance known – no other mineral can scratch them. But they're far from indestructible. Like coal and other forms of carbon, they can burn.

Cut diamonds

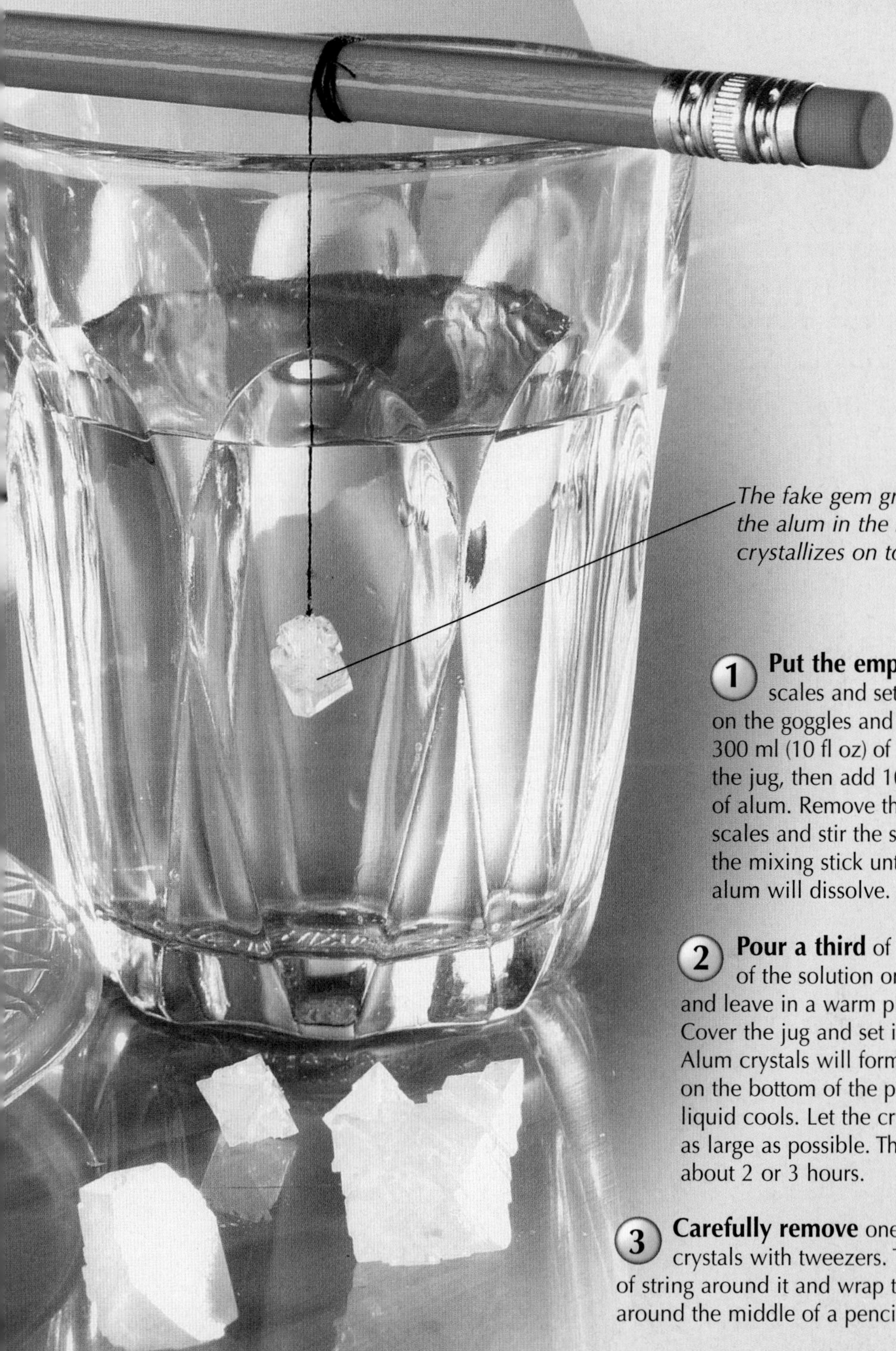
The fake gem grows as
the alum in the solution
crystallizes on to it

1. **Put the empty jug** on the scales and set it to zero. Put on the goggles and gloves. Pour 300 ml (10 fl oz) of hot water into the jug, then add 100 g (3½ oz) of alum. Remove the jug from the scales and stir the solution with the mixing stick until no more alum will dissolve.

2. **Pour a third** of a cupful of the solution on to a plate and leave in a warm place to dry. Cover the jug and set it aside. Alum crystals will form quickly on the bottom of the plate as the liquid cools. Let the crystals grow as large as possible. This will take about 2 or 3 hours.

3. **Carefully remove** one of the best crystals with tweezers. Tie a piece of string around it and wrap the string around the middle of a pencil.

4. **Crystals will also have formed** on the bottom of the jug and you will need to re-dissolve them. Pour the solution into a pan and heat it, then pour it back into the jug and swish it around until all the crystals have dissolved. Let the solution cool for 5 minutes.

5. **Pour some of the solution** into the tumbler and hang the crystal tied to the pencil in the solution. Leave the crystal for a few days to grow into a "diamond".

HANDY TIP

Add red food colouring to make a ruby, or green to make an emerald.

Glittering geodes

In areas where there are porous rocks, you may come across a dull rock shaped like a potato on the ground. These "potato stones" are called geodes and are highly prized by mineral collectors. If the rock is sliced in half, inside is a cavity lined with crystals. You can make a fake geode in a grapefruit skin, using the chemical alum to form the crystals.

WHAT YOU WILL NEED

- Grapefruit or orange
- Aluminium foil
- Plaster of Paris
- Bowl
- Spatula
- Protective goggles
- Protective gloves
- Alum (available in crystal-growing kits or from some grocers' as a pickling salt)
- Hot water
- Measuring jug
- Measuring scales
- Red and blue food colouring (optional)

Ask an adult to supervise the use of alum.

1 Cut a grapefruit or large orange in half and remove the flesh. Line the fruit with some aluminium foil.

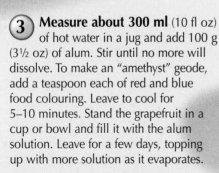

2 Mix about a cupful of plaster of Paris powder in a bowl, following the instructions on the packet. Leave for 10 minutes, or until it thickens, then spread it over the foil inside the grapefruit with a spatula to form a thick, irregular layer. Before it sets, put on the goggles and gloves, and sprinkle over some alum crystals. Leave for half an hour to harden.

3 Measure about 300 ml (10 fl oz) of hot water in a jug and add 100 g (3½ oz) of alum. Stir until no more will dissolve. To make an "amethyst" geode, add a teaspoon each of red and blue food colouring. Leave to cool for 5–10 minutes. Stand the grapefruit in a cup or bowl and fill it with the alum solution. Leave for a few days, topping up with more solution as it evaporates.

HOW GEODES FORM

Geodes form in cavities in porous rock. Fluids rich in dissolved minerals, such as quartz, seep into the cavity. The quartz crystallizes on the inner surface, and the crystals can grow big enough to fill the geode. When the rock erodes, a chunk may break off. The hard crystals hold the chunk together, while the outside wears down to form a dull-looking, potato-shaped rock.

Amethyst geode ▶
This geode is full of amethyst crystals – a purple form of quartz. The crystals are translucent and shaped like pyramids.

4 **After several days**, pour off the solution and peel away the rind and foil to reveal your beautiful "geode"!

You can paint the outside to make it look more like a rock

IMPORTANT

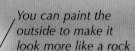

Do not swallow alum. If some should splash on to your skin, wash it off immediately with lots of cold water. Wear goggles to protect your eyes from splashes, and wear protective gloves when handling the alum solution.

Make paint from minerals

Since the earliest times, people have used colourful minerals to make paint. Unlike paints made from plants and animals, mineral paints hold their colour well over time. But they can be difficult to make, especially if the mineral is rock hard. Soft minerals, like red ochre and chalk, are the simplest to make into paints because they are easy to crush. Harder minerals, like azurite and malachite, are difficult to crush, but they produce brilliant blue and green colours.

WHAT YOU WILL NEED

- Dust mask
- Soft minerals, such as red ochre, chalk, and charcoal
- Pestle and mortar
- 2 shallow bowls
- Egg
- Kitchen towel
- Mixing stick
- Paintbrush and paper

Wear a dust mask when crushing minerals – some may be an inhalation risk.

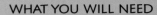

Look up cave paintings in books or on the Internet and find one you want to copy

1. **Wearing a dust mask**, grind a mineral (red ochre here) with a pestle and mortar to make a fine powder. The finer you grind the powder, the smoother the paint will be.

2. **Tip the powder** into a shallow bowl and add a few drops of water. Stir the powder and water together with the pestle until it becomes a smooth paste.

3. **You need to add** a binding agent to the paste to stop it turning to dust when it dries. Egg yolk works well, but it has to be separated from the egg white. Crack open an egg and carefully tip out the white, leaving the yolk in the shell. Roll the yolk very gently in kitchen towel to clean it, then tip it into a bowl.

PIGMENTS AND DYES

Pigments and dyes are substances used to create intense colours. Dyes dissolve in water and soak into absorbent materials like fabric, colouring them throughout. Pigments work in a different way. They don't dissolve, so they are ground into powder and used to make paint. Most modern pigments and dyes are synthetic.

Azurite, once an important source of blue paint

HANDY TIP

White craft glue can be used as a binding agent instead of egg yolk.

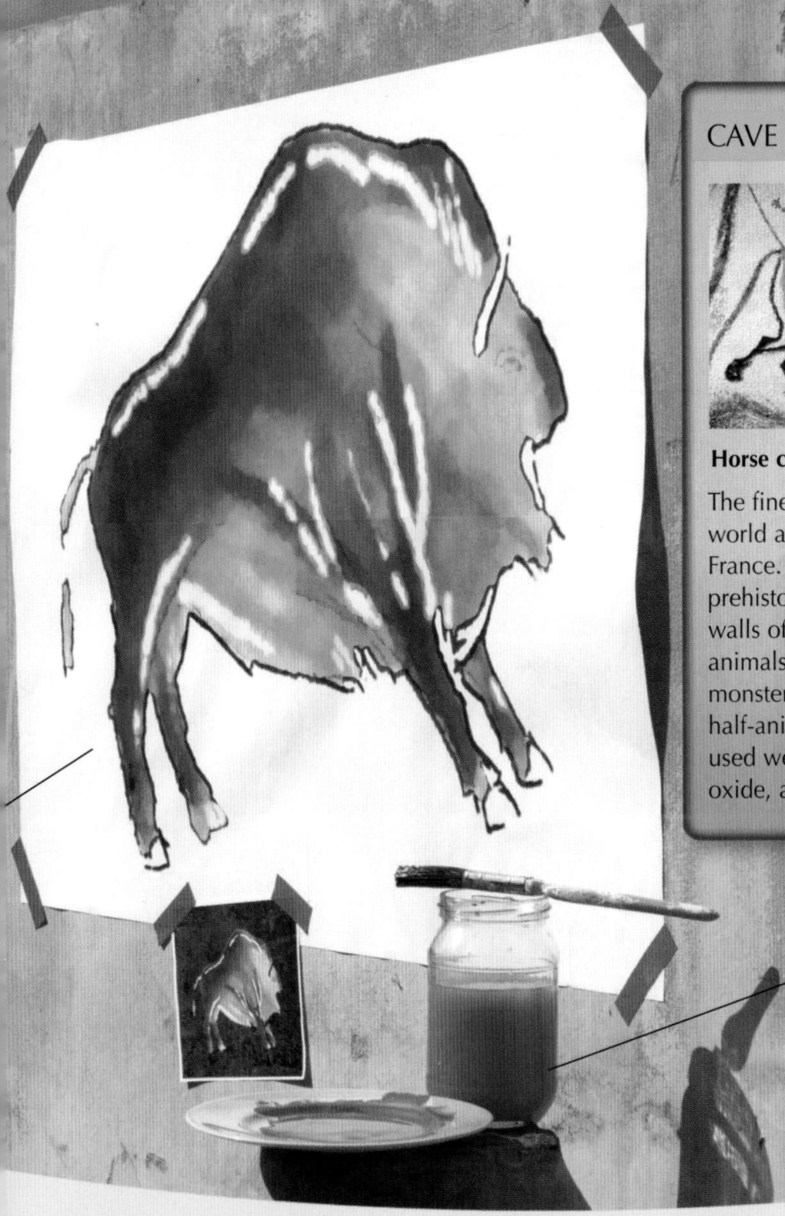

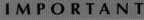

Dip your paintbrush in water if your paint starts to dry out

CAVE PAINTINGS

Horse cave painting, Lascaux, France

The finest cave paintings in the world are in Lascaux, western France. About 17,000 years ago, prehistoric painters decorated the walls of the cave with wild animals, mysterious symbols, and monsters that were half-human and half-animal. The paints that they used were made from ochre, iron oxide, and charcoal.

4 **Add a tiny amount** of yolk to the paste – about one-third the amount of paste. Stir it in with a mixing stick. Your paint is now ready to use.

IMPORTANT

If you make paint from very hard minerals, ask an adult to crush them. Don't use any yellow or orange minerals, which can be toxic.

5 **Try making** a prehistoric cave painting with your mineral paints. Use clay or red ochre for the red paint, chalk to make white paint for highlights, and charcoal to make black paint for shadows and outlines.

Rocks from space

Every day, about 500 tonnes of dust and rock from space collide with planet Earth. Much of this space debris burns up as it enters the atmosphere, producing streaks of light called shooting stars. However, particles smaller than 1 mm (0.04 in) wide can sometimes slip through the air without getting hot enough to burn. These micrometeorites float through the sky as dust, and they fall to the ground in rain. With a powerful magnet – and a bit of luck – you stand a real chance of finding one.

WHAT YOU WILL NEED

- Magnet
- Paper cup
- String
- Sheet of white paper
- Magnifying glass
- Tweezers
- Microscope
- Glass slide

1 **Place a powerful magnet** in a paper cup and tie a loop of string to the top of the cup to make a micrometeorite collector. Take the collector outside on a dry day and gently tap it over areas of ground that are dry (but which do get wet after rain) and seldom disturbed by people or vehicles. Good places to try include the ground around drainpipes and undisturbed lawns.

2 **When black specks** have appeared on the bottom of the cup, take it indoors and place the cup on some clean white paper. Remove the magnet and tap the cup to shake off the specks.

3 **Use a magnifying** glass and tweezers to pick out particles that look spherical and less than 0.5 mm (0.08 in) wide. These could be micrometeorites made of iron or nickel, which are magnetic. Particles that are not spherical will be flecks of iron from other sources.

HANDY TIP

Don't touch the dust with the magnet as it will stick to the magnet and be hard to remove.

The loop of string makes a handle
Use the most powerful magnet you have
Place the magnet in the bottom of the cup

WHAT IS A METEORITE?

Artist's impression of a meteorite hitting Earth

Space rocks that land on Earth's surface are called meteorites. Most are fragments of broken asteroids (colossal rocks that orbit the Sun); those made of iron come from the cores of asteroids. Only about 500 meteorites bigger than a football hit Earth each year and most of these end up in the sea.

4 **If you have a microscope**, put the best particles on a glass slide and examine them. Micrometeorites often look smooth because the surface melts as they enter Earth's atmosphere. You can also use a microscope to search for micrometeorites in the dust that appears on cars after rain. This dust comes from high in the sky and contains desert sand and volcanic ash, which may have travelled thousands of kilometres, as well as micrometeorites.

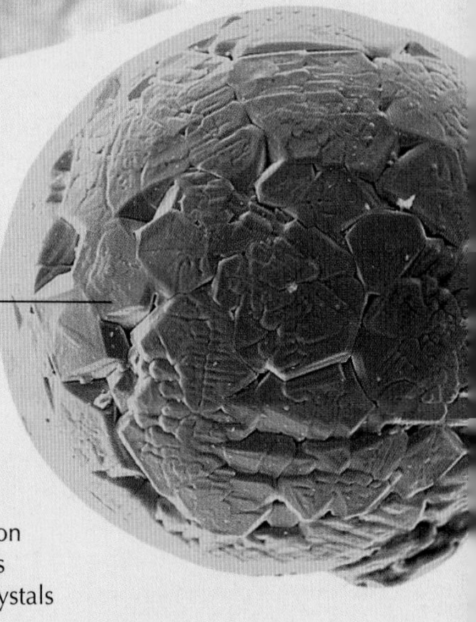
Iron crystals in micrometeorite

Under the microscope ▸ This is what an iron micrometeorite looks like through a powerful electron microscope. The surface is smooth and round, but crystals of metal are visible.

Stalactites on string

Stalactites and stalagmites are made of the mineral calcite, which comes from limestone. Since rain is mildly acidic, it dissolves calcite as it seeps through the ground, hollowing out tunnels, potholes, and caves. Dripping water then re-deposits the calcite in icicle shapes. With Epsom salts, you can recreate this process in miniature.

HANDY TIP

Don't use nylon or polyester string because it won't absorb the liquid so well.

The string soaks up the Epsom salt solution
Paper clip attached to end of the string

1 **Pour the hot water** and Epsom salts into the jug. Stir for several minutes until no more Epsom salts dissolve (there should be a residue of Epsom salts at the bottom of the jug).

2 **Pour the solution** into the jars. Cut a length of string or wool, dunk it in a jar, then run it between your fingers to remove any excess liquid. Attach paper clips to each end, and place one in each jar. Position the jars so the string sags in the middle. Place a saucer underneath to catch the drips.

3 **After an hour**, a drip of liquid – the start of the stalactite – should have formed where the string sags. If the string is completely dry, replace it with a more absorbent type of string or wool. If the saucer is full of liquid, replace the string with a less absorbent material or remove a little liquid from each jar.

4 **Let the experiment run** for a few days, checking the string daily to see how long the stalactite has become.

WHY DO STALACTITES FORM?

Your Epsom salt stalactite formed because some of the water evaporated as it dripped off the string, causing dissolved Epsom salts to turn back into crystals. A similar thing happens in limestone caves. As cave water drips through air, some of it evaporates. As a result, calcite crystallizes out of the solution and grows into a stalactite.

What's the difference? ▶
The following saying might be useful: StalaC***tites*** cling ***tight***ly to the Ceiling. StalaG***mites*** grow from the Ground and ***might*** reach the stalactites.

A stalactite grows from the top down
A stalagmite grows from the bottom up

WHAT YOU WILL NEED

- Gloves and goggles
- 2 cupfuls of Epsom salts
- 2 cupfuls of hot water
- Large jug
- Mixing stick
- 2 glass jars
- Cotton string or wool
- 2 paper clips
- Saucer

⚠ Wear gloves and goggles when using Epsom salts.

Sandstone sandcastles

Sandstone is a common type of sedimentary rock. It forms when buried sand slowly solidifies as minerals crystallize between the sand grains, gluing them together. You can recreate this process with sand, water, and a range of different binding agents.

WHAT YOU WILL NEED

- 6 plastic cups
- Sand
- 5 clear plastic bags
- Dessertspoon
- Salt
- Water
- Newspaper
- Tray
- Marker pen
- Plaster of Paris powder
- Cornflour
- Garden soil
- Jug of water

Salt plus sand

Plaster of Paris plus sand

THE SAND CYCLE

Sand comes from rocks that have been slowly broken down (weathered) by rain, ice, heat, and other forces. Many minerals in the rocks break down into clay, but quartz, which is very tough, survives as sand grains. Rivers wash these away and dump them in seas and lakes, where they build up in layers. Over long periods, water trickling through the layers deposits minerals such as silica and calcite, which crystallize and cement the grains together. And so the sand turns back into new rock: sandstone.

The sands of time ▼
As rocks weather over thousands of years, they crumble into smaller and smaller particles. Eventually, only tiny grains of sand are left.

ROCK BANDS

Sedimentary rocks form layer by layer as debris settles on the floor of a lake or sea, or as wind-blown sand or dust settles on the ground. When the rocks are exposed again at the surface millions of years later, the layers are often visible as bands, or strata, with the youngest strata nearest the top. Geologists can work out the relative age of the strata by identifying any fossils in them.

Vermilion Cliffs in Arizona, USA, formed from desert sand dunes

IMPORTANT

As this activity can be very messy, especially the final step, it is best to do it outdoors.

1 Almost fill a plastic cup with sand and empty it into one of the bags. Add 2–3 dessertspoons of salt. Shake the bag. Add 4–5 dessertspoons of water. Mix the contents by squeezing the bag until the mixture is wet enough to form a sandcastle.

2 Fill a plastic cup with the mixture and press down on the top to make it even. Place a thick layer of newspaper on a tray and tip out the sand to form a sandcastle. Label it "Salt plus sand".

3 Repeat these steps to make three more sandcastles, but instead of adding salt to the sand, use plaster of Paris, cornflour, and then soil. Crumble the soil well with your hands and remove any stones. Finally, make a fifth sandcastle with just sand and water.

4 Leave the tray somewhere dry until the sandcastles dry out completely and harden. Touch them carefully with your fingers. The plaster of Paris castle will feel the most solid, while the sand and water castle will feel the most fragile.

5 Place the tray carefully on the ground. Fill a jug with water and gently pour about the same amount of water over each sandcastle. Which ones wash away most easily? Which is the toughest? When you know the answer, why not make a long-lasting sand sculpture?

Fossil spotter

If you go hunting for fossils, it helps to know what to look out for. The most common fossils are not bones of land animals like dinosaurs, but the remains of small sea creatures. Sea animals fossilize more easily because the muddy sea floor can preserve them. Usually only the hardest body parts survive, such as shells, teeth, and bones.

▲ Brachiopod
Most fossils with two hinged shells are bivalves or brachiopods. Both sides of a brachiopod's shell are symmetrical; bivalves have left and right shells that are mirror images.

◀ Belemnite
Bullet-shaped fossils are the internal shells of animals called belemnites, which were very much like modern squid. Like squid, they had long, torpedo-shaped bodies, ten arms, and an ink sac.

Ammonites were very common during the age of the dinosaurs

◀ Ammonite
These sea animals look a little like snails, but were in fact fast-swimming predators. Their shells were divided into compartments, with the animal in the largest, outer compartment. As the animal grew, it added new compartments, forming a spiral. The largest ammonites grew to 2 m ($6^1/_2$ ft) wide.

▲ **Fish fossil**
It's rare to find a whole fossil fish, but fossilized teeth – especially shark teeth – are very common. This fossil is of a bony fish that lived about 50 million years ago. Our backbones first evolved in a group of primitive fish more than 500 million years ago.

Crinoids used feathery arms to trap tiny sea creatures drifting through the water

▲ **Crinoid**
Crinoids, or sea lilies, look like flowers, but they are animals related to starfish. They still exist but were more common in the past. They anchor themselves to the sea floor by a long stalk.

Armour-plated bodies protected trilobites from attack

◀ **Trilobite**
Trilobites scuttled around on the sea floor like lobsters 590–250 million years ago. Their fossils are common because they moulted as they grew. Many had large eyes made of transparent crystals of the mineral calcite.

HOW FOSSILS FORM

Special circumstances are needed for fossils to form. As a result, only a tiny fraction of the prehistoric animals that lived on Earth became fossilized (and only a tiny fraction of those have been found). The pictures below show how a fish might become fossilized on the sea floor.

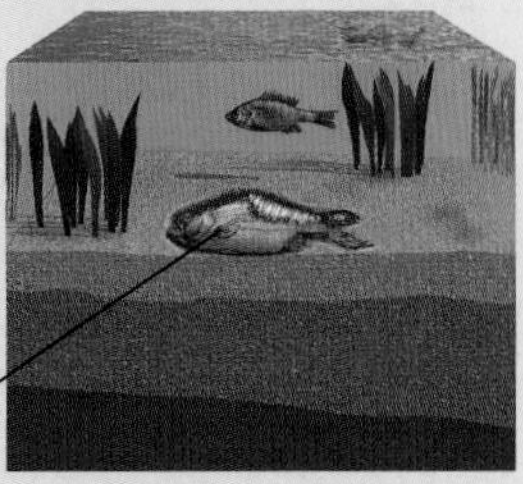
The dead fish settles in mud on the sea floor

▲ **Death**
The fish dies and sinks to the sea floor. Worms and microbes eat the soft parts of its body as it sinks into the mud.

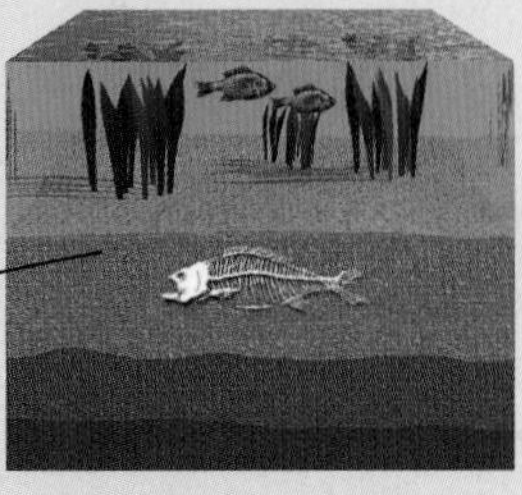
A layer of slimy mud buries the skeleton and helps preserve it

▲ **Burial**
Silt and sand build up over the skeleton, burying it. Deep in the mud there is less oxygen, so the decaying process slows down.

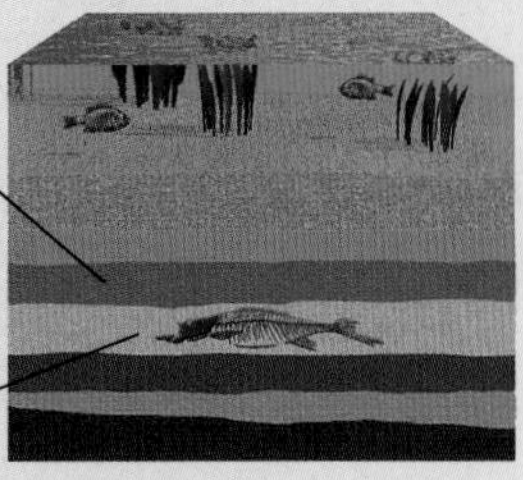
New layers of sediment build up on top
The mud is compressed into rock

▲ **Rock formation**
Over thousands of years, the mud turns into rock, such as shale or limestone. The skeleton is slowly replaced by minerals and turns into rock.

Fossil becomes visible as the rock erodes

▲ **Discovery**
Millions of years later, movements in Earth's crust have brought the rock to the surface of the land, where the fossil may be discovered.

Hunt for fossils

Hunting for fossils is a great hobby. Providing you choose the right site, fossils are surprisingly easy to find. To find a good site in your area, check the Internet or contact a local museum. The best sites are often places where sedimentary rocks are eroding rapidly, such as beaches, cliffs, and quarries. These sites can be dangerous, so be sure to follow the safety precautions on pages 132–133.

Fossil fern
Look for interesting patterns in the rock, such as this fossil fern in sandstone. You can also find good fossils in limestone, clay, and chalk.

IMPORTANT

Some fossil sites are private or have protected status. Don't enter the site without permission. Don't collect or keep fossils until you've checked the rules for the site.

1. **Depending on the site** you choose, you might find fossils by walking slowly and scanning the ground, by cracking open soft rocks, or by scraping mud. Excellent fossils are often found lying among gravel.

2. **Wrap your fossils** carefully in paper or cloth to protect them and put them in a bag. Jot down where you found each fossil. When you get home, clean the fossils gently with a toothbrush. Remove any stubborn grit with a penknife. Soak fossils from a beach in cold water to remove salt. Broken fossils can be mended with craft glue; fragile fossils can be painted with diluted craft glue to seal the surface.

This sea snail lived 300 million years ago

Field guides help you identify fossils

WHAT YOU WILL NEED

- Paper or cloth
- Notebook and pen
- Shoulder bag
- Toothbrush
- Craft glue
- Bucket of water
- Highly visible clothing
- Stout boots

Make sure you are accompanied by an adult and follow the code of conduct on page 135.

VISITING MUSEUMS

A good way to find out about the fossils in your area is to visit a natural history museum. Large museums don't just have dinosaur skeletons – they also have dozens of small fossils of the kind you're likely to find on beaches or in quarries. Museum exhibits may show you what the animals used to look like, how they lived, and the kind of environment they inhabited. Museum staff may help you identify your fossils and will tell you if they're valuable.

Tyrannosaurus rex reconstructed from fossilized bones

③ To identify your fossil, look in a field guide or take it to a local museum. You need to keep a record of where you found the fossil because the location is an important clue to the age of the fossil and its identity, which makes it more valuable.

GEOLOGICAL TIMESCALE

Sedimentary rocks are laid down in strata (layers), with younger strata on top of older ones. By studying sedimentary rocks across the world, geologists have identified a sequence of major strata, each containing a distinctive group of fossils. The names of these strata correspond to major periods in Earth's history. Together they form what scientists call the geological column.

	Period	Million years ago
Ice Age; humans emerge	Quaternary	1.8
Continents take present shape; birds and mammals replace dinosaurs	Tertiary	65
Dinosaurs disappear at the end of the Cretaceous period	Cretaceous	145
Age of the dinosaurs (Cretaceous–Triassic)	Jurassic	200
	Triassic	251
Reptiles become common	Permian	299
Swampy tropical forests cover land	Carboniferous	359
Insects and land plants evolve	Devonian	416
Fish are common; first land animals	Silurian	443
Brachiopods and trilobites are common	Ordovician	490
Shelled animals suddenly become common	Cambrian	542
For billions of years, most life is microscopic	Precambrian	4500

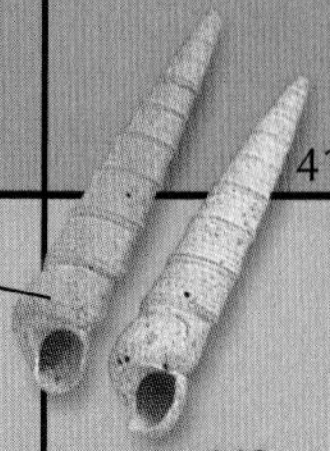

Fake fossils

Most fossils are not ancient, hardened bodies but mineral replicas. They normally take millions of years to form, but you can make your own rocky replica in just a day from plaster of Paris. Use this technique to make copies of real fossils, or to "fossilize" anything from plastic toys to your own hand print.

WHAT YOU WILL NEED

- Plasticine or modelling clay
- Rolling pin
- Petroleum jelly
- Objects to fossilize, such as seashells, plastic toys, or a real fossil
- Thin card • Water
- Plaster of Paris
- Small plastic container
- Yellow food colouring or black ink

HANDY TIP

If you use modelling clay for your mould, keep it and let it harden to make an "imprint" fossil.

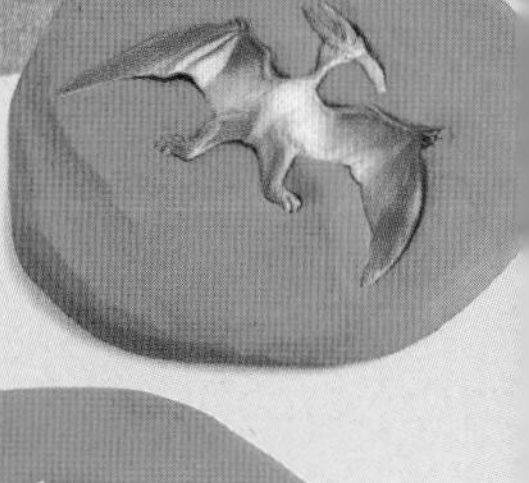

1 **Knead a large piece** of Plasticine until it becomes soft and easy to shape, then make a thick, round shape out of it. Flatten the top with a rolling pin and smear petroleum jelly over the top.

2 **Press the object** you want to fossilize into the Plasticine. (If you use a real fossil, wrap it in cling film to stop it from picking up petroleum jelly or Plasticine.) Remove the object from the Plasticine, taking care not to damage the mould. The mould is now ready to use.

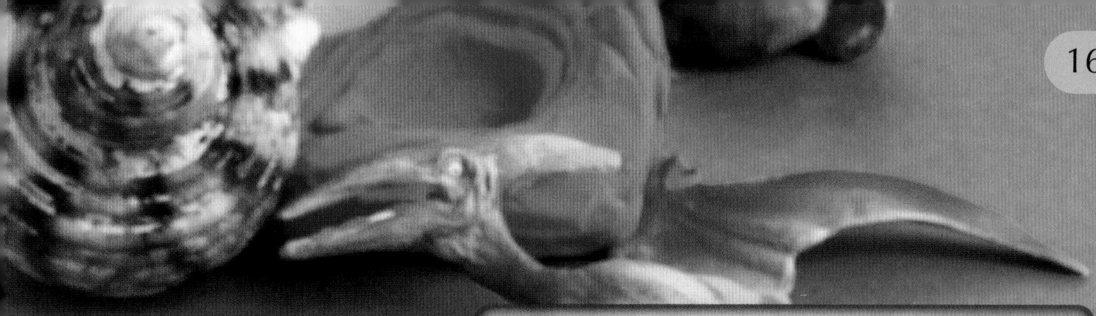

IMPRESSIVE FOSSILS

Many fossils form in exactly the same way as you made your fake fossils with a mould and cast – as impressions in clay, mud, or other soft sediments. The impression fills up with a different kind of sediment, gets buried, and hardens over time to form rock. Fossil impressions can preserve all sorts of structures, from dinosaur footprints to delicate leaves and the feathers of the very first bird.

Fossilized leaves ▶
This fossilized impression of a horsetail plant was formed around 300 million years ago.

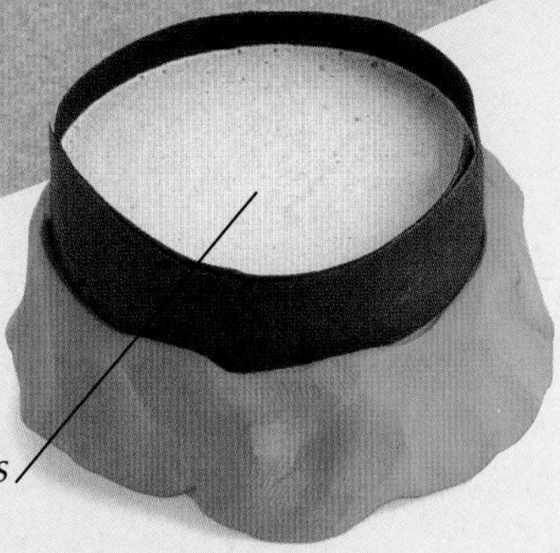

3 **Cut out a strip** of card about 5 cm (2 in) wide and 30 cm (12 in) long. Gently push it partway into the Plasticine to form a circle around the mould.

4 **Mix the plaster of Paris** with water, following the instructions on the packet, in the container. Add yellow food colouring for a sandy colour, or black ink to make it grey. For a gritty texture, add sand.

5 **Wait for the plaster** to thicken, then pour it into the mould. Leave for a day to set, then carefully remove your fossil. To make the fossil look more realistic, paint it a slightly different colour from the base. Chip the edges off the base so that it looks more like a real rock.

Trapped in amber

The most perfect fossils of all form when animals get trapped in pine resin – the sticky gum that oozes from wounded trees. Pine resin forms an airtight seal that preserves an animal's body. Over thousands of years, the resin turns into a hard golden material called amber. With modelling resin, you can make an "amber" fossil of an insect overnight.

Trapped insect in real amber

WHAT YOU WILL NEED

- Dead insects
- Plasticine or modelling clay
- Pebble
- Petroleum jelly
- Protective gloves
- Clear modelling resin (available from art shops)
- Yellow food colouring or turmeric
- Cocktail stick

Modelling resin must be handled with great care and not ingested. Ask an adult to mix the resin.

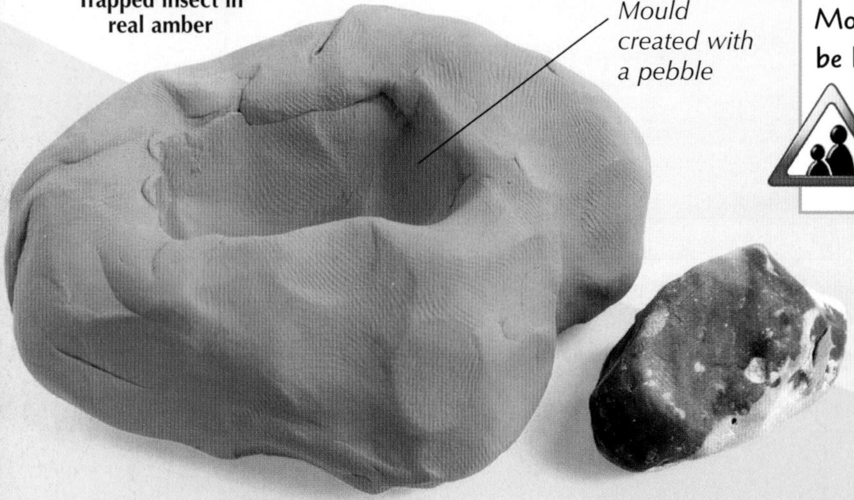
Mould created with a pebble

1 Collect a few dead insects and choose the most intact specimen. Good places to look for dead insects are cobwebs and indoor windowsills.

2 Create a pebble-shaped mould with Plasticine or modelling clay. Do this by pushing a smooth pebble into the clay, pulling it out, and then widening the bottom of the cavity with a finger. Take care to keep the inner surface of the cavity smooth. Line the inside of the mould with a little petroleum jelly.

3 Get an adult to mix the modelling resin, following the manufacturer's instructions carefully, and wearing protective gloves. Usually there are two parts to the mixture – the resin and a hardener – which need to be stirred.

4 To colour the resin yellow, add a tiny drop of yellow food colouring, or a very, very tiny pinch of turmeric. Turmeric will give a slightly less clear "amber".

HANDY TIP

If the insect is fragile, half-fill the mould with resin, put in the insect, then fill to the top.

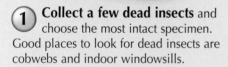

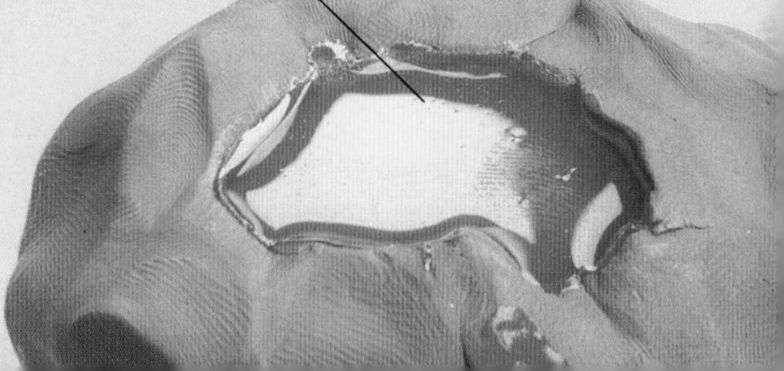
Almost fill the mould with resin

BRINGING BACK THE DINOSAURS

In the film *Jurassic Park*, a scientist extracts dinosaur DNA from a mosquito in amber and brings dinosaurs back to life. This could never happen in reality because DNA disintegrates in fossils. Other body parts, however, are superbly preserved in amber. Insects 100 million years old look as if they died only yesterday, and their tiny mouthparts and wings appear intact under a microscope. Even small lizards and frogs have been preserved in amber. Thanks to amber fossils, scientists know that bees, ants, flies, and all the other main types of insects were present on Earth 100 million years ago.

Hatching dinosaurs (a scene from *Jurassic Park*)

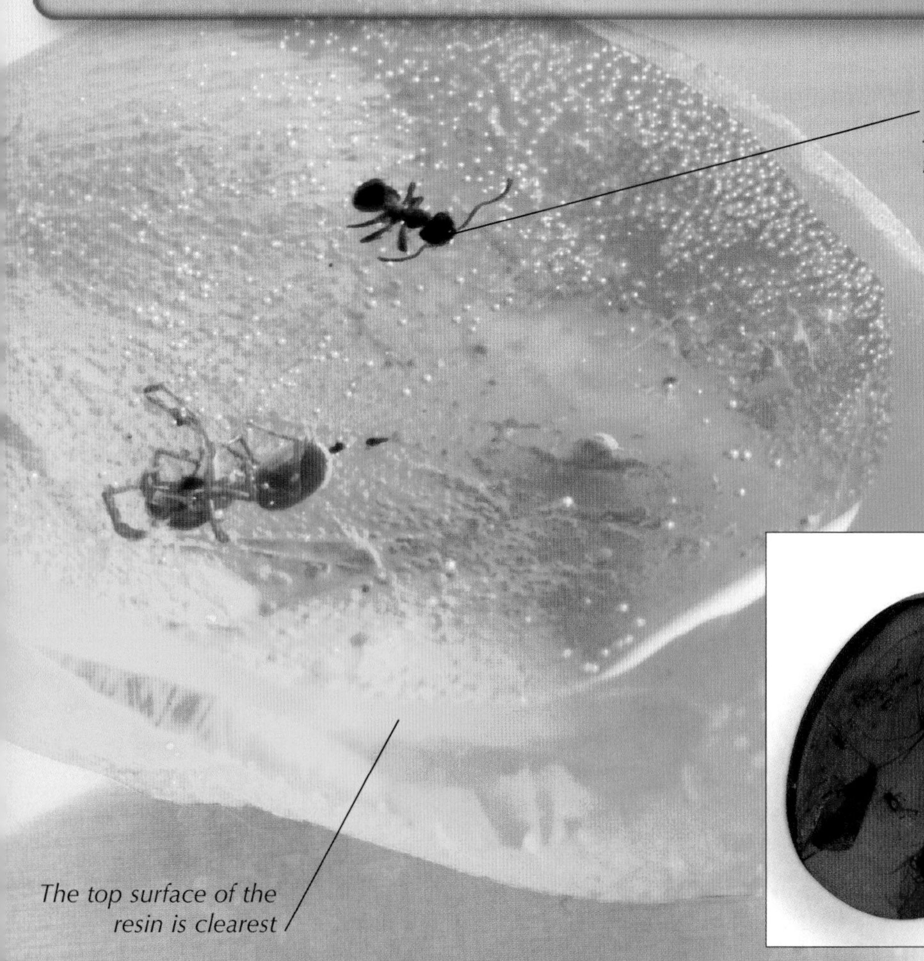

This ant will stay preserved for years

The top surface of the resin is clearest

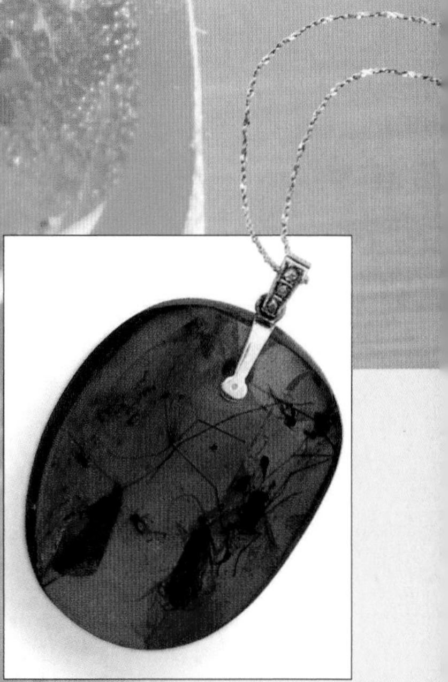

5 **Pour the resin** into the mould, taking care not to overfill it. Drop the insect on the surface and push it down very gently into the resin with a cocktail stick.

6 **After 24 hours** (or when the manufacturer's instructions say that the resin is solid), remove the amber stone from the mould and wash it with soapy water.

Amber jewellery
You can turn your amber fossil into a necklace or keyring. Ask an adult to drill a small hole through the fossil so that you can attach a chain to it.

Fossil mud pie

Professional fossil hunters (palaeontologists) spend weeks at a time digging through soil, sand, and rock for fossils. To protect the fossils, they scrape away the soil very gently, removing it layer by layer. To find out how to dig for fossils, make a fossil mud pie. This is more fun if you do it with a friend and swap mud pies. But don't let your friend see what you hide in yours!

WHAT YOU WILL NEED

- Objects to bury (see step 1 for examples)
- Garden soil (clay-rich soil works best)
- Garden spade
- Bucket
- Mug
- Old mixing bowl or large plastic container
- Water
- Trowel or screwdriver
- Paintbrush
- Cocktail stick or tweezers

An adult may need to help you dig up the soil.

This mud pie is flat, but yours can be any shape

Excavate your fossils slowly and carefully, working from the edge of the mud pie

1 Search your home or garden for hard, dead objects that might make fossils in the future, such as bones, shells, seeds, and pebbles. Include a few human artefacts as well, such as coins, marbles, and small plastic models.

2 Collect three or four spadefuls of soil in a bucket. Ask an adult to break up the soil with the spade, then use your hands to crumble it as finely as possible. Remove any stones or bits of wood, and break up any lumps of soft clay with your fingers.

3 Transfer about six mugfuls of the broken-up soil to an old mixing bowl or plastic container. Add half a cupful of water and mix with your hands to form a very thick mud. Add more water as necessary until the mud is thick enough to form into a solid lump, but isn't runny.

4 Mould the mud into a large clod and bury your "fossils" inside it. Leave it to set in the bowl or container in a dry place for a few days.

HANDY TIP

If your soil is very crumbly or sandy, add flour and water to make it stickier.

5 Once your fossil mud pie has set, swap it with your friend's. Carefully excavate the fossils with a trowel or screwdriver, brushing the soil away gently with a paintbrush. If you find a small delicate item, use a cocktail stick or tweezers to remove it gently from the pie.

IMPORTANT

Check with an adult that the mug and mixing bowl you use for the experiment are not still used for drinks and food. It's best to do this experiment outdoors as it can be messy.

RECONSTRUCTING THE PAST

Digging for fossils is only one part of a palaeontologist's job. When a skeleton has been excavated, the palaeontologist must put together the pieces of the skeleton like a jigsaw puzzle. The bones are analysed for any signs of disease or injury, and the rock around the bones is searched for clues about when and where the animal or person lived, and the probable cause of death.

Fossil rhinoceros ▶
Palaeontologists excavate a 10-million-year-old rhino in Nebraska, USA. It was killed by a cloud of volcanic ash, which hardened around the body, preserving it.

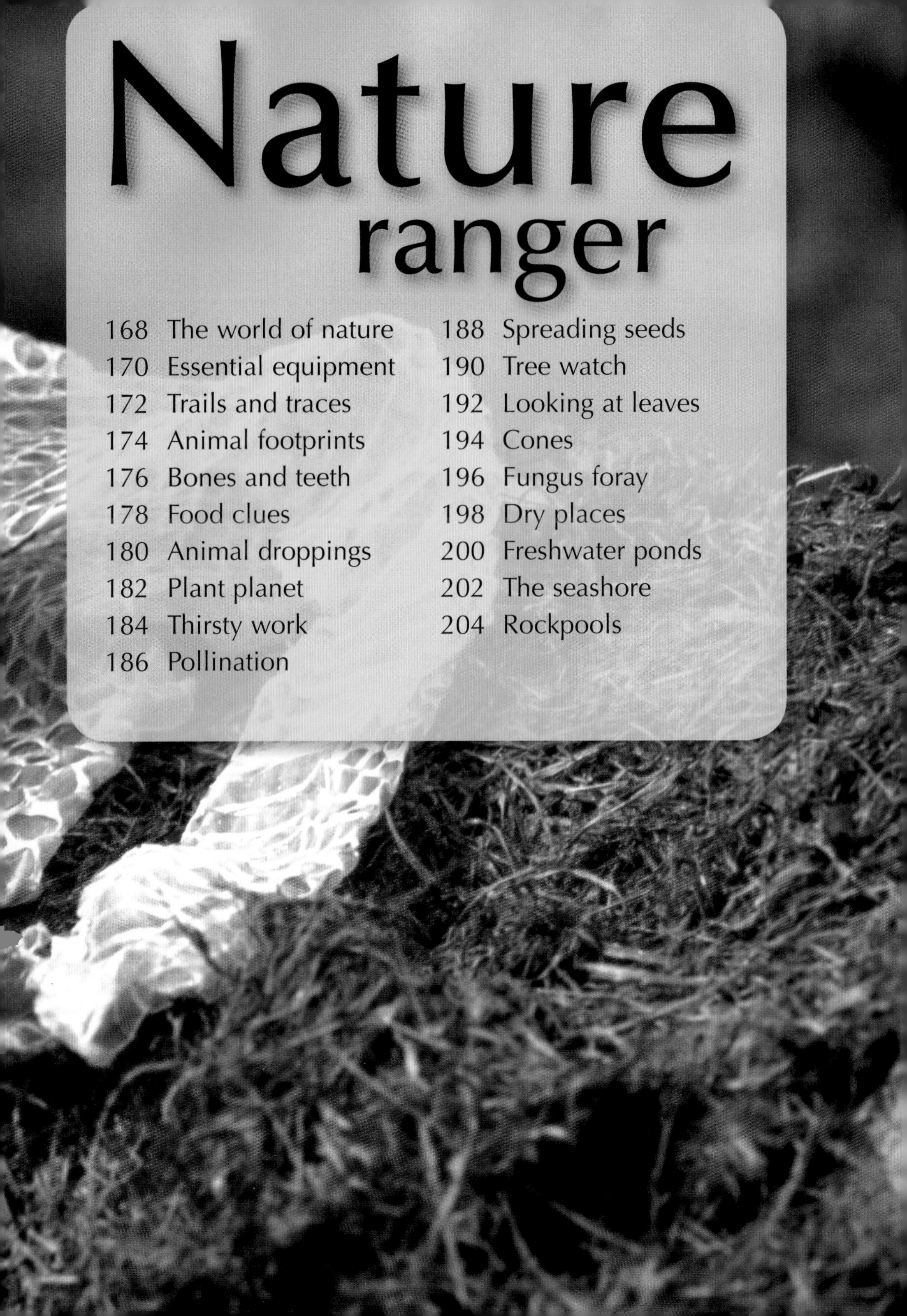

Nature ranger

The world of nature

We are surrounded by an amazing world of nature – an incredible array of animals, plants, and other living things that live in gardens, woodlands, meadows, lakes, rivers, and a host of other places. It doesn't matter whether you live in a city, town, or in the countryside, you can find out lots about this magical world by becoming a nature ranger. It's fun and fascinating, and details of how to do it can be found in the pages that follow.

Harsh conditions
Even the harshest conditions do not deter some organisms. These orange lichens – a combination of fungus and alga – have colonized bare rocks on a windy cliff top.

Plant competitors
Providing it's not too cold, plants grow wherever there is water and light. Plants, unlike animals, do not move around, and they make their own food using sunlight energy. So light is essential for survival, and plants, such as these bluebells in a woodland clearing, compete with their neighbours to make sure they get access to it.

PLANET EARTH

View from space ▲
Taken by a satellite, this photo shows blue oceans, green landmasses, and polar ice.

As far as we know, Earth is the only planet with living organisms. They live in its air, water, on land, and in soil. Earth has water that is vital for life. It has an atmosphere that contains essential oxygen. Its temperatures are neither too hot nor too cold. Earth also supports plants, which harness sunlight to provide an energy source for themselves and all other organisms.

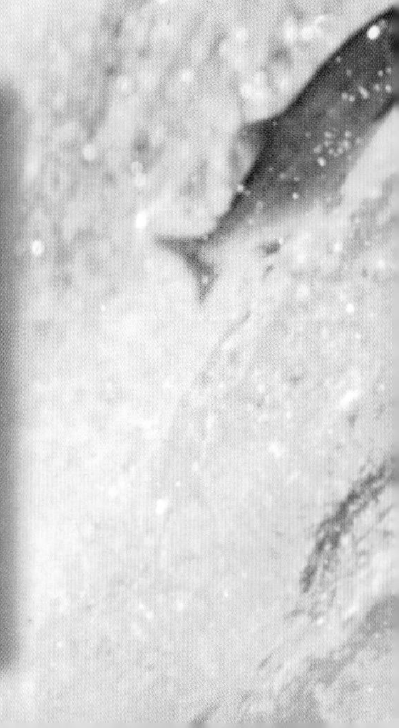

STUDYING NATURE

Scientists who study the living world are called biologists. The two main branches of biology are zoology (the study of animals) and botany (the study of plants). But there are lots of other branches, too. While some biologists work in laboratories, others do more of their research outdoors. They include ecologists, who investigate how living things interact with their surroundings.

◀ **Puffin researcher**
A Norwegian ecologist measures a puffin chick, called a puffling. This is part of his research into Atlantic puffin populations in their cliff-top nesting sites.

Active animals

From termites to tigers, animals form the largest and most varied group of living things. Animals feed on plants or other animals. To find food they move actively and use their senses, just like this grizzly bear, which has caught a migrating salmon.

Essential equipment

Nature ranging is something that might take a few minutes or a whole day. But you can often make the experience more interesting by having the right equipment at the right time. For example, there's nothing more frustrating than spotting a distant bird or mammal that you cannot identify because you haven't got a pair of binoculars.

FIELD KIT

Here you can see some useful nature-ranging equipment. Use this field kit to spot, record, and collect wildlife. You won't need to take all these items with you at the same time. Sometimes you may need other equipment such as dip nets (see opposite).

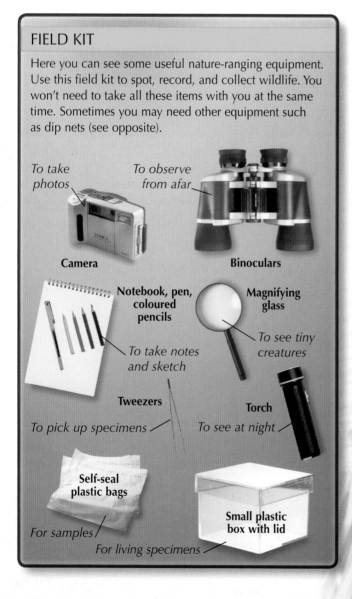

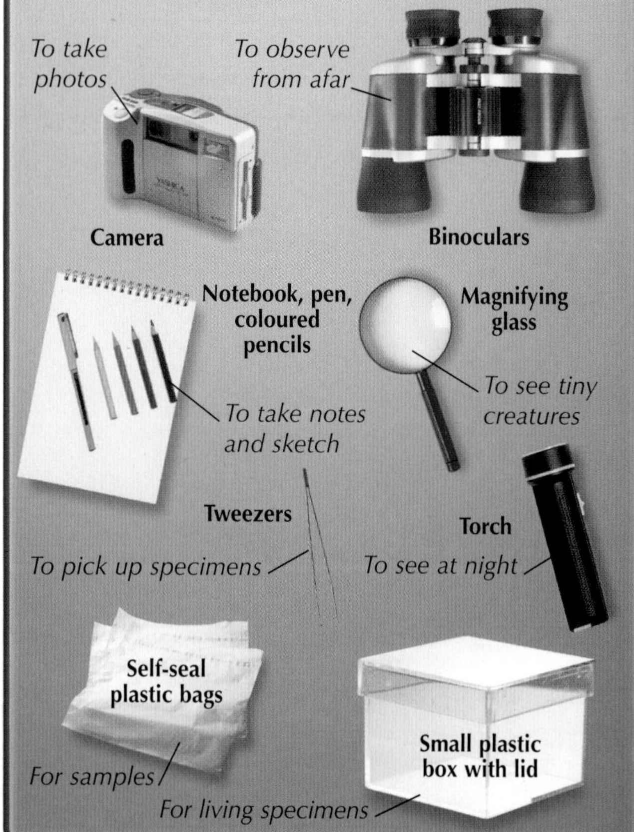

NATURE RANGER'S CODE

When you are nature ranging, do not harm any wildlife or yourself. Always follow these five rules:

- Don't touch any animal or fungus with your bare hands unless you know it is harmless.
- Don't pick wild flowers. You can draw or photograph them instead.
- If you take any animals, return them to their homes after studying them.
- If you move logs or rocks, return them carefully to their original position.
- In the countryside, always close any gates and keep to footpaths.

Nature expedition

It's often more fun, and safer, to go on a nature expedition with some friends. You can compare notes and share information about what you find. These children are doing some pond dipping in search of freshwater animals. They are using dip nets and buckets.

ON SCREEN

Got a digital camera and a computer? Then take pictures of the wildlife you find when you go nature ranging. You can store these on your computer. It's a great way to keep a record of your expeditions.

Pond skater ▶
You can enlarge images of the creatures you photograph. This is an image of a pond skater, an insect that walks over the surface of ponds.

Trails and traces

Whether active at night or during the day, many wild animals are creatures of habit. They follow the same trails and pathways whenever they go in search of food. If you discover a trail, you may get clues as to the animal's identity from the size of the trail or from any traces that the passing animal has left behind, such as a scrap of fur. Even animals that have visited an area only once may accidentally deposit vital evidence. It's up to you to spot these trails and traces.

Animal runways
Some mammals, including this nocturnal badger, follow regular paths that can wear away grass and undergrowth, leaving a visible path or runway.

TRACKING ANIMALS

At one time, the only way to study the movement and behaviour of an animal was to follow it. Today, biologists can track animals by fitting them with radio collars. These send out radio signals, which are picked up by aerials or by satellites. The radio signals allow researchers to map an animal's movements without going anywhere near it.

Radio collars ▲
A lightweight radio collar doesn't stop this harvest mouse clambering up grass stems and behaving normally.

ANIMAL UNDERPASSES

Millions of animals world-wide are killed each year crossing roads. They may be following a regular path in order to feed, or, like toads and some other animals, making an annual migration in order to breed. In some places, special tunnels have been built to help animals avoid roads.

◀ Toad tunnel
A toad emerges from an under-road tunnel in Sussex, England. Toads cross roads when returning to their home ponds in spring to breed. Tunnels like this one greatly reduce the numbers of toads killed by traffic.

WHERE TO LOOK

Wherever you go, be on the lookout for trails and traces.

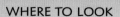

- Gardens
- Woodlands and forests
- Edges of fields
- Open heath and moorland
- Dry scrub
- Coastal areas

ANIMAL TRACES

Whenever you go out nature ranging, keep an eye out for anything that may have been left behind by a passing animal. Even a tiny scrap of fur left on a fence or bush can help you to identify a recent visitor. Other things to look out for are feathers from a moulting bird or even a discarded snake skin. These vital clues can help you put together a picture of the animals that live in your area, even though you may rarely spot the animals themselves.

Snake skin ▶
This grass snake has just shed its scaly skin. Snakes do this when their skin gets too small for their growing body. Look out for snake skins and see if you can identify their owners.

Fur deposit ▶
When they are on the move, mammals rub against sharp objects, such as thorns, leaving behind tufts of fur that can identify them. Here, a rabbit has left some of its fur on a barbed wire fence.

Snail trail ▶
A shiny, silvery trail is a sure sign that a snail or slug has recently passed that way. They produce a film of slippery mucus that helps them to glide over paths, walls, or leaves.

Missing bark ▶
Some mammals use trees as itching posts. This red deer is using a branch to rub the "felt" off its growing antlers. Such rubbing leaves tell-tale marks, but also damages the bark.

Animal footprints

Wild mammals tend to stay out of sight, and some come out only at night. But even if you don't see an animal, you can detect its presence by the tell-tale footprints it leaves. By identifying tracks you can discover which animals live in your neighbourhood or the places you go nature ranging. Tracks also tell you how animals move. You can produce a permanent record of mammal and other animal tracks by making casts of them using plaster of Paris.

WHAT YOU WILL NEED

- Strip of thin cardboard 25 cm (10 in) long and 4 cm (1.5 in) wide
- Paper clips
- Jug of water
- Mixing bowl or bucket
- Plaster of Paris
- Spoon
- Water
- Old toothbrush

1 **Find some** animal tracks. Good places to look are shady woodlands or near ponds where there is moist, firm mud or sand. When you find some tracks, look for the clearest ones. Shown above are clear examples of deer footprints.

2 **Remove any** loose twigs or leaves from the footprints. Shape the strip of cardboard into a ring, securing it with the paper clips. Push the ring downwards so it surrounds the footprints. Make sure there are no gaps around the bottom.

3 **Put some** plaster of Paris into the bowl. Slowly pour water from the jug into the bowl, stirring the mixture continually with the spoon. When you have smooth, slightly runny plaster, pour it into the cardboard ring.

OBSERVING TRACKS

When you come across tracks, count the number of toes, and look out for claw marks. Also look at the shape of the footprints. Some mammals, including dogs and cats, walk on their toes, while others walk with their heels flat on the ground.

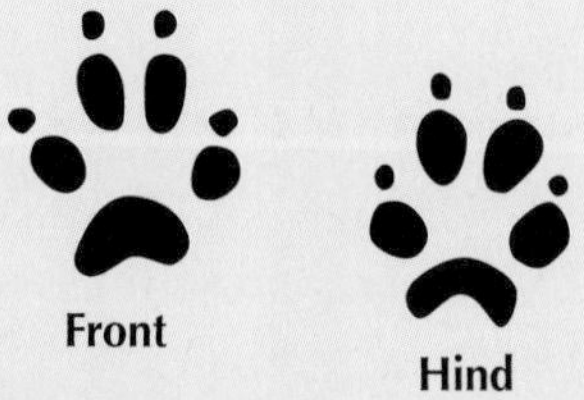

Dog family ▲
Members of the dog family, such as foxes and wolves, show four toes in both front and hind feet. They also leave claw marks.

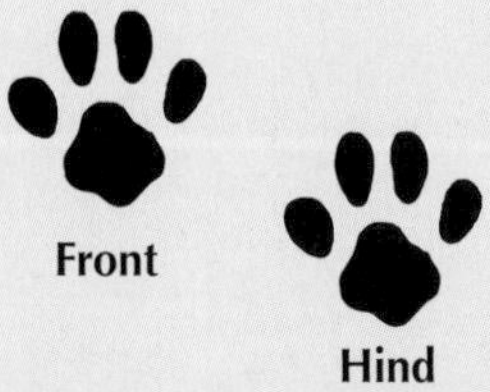

Cat family ▲
Cat footprints, such as lynx and bobcats, show four front and hind toes. There are no claw marks – claws are pulled in when walking.

FOOTPRINTS IN THE SNOW

A snowy winter's day can provide a good opportunity to search for animal tracks. Snow is a great surface for spotting footprints – in this case, those of a snowshoe hare. Hares and rabbits move by hopping or bounding. They push off with their long, powerful hind feet and land on their smaller front feet. Their hind feet land just ahead of their front feet ready to push off again.

Snowshoe hare tracks

Deer

These animals belong to the group of even-toed, hoofed mammals that also includes pigs and cattle. The twin, hoofed toes on each foot leave an easily recognized footprint.

4 **Leave the plaster** to set for about 15 minutes. Then, lift up the plaster – complete with the cardboard ring – take it home, and leave for a further 24 hours to set completely. Brush off any remaining mud with the old toothbrush. Try to identify which animal made the print.

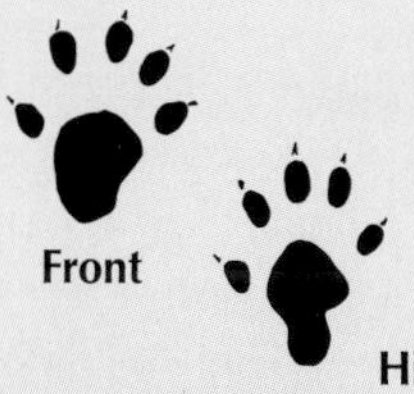

Mustelid family ▲
Animals of the mustelid family, such as otters and badgers, have five front and hind toes. They also have extended claws.

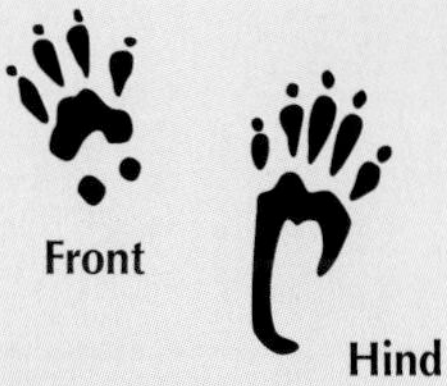

Rodents ▲
Squirrels and other rodents walk flat on their feet. They have four front and five hind toes. They also have claws.

Rabbits and hares ▶
With four toes, front and rear, rabbit and hare tracks are easy to identify because the hind foot is much longer than the front.

Bones and teeth

When animals die, their skin, muscles, and other soft parts soon rot away or are eaten by other animals. But their bones and teeth remain – and can tell you a lot about the animal they once belonged to. When you go nature ranging, look out for skulls and other bones and see if you can tell what animal they came from. Some biologists clean the bones from dead animals and rebuild their skeletons for further study.

IMPORTANT

When handling bones always wear rubber gloves and wash the gloves afterwards.

Necrophagous beetles

The word necrophagous means "eating the dead" and that's exactly what these beetles do. Here you can see one feeding on a dead shrew. Some biologists use these beetles to strip soft tissues from animals that died naturally in the wild, so that only the skeleton is left.

BONE STRUCTURE

If you find long bones, such as leg bones, you may be able to tell whether they come from mammals or birds. Bird bones are lighter for their size because they are either hollow or contain air spaces reinforced by a honeycomb of struts. A bird's light skeleton makes flight possible.

Mammal and bird bones ▶
As you can see, the structure of a mammal bone is thicker and heavier than that of a bird bone. A bird bone only has a thin outer layer surrounding a large space.

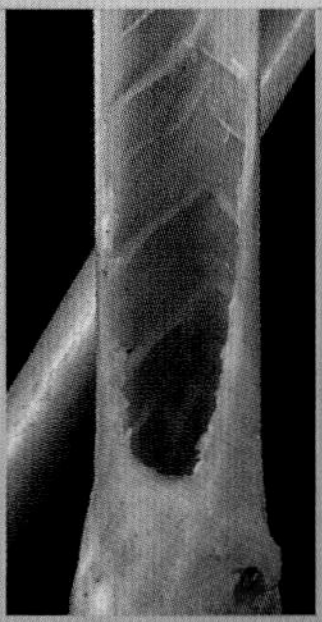

Bird bone

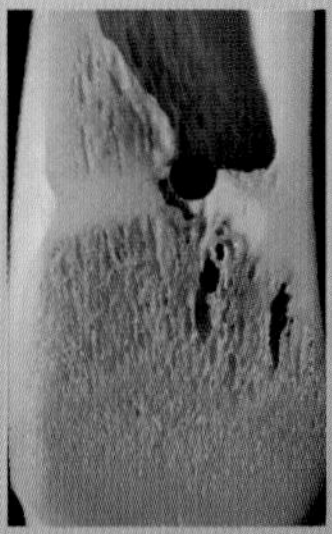

Cow bone

DENTAL CHECK

In open country or woodland you may find a mammal skull, such as the ones shown here. The shape and teeth can identify its owner and its diet. There are four types of mammal teeth. Incisors at the front bite and slice. Canines pierce and grip. Large premolars and molars at the back grind or cut.

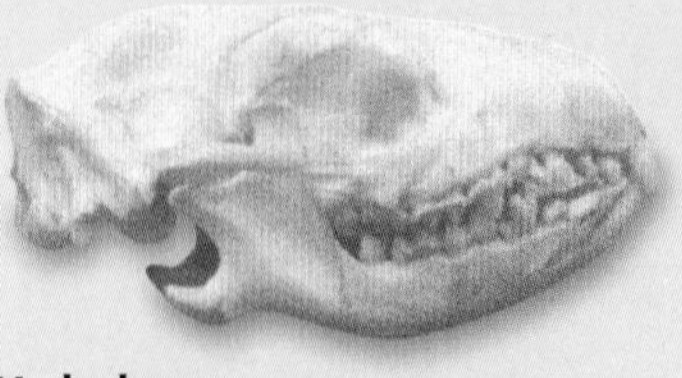

Hedgehog ▲
The hedgehog's big incisors and sharp, biting premolars and molars are ideal for its varied diet, which includes beetles, worms, and slugs, as well as birds' eggs and carrion.

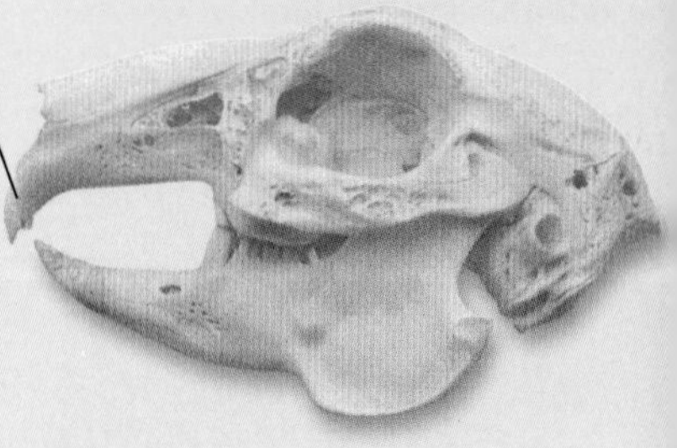

Rabbit ▲
Hares and rabbits are herbivores with long, gnawing incisors. These teeth grow constantly so they don't wear down as they slide past each other to slice off pieces of grass.

SKELETONS

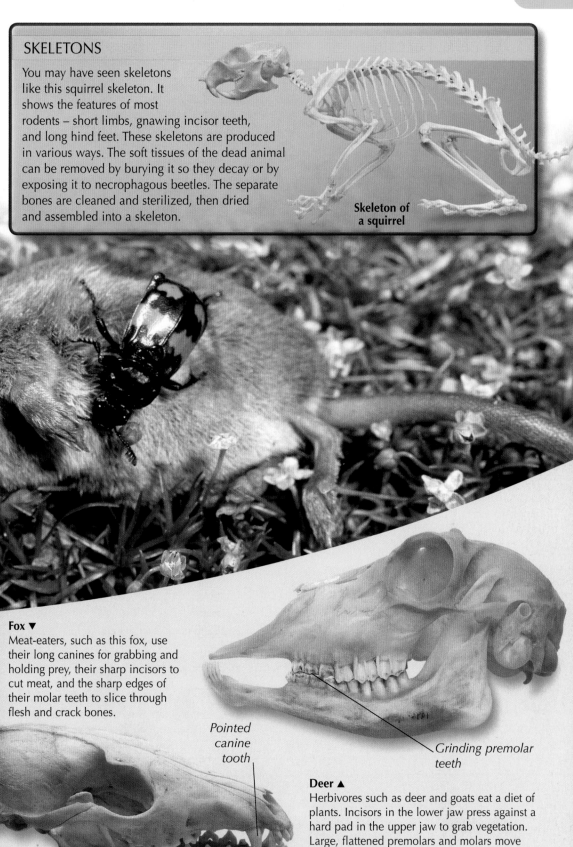

You may have seen skeletons like this squirrel skeleton. It shows the features of most rodents – short limbs, gnawing incisor teeth, and long hind feet. These skeletons are produced in various ways. The soft tissues of the dead animal can be removed by burying it so they decay or by exposing it to necrophagous beetles. The separate bones are cleaned and sterilized, then dried and assembled into a skeleton.

Skeleton of a squirrel

Fox ▼
Meat-eaters, such as this fox, use their long canines for grabbing and holding prey, their sharp incisors to cut meat, and the sharp edges of their molar teeth to slice through flesh and crack bones.

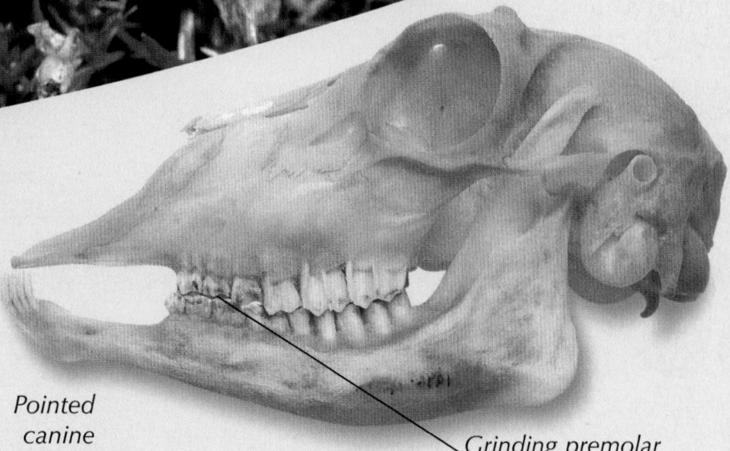

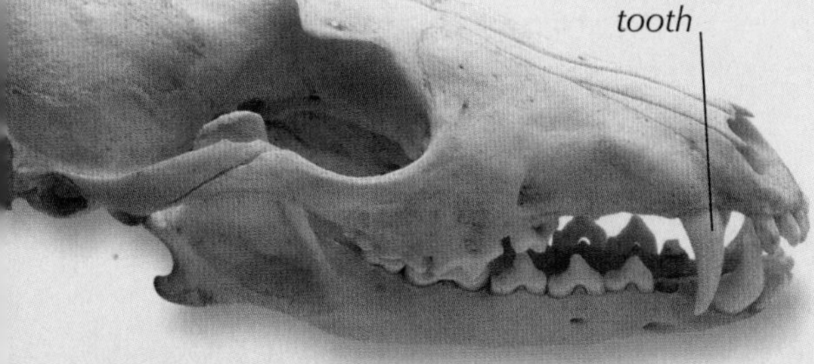

Deer ▲
Herbivores such as deer and goats eat a diet of plants. Incisors in the lower jaw press against a hard pad in the upper jaw to grab vegetation. Large, flattened premolars and molars move side to side, grinding tough plants into pulp.

Food clues

When some animals feed they leave behind no traces of what they ate. Many animals, however, are much messier, and leave clues that show what they are and what they've been eating. Look carefully when you're exploring nature and you'll soon notice plenty of these clues, enabling you to build up a list of the animals that live in an area. For example, if you find an animal corpse, a quick look may reveal what kind of animal made the kill. If you find chewed leaves or nuts, you may even be able to tell which animal did the chewing.

Wings are tough and rarely eaten

Just wings
Bird wings can indicate a kill by a fox or coyote, or by a bird of prey. Wings are often left behind because they contain little meat. These wings mark the spot where a fox killed a jay. A bird of prey usually leaves a ring of neatly plucked feathers.

Chipmunk gnaws a nut held in its front paws

Gnawed nuts
Rodents use their chisel-like teeth to gnaw into hard nuts to reach the seed inside. The remains of the shell can identify which rodent was feeding. Chipmunks and squirrels, for example, split nuts cleanly in half.

IMPORTANT

If you find a dead animal or part of one, look at it but do not touch it.

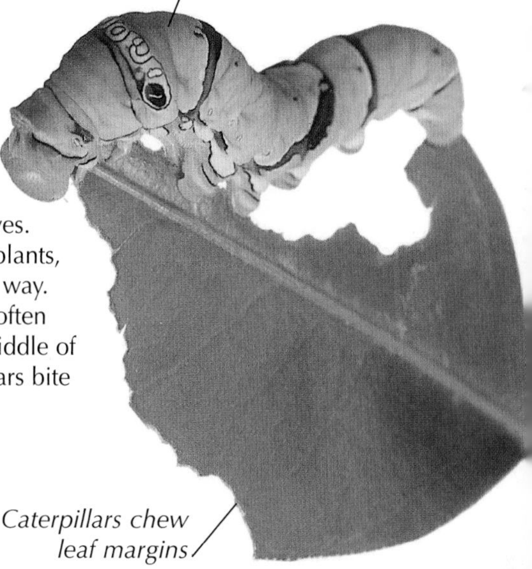

Chewed leaves

Lots of insects eat leaves. Many favour specific plants, or feed in a particular way. Beetles, for example, often cut pieces from the middle of leaves, while caterpillars bite bits from the edge.

Fish heads

You may find fish heads, tails, or other chewed remains on the banks of clean freshwater streams or ponds, or on some isolated seashores. This can indicate the presence of otters.

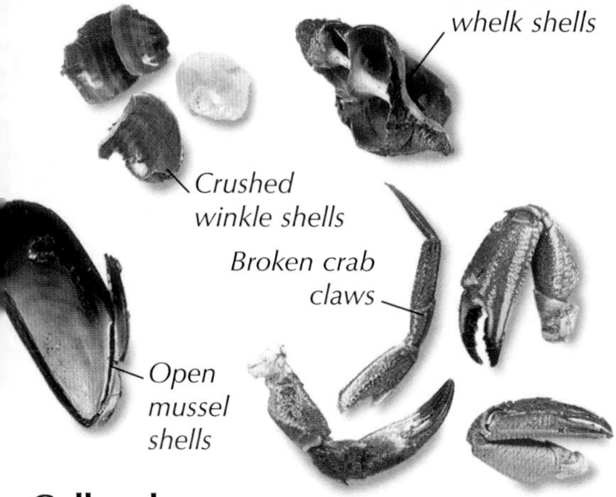

Gull garbage

On rocky shores many animals are encased in a shell or hard case. Hungry gulls get around this by dropping their prey on to rocks to smash the outer covering so the juicy flesh can be extracted.

FOOD STORES

Some animals cache, or store, food for future use. In summer and autumn, for example, you may see squirrels or jays burying seeds and nuts that they will retrieve in winter when food is in short supply. Orb web spiders wrap up prey in silk packages for eating later. If you come across a small animal impaled on a thorn or the spike of a barbed wire fence, you may have found a shrike's larder.

Shrike's larder ▲

Great grey shrikes feed on small mammals, reptiles, amphibians, and insects. Here, one has impaled a sparrow on a tree thorn, which will act as a "larder" until the bird is ready to eat its prey.

Animal droppings

All animals leave behind droppings, or scats, as they're sometimes known. For nature rangers, droppings are a mine of information, and it's quite safe to study them as long as you don't touch them with bare hands. A professional naturalist can tell which animal produced droppings and when, what the animal had eaten, how big it was, and what sex. Don't expect to be able to do this when you start, but you will soon be able to tell the difference between different types of mammal droppings.

WHAT TO LOOK FOR

- Tube-shaped droppings, perhaps with pointed ends (fox, raccoon, skunk, opossum, or bear)
- Thinner, rounded tube (cats, such as lynx)
- Long, thin (weasel or stoat)
- Rounded with plant fibre content (deer, rabbits, or hares)
- Rice-grain shaped (rats and other rodents)

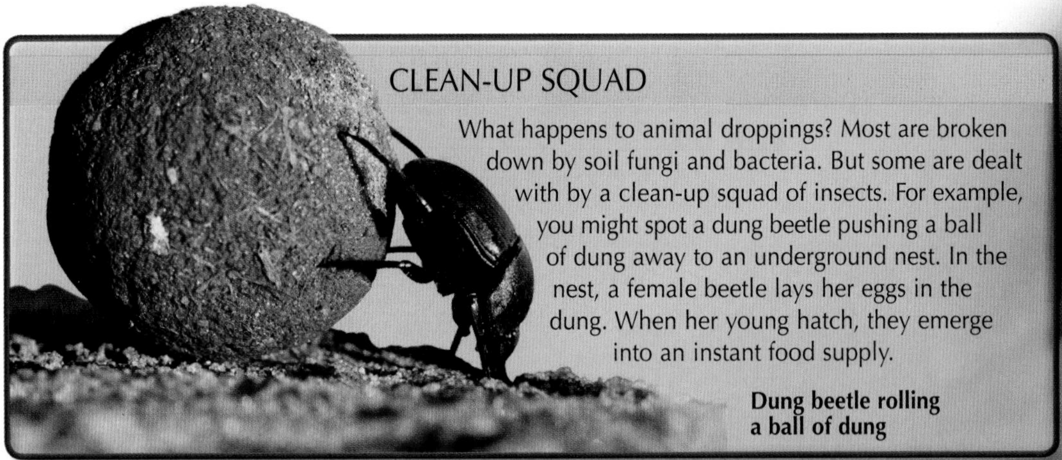

CLEAN-UP SQUAD

What happens to animal droppings? Most are broken down by soil fungi and bacteria. But some are dealt with by a clean-up squad of insects. For example, you might spot a dung beetle pushing a ball of dung away to an underground nest. In the nest, a female beetle lays her eggs in the dung. When her young hatch, they emerge into an instant food supply.

Dung beetle rolling a ball of dung

DROPPINGS GALLERY

By examining droppings you can get a good idea of which animal passed by recently and what it ate. Herbivore droppings are rounded with traces of indigestible plant fibres. Carnivore droppings are usually long and may contain fur, bones, and other prey remains. Here are some common examples of droppings to look out for.

Rabbit droppings ▲
These spherical droppings are very common and are often found in small clumps. Rabbit droppings are dark brown when fresh, but turn greener and paler as they age and dry out.

Deer droppings ▲
The droppings left by deer are dark and cylindrical. Deer eat low-nutrient vegetation so they have to eat a lot to derive any benefit. Hence, they leave behind large amounts of droppings.

Animal latrine

Some mammals leave their droppings in specific locations called latrines. These smelly piles mark out the boundary of that particular animal's territory (in this case, a badger's) and warn other members of the same species to stay away.

BIRD PELLETS

At first glance, bird pellets might look like droppings, but they are not. So what exactly are they? Birds don't have teeth, so they can't chew their food. Some birds swallow food whole, then regurgitate the hard, indigestible parts of their meal as a soft package called a pellet. Perhaps the most interesting pellets are produced by owls. You can look for these at the bottom of trees or fence posts, or in old barns, where owls roost. Owl pellets can be moistened and gently pulled apart to reveal tiny skulls, bones, and fur.

Owl pellet

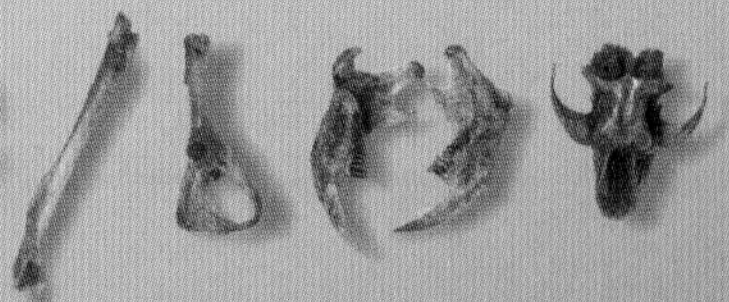

Bones found in pellet

Buried droppings

Have you noticed how domestic cats dig a shallow hole to defecate into, then carefully cover their droppings with soil? The same is true for wild species of small cats, such as this bobcat. Sometimes, droppings may also be left in a latrine to mark territory.

IMPORTANT

Never handle animal droppings or pellets with your bare hands. Always wear rubber gloves, which should be washed afterwards.

Otter droppings ▲
Spraints, or otter droppings, are often found on riverbanks. They are irregular in shape, black and sticky when fresh, and contain fish and insect parts. They may be used to mark territory.

Fox droppings ▲
Foxes are omnivores (they eat both plants and meat), so their tubular, sometimes twisted, droppings may contain the fur of small animals, insect wings and casings, or wild fruit seeds.

Wild cat droppings ▲
Cats feed only on other animals. Their droppings can have rounded or tapering ends, and may be divided into smaller pieces. Droppings may contain animal fur.

Plant planet

The Earth's land surface provides a home for an astonishing variety of plants. They have the unique ability to make their own food by photosynthesis. This is the process by which plants use the green chlorophyll that colours their leaves to trap the Sun's energy to make sugars. Photosynthesis also releases the oxygen that you and other organisms breathe in. You can use pondweed to see the process in action.

Test tube is full of water at the beginning of the experiment
In sunlight, the pondweed slowly releases tiny oxygen bubbles
Pondweed in upside-down funnel

1 **Half fill** a sink with cold water. Hold the jar underwater, put some pondweed in it, then place the funnel upside-down inside the jar to trap the pondweed.

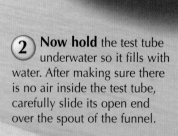

2 **Now hold** the test tube underwater so it fills with water. After making sure there is no air inside the test tube, carefully slide its open end over the spout of the funnel.

3 **Keeping the jar**, funnel, and test tube upright, remove them together from the water in the sink. Carefully tip a little water from the jar so it does not spill over. Place the assembled equipment indoors on a sunny windowsill.

WHAT YOU WILL NEED

- Glass jar
- Test tube
- Wide-necked funnel
- Pondweed, such as hornwort or elodea
- Wooden splint or taper
- Matches
- Water

An adult should help you when you use the matches and splint.

After a few hours in sunlight, the test tube fills with oxygen

PLANT CENSUS

Wherever you look, there are often many different plants living side by side. You can find out how many by carrying out a plant census. You need a measuring square called a quadrat. Throw the quadrat at random over an area of ground, then record the plants in each small square to make a quadrat map.

Quadrat ▲
A quadrat consists of a square wooden frame divided into 16 smaller squares by six pieces of string or wire.

4 **When the tube** is nearly filled with oxygen, put your thumb over the end of the tube and remove it from the jar.

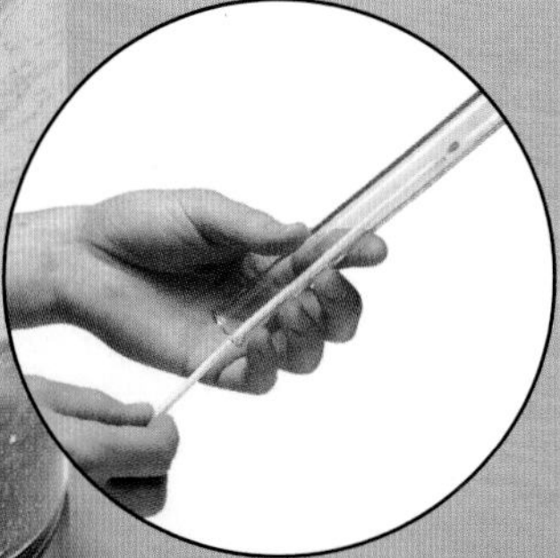

5 **Ask an adult** to light the splint, blow it out, then put the glowing tip into the test tube. It will relight, showing that pure oxygen is present.

THE WORLD OF PLANTS

There are 300,000 different plant types on Earth, but most belong to one of four groups that you will easily recognize.

Flowering plants ▼
Around 80 per cent of all plants reproduce using flowers that produce seeds. The biggest are broad-leaved trees, such as oaks. The smallest is tiny duckweed, which floats on ponds.

Dog rose

◀ Conifers
Pines, firs, spruces, cedars, and other conifers produce seeds in cones instead of flowers.

Scots pine

Ferns ▶
Fond of damp, shady places, ferns have fronds, or leaves, divided into leaflets. They reproduce by releasing spores.

Buckler fern

Mosses and liverworts ▼
These small, delicate plants grow in clumps in damp and wet places. They have no true roots or leaves, and reproduce using spores.

Moss

Thirsty work

WHAT YOU WILL NEED

- Two drinking glasses
- Food colouring
- Water • Spoon
- Pale-coloured flower with a long stem, such as a white carnation
- Sticky tape
- Sharp knife
- Chopping board

Ask an adult to split the stem.

Plants need lots of water to grow and stay alive. Water also keeps plant cells firm, holding plants upright and in shape. Without water, plants wilt and die. Plants take in water through their roots. It travels up microscopic pipelines in their stems to leaves and flowers. From here, much of the water evaporates into the air as water vapour. This process, called transpiration, provides the "pull" that draws up more water through roots and stems. You can see water moving up a plant in this simple experiment.

1 **Lay the flower** carefully on a cutting surface. Ask an adult to slice its stem in two, working from the base of the stem to around halfway up.

2 **Wind some** tape around the stem just above the top end of the cut. This prevents the stem from splitting any further. Each half-stem contains water-transporting tubes.

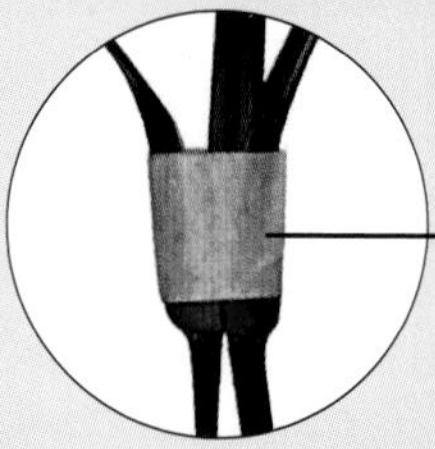

Sticky tape prevents upper part of stem from splitting

3 **Pour water into** both glasses until they are three-quarters full. Add food colouring to one glass and stir well.

STORING WATER

While most plants need a constant supply of water, some plants have an amazing ability to store water for long periods of time. The most obvious are desert plants such as cacti, which store water from infrequent rain in their thick, expandable stems. Some rainforest plants also store water. These stores can sometimes provide a life-saving drink of clean water for people able to identify the right plants.

Water vine ▸
A forest dweller drinks water from a water vine in the Amazonian rainforest in Brazil. He has cut into the vine to release the fresh, clean water.

Food colouring left behind in petals as water evaporates into the air
These petals stay white because they receive plain water from the left-hand glass
Separate mini-tubes in stem carry plain water and coloured water
Tiny tubes carry water and food colouring up this half of the stem
Red food colouring is dissolved in this glass of water
Glass contains plain water without any food colouring

MAKING WEATHER

Around the equator, where temperatures are high all year, tropical rainforests create their own weather. When daily rain soaks the forest soil, millions of trees, shrubs, and plants take up the water. This water evaporates from their leaves as water vapour, which forms clouds above the rainforest. Eventually, more rain falls from these clouds.

Tropical rainforest ▲
This aerial view of a lowland rainforest in the Danum Valley in Borneo shows rain clouds forming above the treetops following heavy rain.

4. **Put each half-stem** into one of the glasses. Support the flower by leaning it against a wall or window. Leave the flower to take up water. Come back every 15 minutes to look at the petals.

5. **Within one hour** you should see half of the flower changing colour. This indicates that water is travelling up the stem and into the flower. This is happening along both half-stems but is only visible on the coloured side where the water reaching the flower contains the food colouring.

Pollination

Flowers don't grow just for us to admire. They make pollen, which is carried to other flowers of the same kind. This is called pollination. The pollen is used to make seeds. Some flowers use wind to spread pollen, but many depend on animal visitors, such as insects, to pollinate their flowers. Attracted by a flower's bright colours and strong smells, animals come to feed on nectar, a sweet-tasting liquid food. While they are there, animals pick up pollen and carry it to other flowers. When animals pollinate flowers they are often too busy to worry about being watched, so you may be able to observe them quite closely.

Long tongues
Look out for butterflies visiting sweet-smelling flowers, such as buddleia or this marjoram. They uncoil their tongues to reach the nectar at the bottom of narrow, tube-shaped flowers.

IMPORTANT

Don't touch or get too close to bees while they are visiting flowers because they may sting you.

ALL ABOUT POLLEN

Pollen consists of tiny specks called pollen grains made by anthers, the male parts of the flower. In wind-pollinated flowers the grains are light and dusty, but in animal-pollinated flowers they are often sticky. During pollination, pollen grains are carried to the female part of the same kind of flower, where seeds are made.

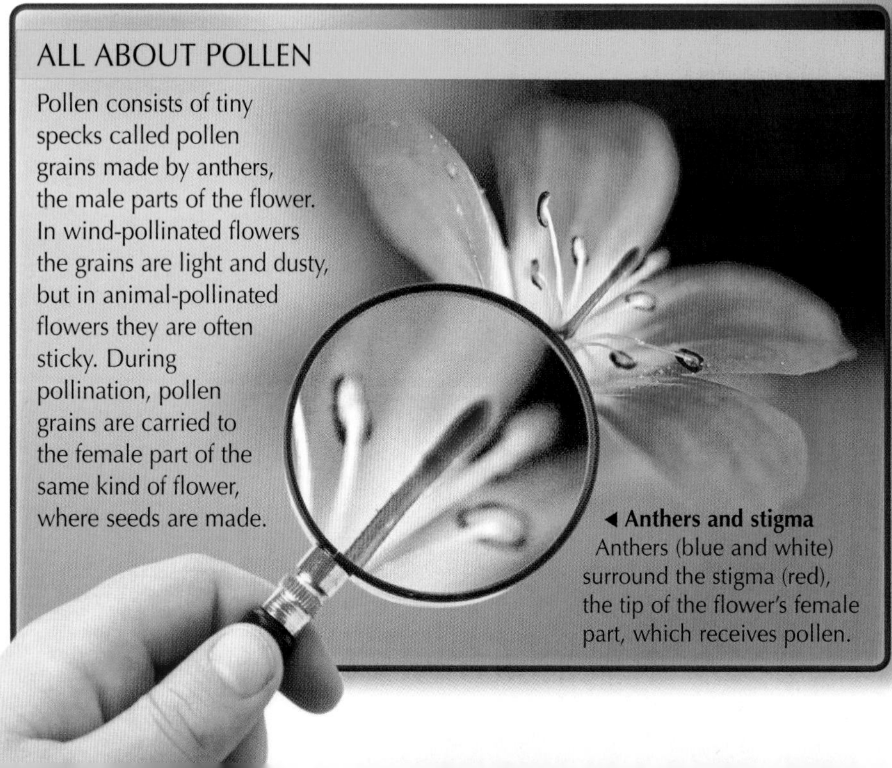

◀ **Anthers and stigma**
Anthers (blue and white) surround the stigma (red), the tip of the flower's female part, which receives pollen.

Blowing in the wind

On dry, summer days look out for grasses shedding clouds of pollen. Grasses and other wind-pollinated plants release thousands of pollen grains into the wind. Their flowers are small, drab, and smell-free because, being wind-pollinated, they don't need to attract insects.

POLLINATING BIRDS

In some parts of the world – the Americas, Africa, Asia, and Australia – birds as well as insects pollinate flowers. Some, such as honey creepers, clamber over flowers as they search for nectar, accidentally picking up pollen at the same time. But hummingbirds feed while hovering in mid-air. Spotting bird-pollinated flowers is easy. Most of them are yellow or red, and they rarely smell.

Hummingbird ▶ A summer visitor to eastern North America, this ruby-throated hummingbird hovers as it feeds on the flower's nectar.

Honey guides

Pollinating insects, such as this bumblebee targeting a foxglove, are helped in their search for nectar. They are often directed towards a flower's nectar stores by dots or lines on its petals called honey guides.

WHERE TO LOOK

- Look for bees on bright, showy flowers, especially blue, purple, or yellow ones
- Look for butterflies on buddleia or other tube-shaped, scented flowers
- Look for birds on red and yellow flowers, such as poinsettia

Spreading seeds

Plants need to disperse, or spread, their seeds far and wide so they have enough space, water, and light to sprout and grow. Seeds develop inside fruits that help them to disperse by various routes – wind, animals, water, and even by explosive force. In summer, look for tricks used by plants to spread seeds. Some seeds spread by sticking to fur or feathers – or to your socks and shoes. After a nature-ranging walk, find out whether you have given any seeds a lift home.

WHAT YOU WILL NEED

- Metal baking tray
- Oven gloves • Compost
- Blunt knife or screwdriver
- Water sprayer or indoor watering can
- Cling film or polythene bag

Ask an adult to supervise putting the tray into, and removing it from, the oven.

1 **Put a layer** of compost in the baking tray. Preheat the oven to 100°C (210°F). Place the tray in the oven and "bake" the compost for 30 minutes. This will kill any seeds that are already in the compost.

2 **Using oven gloves,** remove the baking tray from the oven. Leave it to cool in a safe location.

3 **Use the knife** or screwdriver to scrape the soles of your walking shoes on to the compost. Water the compost, seal it with the bag or cling film, and put it on a sunny windowsill.

Grass grows from the picked-up seeds

HANDY TIP

Wear trainers or walking boots so that seeds get trapped in the treads.

TASTY FRUITS

Some plants produce sweet, juicy fruits that attract and provide food for many birds and mammals, including ourselves. Once eaten, the fruit is digested, but the seeds pass unharmed out of the animal's body in its droppings. Animals are always on the move and so the seeds are deposited well away from their parent plant – and in a "starter kit" of natural fertilizer.

◀ **Berry eater**
A young northern mockingbird eats the juicy, purple berries of the pokeweed plant. The seeds in the bird's droppings will be deposited elsewhere, allowing new pokeweed plants to thrive.

4 **During the next** 10 days, check the tray regularly and keep the compost moist. You should soon see new plants sprouting from the seeds picked up by your shoes.

Newly sprouted plant grows towards the light

SNAPPING, DRIFTING, AND FLOATING

Not all seeds are spread by animals. Some are flung explosively into the air, blown by wind, or dispersed by oceans and rivers.

Snapping pods ▶
On warm summer days, listen for sharp snapping sounds coming from overgrown places and shrubs. These sounds are made by pods (fruits) that snap open as they dry out, flinging their seeds through the air.

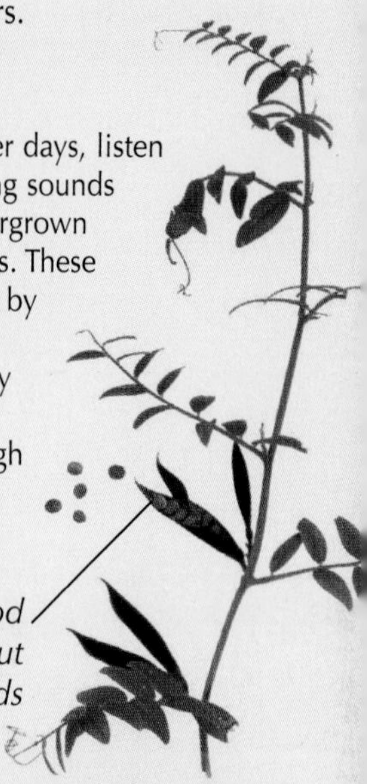

Exploding pod throws out the seeds

Cow vetch

Drifting away ▲
Many plants produce fruits with wings, fluffy sails, or – like this dandelion – individual parachutes. In dry weather, the seedheads open out, and seeds drift away in the wind.

Floating seeds ▶
A few plants depend on water to help them spread their seeds. You might see them washed up on a beach. Their fruits are designed to float, sometimes – as with this sprouting coconut – over long distances.

Tree watch

Trees form a vital part of the living world. They release oxygen into the air and absorb carbon dioxide, and their branches, leaves, and seeds provide shelter and food for many animals. Trees are also the tallest and longest-lived plants in the world. Here, you can find out the height and age of a tree.

WHAT YOU WILL NEED

- Measuring tape
- Long stick or cane
- Pencil and notebook
- Calculator
- A friend to help you

1 **Choose a tree.** Stand facing, and some distance away from, the tree. Ask your friend to stand at the bottom of the tree with the stick.

2 **Hold out** the pencil at arm's length and line it up so that the top of the pencil is level with the top of the tree. Still keeping the pencil in position, move your thumb down the pencil so it is level with the bottom of the tree.

HOW OLD?

Which trees? ▲
This method works for most trees except for fast growers (firs) and slow growers (horse chestnuts).

One way of working out the age of a tree is to count the growth rings that radiate from the centre of its trunk. Unfortunately, you have to cut down the tree first! So here's a simpler way of estimating a tree's age. Take a tape measure and measure the circumference (distance around) of the trunk in centimetres at a point 1.5 m (5 ft) above the ground. Using a calculator, divide the circumference by 2.5 to get the tree's age in years.

BROAD-LEAVED TREES AND CONIFERS

It's easy to tell whether a tree is broad-leaved or a conifer. Broad-leaved trees, such as oaks, birches, and cherries, have broad, thin leaves and flowers that develop seeds. Broad-leaved trees often shed their leaves in autumn. Conifers, such as firs, pines, and spruces, have narrow, hard leaves that are needle- or scale-shaped. Conifers produce their seeds in cones, are evergreen, and they often smell aromatic.

Oak

Scots pine

Try to find out whether the tree is a broad-leaved tree or a conifer, and what species
This distance is the height of the tree

3 **Keeping your thumb** in place, turn the pencil so it is horizontal. Ask your friend to walk away from the trunk. Tell them to stop when level with the tip of the pencil, and to mark the spot with the stick.

4 **Now measure** with the tape the distance from the stick to the base of the tree and record it in your notebook. This is the height of the tree. Try to find out the name of the tree.

Looking at leaves

WHAT YOU WILL NEED

- Fallen leaves
- Saucepan
- 1 l ($1\frac{3}{4}$ pts) water
- 40 g ($1\frac{1}{2}$ oz) washing soda crystals
- Rubber gloves
- Blotting paper
- Notebook

Ask an adult to help when you heat the water and soda.

Without leaves, trees and other plants would not be able to collect the light they need to grow. Evergreen trees keep their leaves all year round, whereas deciduous trees have more delicate leaves that are shed during the coldest times of the year. Leaves are supported by a network of veins that fan out from a central midrib, which arises from the leaf stalk. Veins carry essential materials to and from the leaf's cells. You can make a leaf skeleton by removing the soft parts of the leaf blade to expose the network of veins.

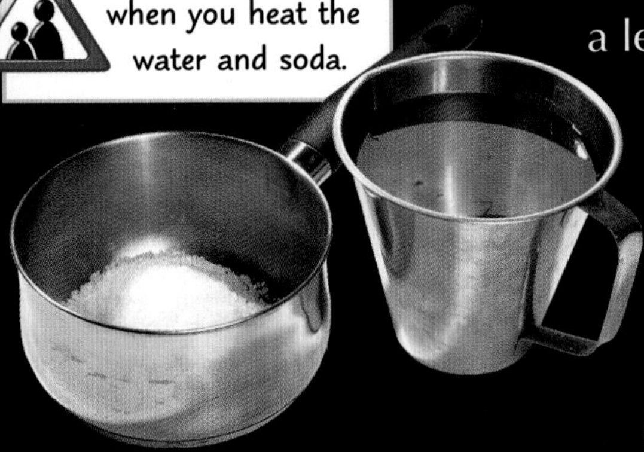

1 **Add the water** to a saucepan along with the washing soda crystals. Heat the pan until the water and washing soda start to boil.

2 **Remove the pan** from the heat. Put the leaves into the hot washing soda solution and leave there for several hours.

3 **Wearing the rubber gloves**, put the saucepan under a tap and rinse the leaves thoroughly in cold water. Washing removes the soft parts of the leaf, so that a skeleton of midrib and veins is left behind. Dry the leaf skeletons on the blotting paper and then stick them into your nature notebook.

AUTUMN COLOURS

In autumn, the leaves of deciduous trees change colour before they are shed. The chlorophyll that colours leaves green breaks down, and is replaced by other pigments that produce yellows, oranges, and reds.

LEAF PRINTS

You can make leaf prints in much the same way you make bark rubbings. To record the different shapes and textures of leaves put a leaf on a smooth surface and cover it with a piece of white paper. Holding the paper in place, rub over the leaf with a soft coloured pencil or wax crayon.

◀ Colourful copies
Leaf prints record not just a leaf's shape but also its pattern of veins. Try to label each rubbing with the tree that the leaf came from.

Veins are visible on e leaf after washing with soda water

LEAF TYPES

The leaves of broad-leaved trees (dicot flowering plants) have branching veins and include simple and compound types. Palm trees have broad fronds. Conifer leaves are narrow and leathery.

Simple leaf ▶
A simple leaf, such as this maple, consists of a single leaf blade that is not divided. Both simple and compound leaves are classified by shape.

Maple

Mountain ash

◀ Compound leaf
This leaf may look like many leaves, but it is actually a single leaf, called a compound leaf. It is divided into many small leaflets attached to a central stalk.

Palm leaf ▶
Palms are trees that belong to a group of flowering plants called monocots. Their leaves are frond-like and have parallel veins.

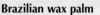

Brazilian wax palm

Santa Lucia fir

◀ Conifer leaf
Mostly evergreen, conifers have hard needle- or scale-like leaves that can tolerate dry or cold conditions. Conifers produce seeds in cones, not in flowers.

IMPORTANT

Washing soda can harm the skin – always wear rubber gloves when handling the soaked leaves.

Cones

Wherever pines, firs, or other conifers grow, it's fun to collect the cones that fall from these trees on to the woodland floor. Some cones are tiny, but others are huge, weighing up to 5 kilos (11 lbs). Just as broad-leaved trees use flowers to make their seeds, conifers use cones to make seeds. Collect some ripe female cones and watch how their scales open with the changing weather.

1 Visit a coniferous woodland (one with trees such as pines, firs, and spruces). Collect some cones in your bag and take them home with you.

2 If possible, identify the cones and put them in a warm, dry place. If the scales of the cones are closed, watch them over several days to see if the scales open. This normally happens in warm, dry weather, ideal conditions for the cone to release its seeds.

SEED EATERS

Conifer seeds are an important food source for forest birds and small mammals. For example, crossbills and nutcrackers have specialized beaks to probe for and extract seeds from cones, while red squirrels get at seeds by stripping off cone scales.

◄ **Crossbill**
This red crossbill's beak has a crossed tip to help it lift the scales of a cone and loosen the seeds.

WHAT YOU WILL NEED

- Bag for collecting cones
- Tweezers

Only go into a woodland when accompanied by an adult.

MALE AND FEMALE CONES

Conifers reproduce using male and female cones, which usually grow separately on the same tree. Male cones tend to be soft and smaller than female cones. If you tap them, they release clouds of pollen. This pollen is carried by the wind to pollinate the female cones, which then produce seeds. Once this has happened, the female cone's scales close and become increasingly woody as the seeds develop, a process that can take up to three years. When the cone is mature, and the weather is neither too damp nor too cold, the scales open and seeds are released.

Scots pine cones ▸ The difference between these male and female cones is clear. Once male cones have shed their pollen, they drop off. Years after pollination, the woody female cone releases its seeds, which spin away.

3 **If the scales** are open, look inside to see if there is a seed. Most conifers have seeds with papery "wings". Use the tweezers to remove a seed without tearing the wing. Hold the seed up in the air. Let it go and watch it spiral to the floor. If caught by the wind, this takes the seed well away from its parent plant.

Fungus foray

Fungi, such as mushrooms and toadstools, resemble plants, but live very differently. They are not green, they don't need light, they feed on dead or living organisms, and they reproduce by scattering millions of microscopic spores. A simple way of recording the fungi you find is to make a spore print.

Billions of spores
A type of fungus known as a puffball (right) can produce billions of spores. The slightest knock causes spores to puff out through a hole in the top of the puffball's cap. If you find a ripe puffball, tap it and watch its spores escape.

1 **Ask an adult** to cut the stalk from the mushroom cap. Look at the underside of the cap to see the spore-releasing gills. Put the cap on a piece of coloured card and cover it with a bowl to keep out draughts. Leave it overnight.

WHAT YOU WILL NEED

- Mushroom or toadstool
- Coloured card (for example, blue, black, or light brown)
- Glass or plastic bowl
- Artist's fixative spray or hairspray
- Knife

Adult supervision required. Spray fixative in a well-ventilated room.

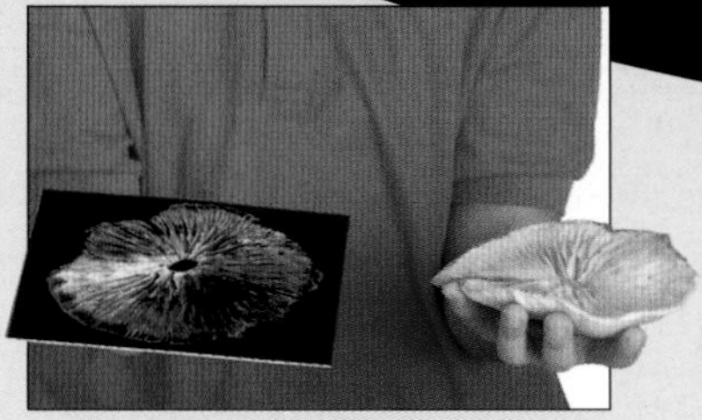

2 **The next day**, remove the bowl and carefully lift the cap. You will see that the spores have made a print that matches the gill pattern of the mushroom.

3 **Carefully spray** the spore print with fixative to stop it from being smudged. If possible, find out what kind of mushroom or toadstool the spores came from.

IMPORTANT

Only handle wild fungi if a knowledgeable adult confirms that it is safe to do so. Always wash your hands after handling fungi.

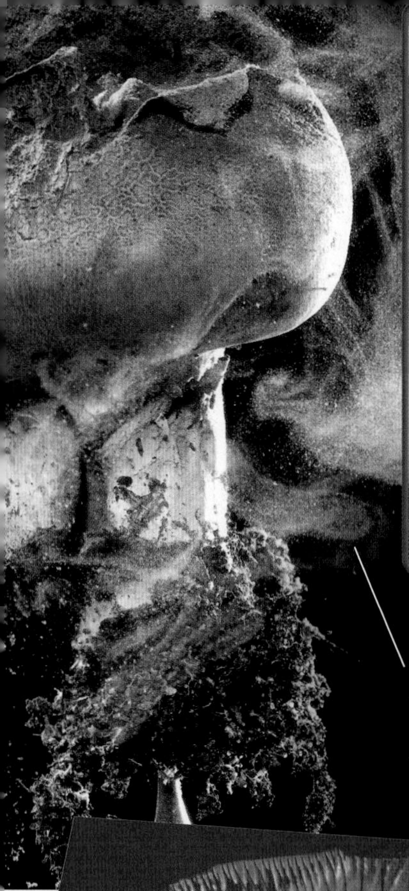

Puffballs may release more than 5,000 billion spores

SAFE OR DANGEROUS?

Some fungi, such as field mushrooms, are good to eat. Others, however, contain poisons. Some of these poisonous species are easily identified, but others can be confused with edible fungi. That is why you should never eat wild fungi unless their identity is confirmed by an expert.

Fly agaric ▶
This toadstool lives near trees, especially birch and spruce. Its bright colour provides a warning that the fly agaric is poisonous.

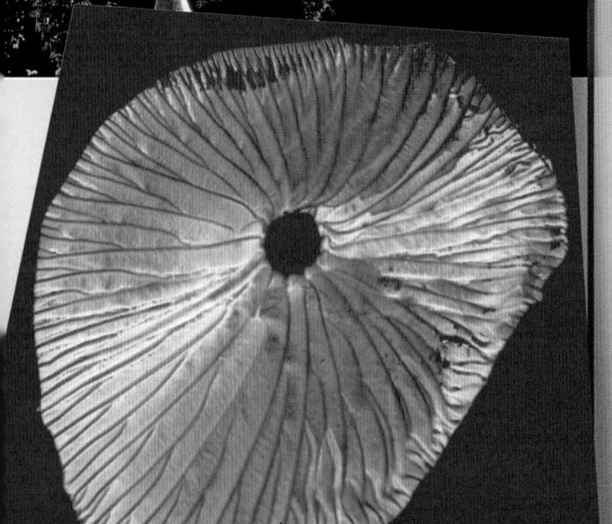

Use a dark card for white spores

4 Repeat using different specimens and card colours. Compare the different spore colours and gill patterns.

NATURE'S RECYCLERS

Many types of fungi, such as bracket fungi, are decomposers. They perform a vital role in nature by disposing of dead plants and animals. A network of slender fungal feeding threads, called hyphae, invade and digest the dead organism, causing it to decay and eventually disappear. This process releases chemicals that are recycled for use by living organisms, such as growing plants.

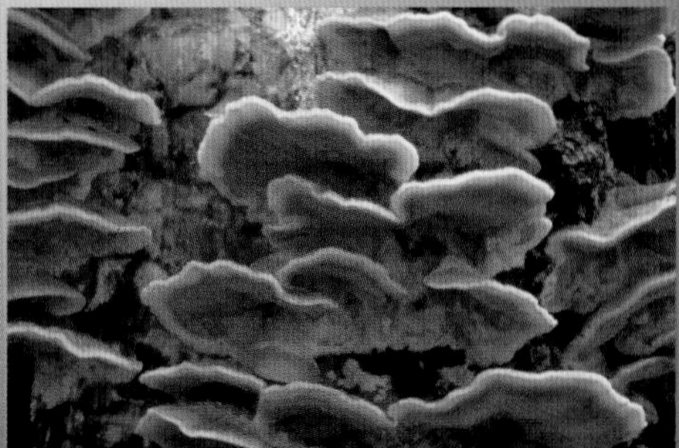

Bracket fungus ▲
On woodland walks, look out for the shelf-like bracket fungi on the trunks of dead trees. Their hyphae penetrate deep inside the tree, causing it to rot and crumble.

Dry places

Deserts and other dry places often seem empty and lifeless. But look closely and you'll find that lots of animals and plants use them as their home. Desert animals are mainly active at night when it is cool. Many desert plants survive fierce sunshine and months without rain by storing water in their fleshy stems. You can create a mini desert by planting cacti and other succulents in sandy soil and growing them in a warm place.

WHAT YOU WILL NEED

- Planting tray
- Trowel
- Spoon
- Small watering can
- Gravel
- Compost
- Sand
- A variety of potted cacti and succulent plants, ideally 5–7 specimens

Gravel covers bottom of the planting tray

1 Cover the bottom of the planting tray with a shallow layer of gravel. Use the trowel to add compost until the tray is about half full. Place the plant pots around the tray to find the best arrangement.

Soil around the roots is loosened before planting

2 Dig a small hole for each plant. Remove the plant from its pot, place it in its hole, and gently press it down. Fill any gaps around the plants with compost. Check that the roots are covered.

A layer of sand covers the compost

3 Use the spoon to cover the compost with sand. Press the sand down firmly with the back of the spoon.

AFTER DARK

Do you like to shelter from the Sun on really hot days? Well, so do most desert animals. They either seek out shade or rest in burrows during the day to escape the intense heat. But at night, when temperatures fall, they become active and emerge to search for food.

◀ Desert jerboa
Emerging from its burrow at night, this rodent uses its big back feet to hop in search of seeds. Its large eyes are typical of many nocturnal animals.

SNAKE TRACKS

Moving across shifting, painfully hot, desert sand is difficult, but not for sidewinding snakes. They launch their bodies sideways in a series of leaps so that only a small part of their body is in contact with the hot sand for a short amount of time. They leave behind a tell-tale trail of parallel tracks. Look out for them if you visit a desert.

Sidewinding snake ▲
A desert adder from the Namib Desert in southern Africa moves across the sand, leaving behind its typical sidewinding tracks.

4 **Give your mini desert** a light water and place it in a warm sunny position indoors. Lightly water it once every week or two weeks, but never let the soil get too wet. Watch your mini desert plants thrive in their dry, warm surroundings.

Freshwater ponds

Pond wildlife ranges from tiny shrimps, looping leeches, and grazing snails of all sizes, to fish, tadpoles, and an array of insects, not to mention algae, pondweed, and other pond plants. Most of you probably know of a pond that you can visit, so here is an ideal nature-ranging opportunity to explore a fascinating habitat.

WHAT YOU WILL NEED

- Dip net with a fine mesh
- Two plastic containers, such as empty ice-cream tubs
- Small, clear plastic dish
- Clean pipette (dropper)
- Fine paintbrush
- Plastic spoon
- Magnifying glass
- Notebook and pencil
- Field guide to pond life

Always go with an adult to a pond, stream, or river and take care on the banks.

1 **Find a clean**, unpolluted pond. Choose a location where you can approach the water's edge safely. Half-fill both containers with clean water from the pond. Now slowly sweep your dip net through the pond.

2 **Turn the net** inside-out over one of the containers to release any animals or plants you have caught. If you haven't had much luck, try dipping through an area of weeds, as more animals tend to gather here.

IMPORTANT

Always return the animals you have caught to the same part of the pond.

DRAGONFLIES

You can't fail to spot these fantastic insects with their long bodies, large wings, and big eyes. Dragonflies are daytime hunters that prey on other flying insects. Their eggs, laid in ponds, hatch into predatory larvae called nymphs that lurk, well-camouflaged, in mud and vegetation, grabbing passing pond animals with their piercing jaws.

Emerging adult ▶
Dragonfly nymphs live underwater for up to five years, shedding their skin as they grow. Eventually, the nymph climbs out of the water and sheds its skin for the last time. Look out for emerging adult dragonflies early on summer mornings.

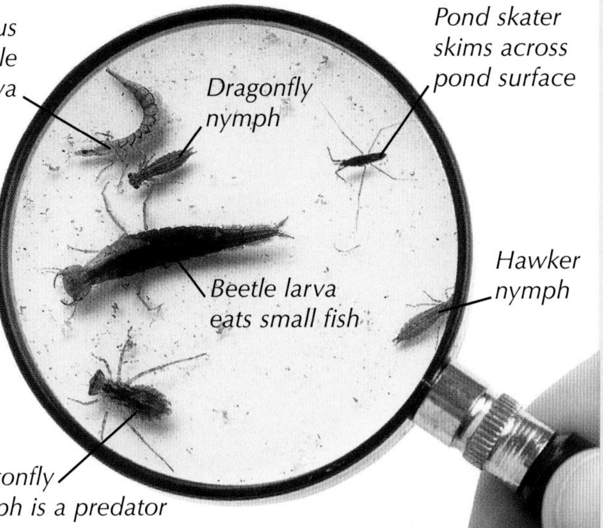
Acilius beetle larva
Dragonfly nymph
Pond skater skims across pond surface
Beetle larva eats small fish
Hawker nymph
Dragonfly nymph is a predator

3 **Carefully transfer** specimens, using the spoon or paintbrush, to the clean water of the second container. Make a note of what you have caught. Using the pipette, transfer any tiny organisms to the small plastic dish. Try to identify them with your magnifying glass.

4 **Compare different parts** of the pond, including open water, places with pond plants, and the bottom of the pond. You should find that the numbers and types of animals you find vary from area to area.

POND LIFE

All of these animals are commonly found in ponds, as are dragonflies, beetle larvae, and pond skaters.

◀ Greater water boatman
Also called the backswimmer, because it swims upside-down, this predatory insect moves using its long, oar-like hind legs.

Pond snail ▶
Like other snails, pond snails have a rasping radula (tongue) that they use to feed on algae, decaying plant remains, and pond plants (where they also lay eggs).

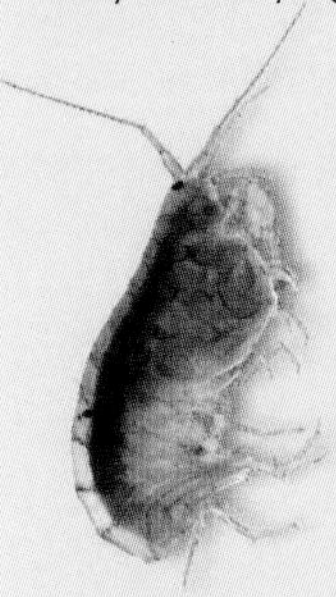

◀ Freshwater shrimp
With long antennae and transparent, flattened bodies, freshwater shrimps live among stones and pond weed. They feed on decaying pond matter.

Freshwater leech ▶
Leeches move through a pond using their front and rear suckers. Some feed on other soft-bodied animals, while others eat decaying plants.

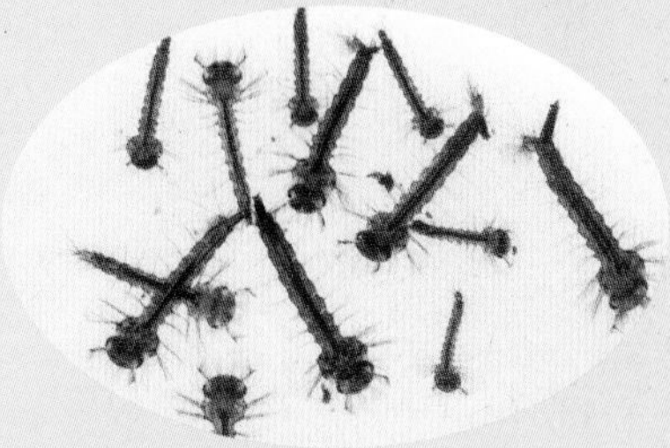

Mosquito larvae ▲
Moving jerkily, mosquito larvae are a common sight just below the pond surface. They form rounded pupae from which adult mosquitoes emerge.

WHAT YOU WILL NEED

- Sheets of thin cardboard
- Pencil or pen
- Ruler • Scissors
- Kitchen paper
- Sticky tape
- Sticky labels
- Plastic or paper bag
- Field guide to the seashore

Only go into the sea if an adult is supervising you.

The seashore

Found where sea and land meet, the seashore is a great place for nature ranging because it is home to an incredible variety of living things. Every seashore – be it sandy, muddy, shingle, or rocky – is a place of constant change, where living things have to cope with the tide going in and out twice a day. One way of investigating the wildlife on seashores is to make a shell showcase. This enables you to identify seashore residents by the shells they used to live in.

1 **Visit a beach**. Look for empty shells on rocks and sand, and in pools. Pick the best of each type, and take them home in a bag.

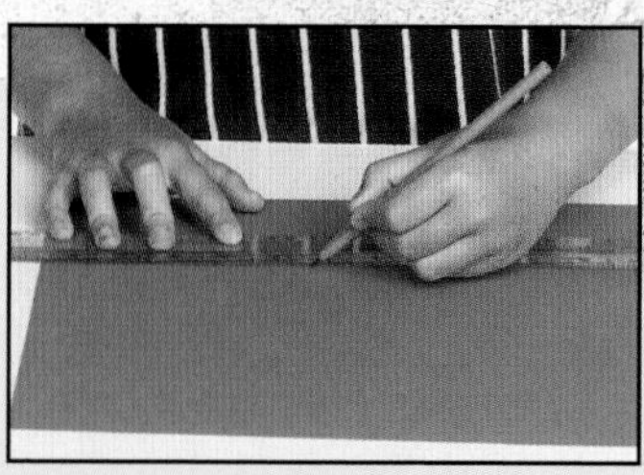

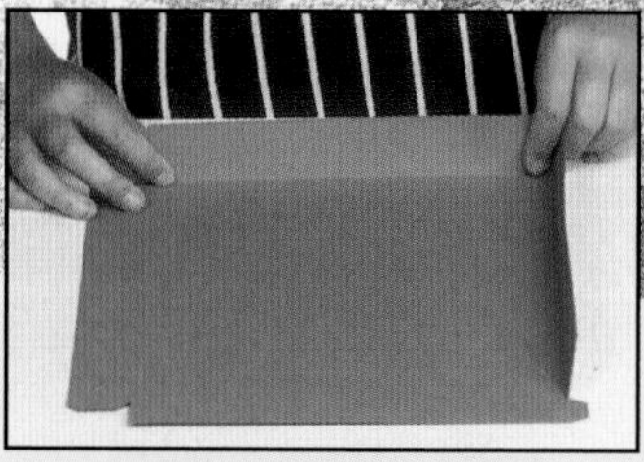

2 **Wash the shells** in cold water to remove traces of sand, seaweed, or small animals. Put them on some kitchen paper, with open surfaces down so that water can drain out. Leave them to dry.

3 **Now make** a simple showcase to display and identify the shells you have collected. First of all, take a sheet of cardboard and mark out a rectangle approximately 40 cm x 30 cm (16 in x 12 in).

4 **Draw a margin** 2.5 cm (1 in) wide around the rectangle. Snip the corners with scissors, then fold up the margin to make four sides. Secure these with tape to keep them upright and form a shallow box.

Dune plants ▲
The roots of this marram grass stabilize dunes by binding sand grains together. Spiky stems trap blown sand, so the dunes grow higher.

SAND DUNES

Visit many sandy beaches and you will see sand dunes lying parallel to the shoreline along the landward side of the beach. Dunes form over many years when sand, carried from the beach by the wind, settles to form ripples, then larger ridges, and finally dunes. Sand dunes are really important because they protect land behind the beach from wind and waves. They also provide a habitat for mammals, birds, lizards, and insects, as well as tough plants that can tolerate the harsh, dry, salty conditions.

UNDER THE SURFACE

At low tide, most seashores appear lifeless. But just under the surface there are millions of animals, including marine worms, molluscs, and crustaceans. These creatures become active when the beach is underwater. Look out for wading birds patrolling beaches at low tide. They'll be probing with their beaks for juicy prey.

◀ **American avocet**
This wader sweeps its upcurved beak from side to side through watery mud or shallow water to locate worms and crustaceans.

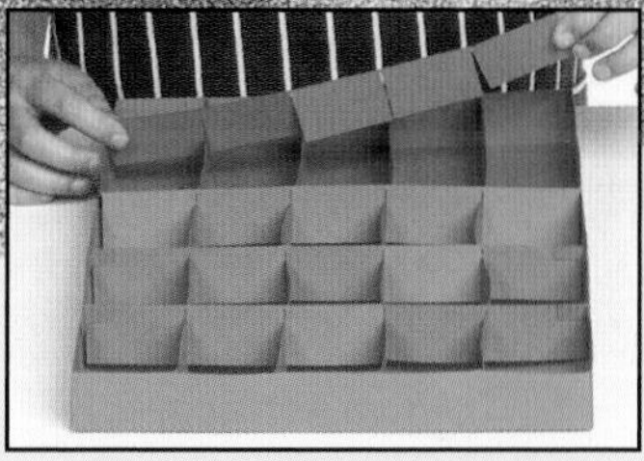

5 **From another cardboard** sheet, cut out eight strips 2.5 cm (1 in) wide – four the same length as the box, and four the same width. Use the strips to divide the box into 25 sections. Tape them in place.

6 **Arrange your shell** collection in the showcase. If you can, use a seashore guide to identify each shell. Add a label to its compartment showing its name and when and where you found it.

IMPORTANT

Only collect shells that are empty. Don't be tempted to collect shells that still contain living animals as they will die very quickly, rot, and smell.

Rockpools

If you visit a rocky shore, spend some time looking in rockpools. They are great places for watching wildlife because you can see a range of creatures in one place, such as sea anemones, shrimps, starfish, sponges, crabs, and fish – and the occupants are unable to swim away. But one of the problems of looking in rockpools is that sunlight is reflected from the pool's surface, making it difficult to see into the water. To get around this, you can make a rockpool viewer. This will give you a clear view of the teeming life in a rockpool.

ROCKY SHORE

Most rocky shores provide shelter for a wide variety of seaweeds and marine animals. But life on the rocks can be tough. Twice each day, when the tide comes in, the rocky shore and its wildlife is battered by the waves. Then, when the tide goes out, the animals and seaweeds – whether or not in rockpools – are exposed to the harsh effects of the Sun and wind.

Waves batter a rocky shore in California, USA

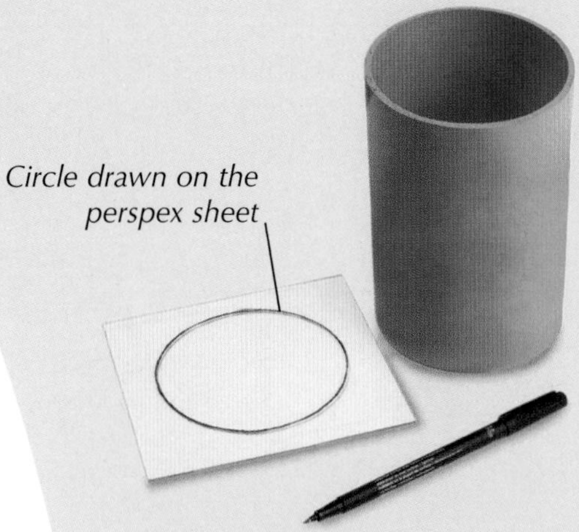

1 Put one end of the plastic pipe on the perspex. Draw around it using the felt-tip pen to get the right size for the viewer's "window".

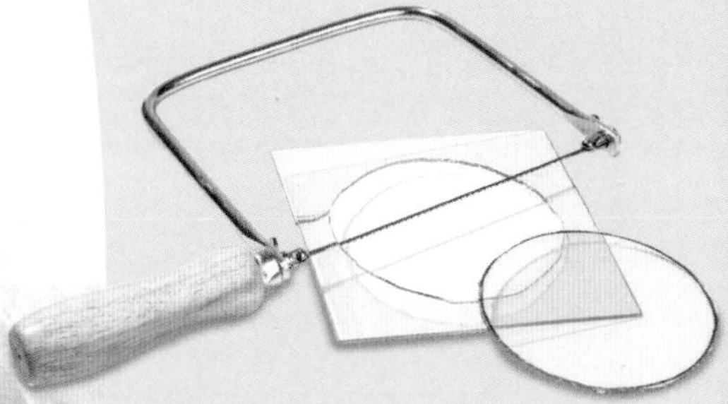

2 Ask an adult to use the hacksaw to cut carefully around the circle you have just drawn.

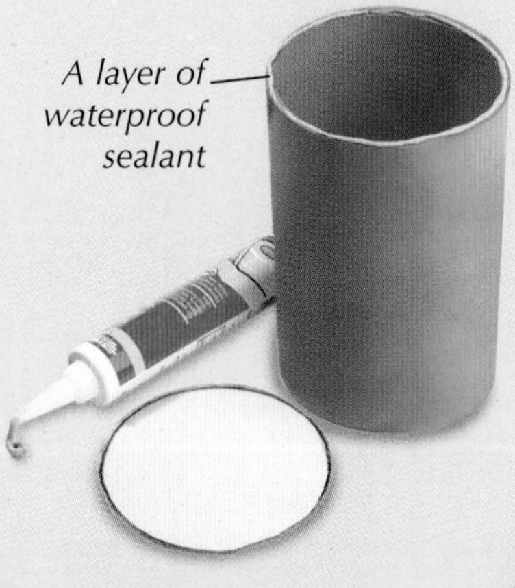

3 Put some sealant around one end of the plastic pipe. Carefully place the perspex disc on top to make a window. Let the sealant set, then check the window is waterproof in a water-filled sink.

WHAT YOU WILL NEED

- Drainpipe or other large diameter plastic pipe 30–40 cm (12–16 in) long
- Perspex sheet
- Felt-tip pen
- Hacksaw
- Waterproof sealant
- Seashore field guide

Ask an adult to cut the perspex.

4 **Kneel down** next to a rockpool and push the window end of the viewer into the water. Look through the window and try to identify the animals you spot.

SEA ANEMONES

They may look like plants, but sea anemones are actually flesh-eating animals. Any small creature that ventures near the anemone's tentacles is stung by a battery of stinging cells, paralysed, and pulled into its mouth. Try feeding an anemone by gently brushing a small piece of meat across its tentacles. Wear rubber gloves in case it's a species that can sting you!

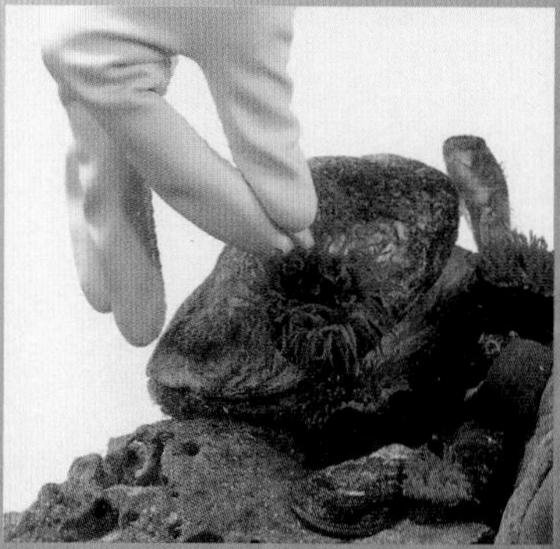

Feeding an anemone ▶ The anemone detects chemicals released by the meat, then extends its tentacles to grab its "prey".

IMPORTANT

Visit a rocky shore only when accompanied by an adult. Check the time of high tide so that you are not cut off when the tide comes in.

Weather watcher

Weather and climate

We are all affected by the weather. At its worst, weather can destroy cities and cause devastating floods. At its best, it can turn a simple picnic into a magical experience. But weather is also fascinating in its own right. Why does the wind blow? How do clouds form? What causes lightning? You can find out by trying a few experiments and building some simple weather-watching instruments. You may even learn how to predict what the weather may do next.

Heavenly beauty
The weather is more than just wind, rain, and snow. It also includes some stunning atmospheric effects that can transform the sky. These include rainbows, sunsets, and flashes of lightning. This glorious sunset was photographed near Tierra del Fuego at the southern tip of South America.

WORLD CLIMATES

The average weather of any place is described as its climate. The weather in California, USA, for example, is usually warm and dry, so it has a warm, dry climate. By contrast, New Zealand has a cool, damp climate. A region's climate is affected by how far it is from the equator, amongst other things. Climates can be described in many ways, but the climates of the world are often divided into five types. These are tropical, dry, warm temperate, cool temperate, and Arctic. Each climate type has many variations.

Tropical climate ▲
Near the equator, the heat and moisture in the air causes the formation of huge clouds and heavy rain. This encourages the growth of lush rainforests. Shown above is a rainforest in Costa Rica.

Dry climate ▲
In many regions, but mainly near the tropics, very dry air prevents the formation of clouds and rain. This leads to the development of deserts, such as the cactus deserts of the southwest USA.

STORM RELIEF

We all know what we mean by good weather and bad weather. For most of us, good weather is warm and sunny, while bad weather is cold and wet. But some people's bad weather is other people's good weather. For example, people who go skiing look forward to winter, and some people even enjoy thunderstorms. Rainstorms can be destructive, but they bring new life to places that suffer drought. In parts of southern Asia, the arrival of heavy monsoon rain at the end of the dry season is a reason for celebration, even though it can cause serious floods.

Monsoon rain ▶
Indian children make the most of a flash flood at the start of the wet season.

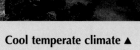

Warm temperate climate ▲
Some regions, for example, southern Australia, enjoy a warm temperate climate, where the weather is usually warm and sunny but there is enough rain to grow crops.

Cool temperate climate ▲
Places such as New Zealand and northwest Europe have cool summers but quite mild winters. The weather tends to be very changeable. Plants grow well because there is plenty of rain.

Arctic climate ▲
In the polar regions the weather is always cold, and temperatures fall well below freezing in winter. This leads to the growth of thick ice sheets, fringed by treeless, grassy land known as tundra.

Moving air

Near the equator, the heat of the Sun makes warm air rise and flow towards the cold polar regions. The rising air is replaced by cooler air flowing from the poles towards the equator. This global air flow cools down the hottest parts of the Earth, and warms up the coldest parts. But the pattern is complicated by more bands of rising and falling air, by the way the Earth spins, and by the way the air masses swirl together to create weather systems.

The sky from space
Rising air often makes clouds form, and these can show how the air is moving. The clouds map out the weather systems that can be seen from space, as in this picture taken from the orbiting Space Shuttle.

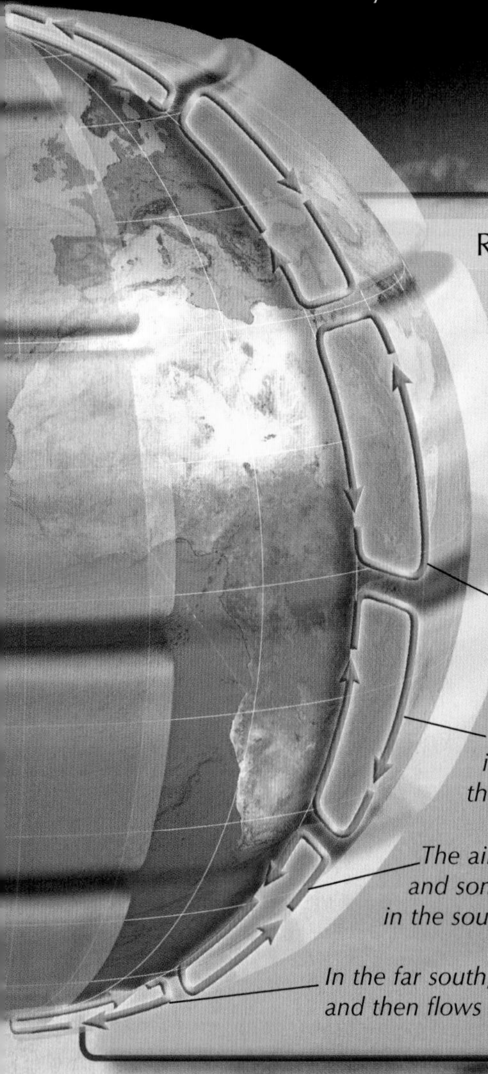
Warm, moist air rises over the rainforest zone and moves away from the equator.
High-level air flows south, in the Hadley cell. North of the equator, the air flows north.
The air sinks in the subtropics, and some flows south at low level in the southern Ferrel cell.
In the far south, cold air sinks over Antarctica and then flows north in the southern polar cell.

RISING AND FALLING AIR

In the troposphere, the lowest level of the atmosphere, air rises and falls in a pattern of convection cells called the Hadley, Ferrel, and polar cells. Warm air rising near the equator sinks over the subtropical deserts. Some of the sinking air flows away from the tropics near ground level, rises again, then sinks at the poles.

THE CORIOLIS EFFECT

As the Earth spins on its axis, it makes moving air masses swerve off course. Instead of heading north or south, the moving air is pushed to the right in the Northern Hemisphere, and to the left in the Southern Hemisphere. This is the Coriolis effect. It creates prevailing winds, such as the trade winds that always blow towards the west over tropical oceans. The prevailing winds carry weather systems with them, and this is why the weather usually comes from the same direction.

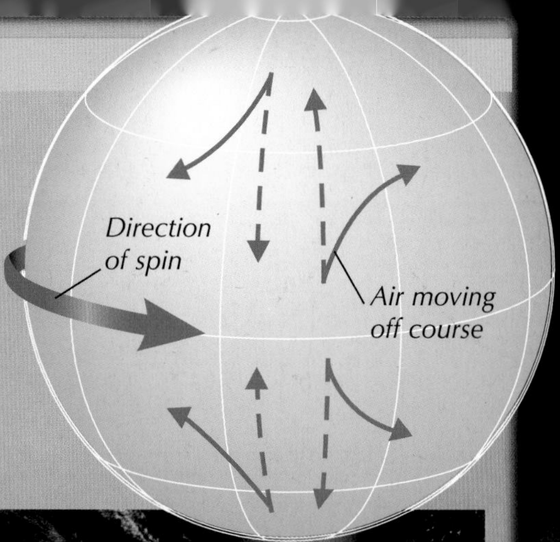

The swirling clouds are carried by winds that spiral into each cyclone and then spill out of the top.

Swirling cyclones ▲
The Coriolis effect also makes local winds swerve off course. These winds blow into regions where warm air is rising. But instead of blowing straight into these regions, the winds veer to one side, then circle around like these tropical cyclones in the Indian Ocean.

Storm clouds rise high into the air, to the bottom of the stratosphere.

The world's weather is powered by the heat of the Sun. This is strongest in tropical regions near the equator, where the Sun's rays are more concentrated. Near the North and South Poles the Sun's rays are spread out, so they do not heat the Earth so strongly. This makes these regions much cooler than the tropics. You can see how this works using a torch and a balloon.

WHAT YOU WILL NEED

- Large round balloon (any colour)
- Black marker or felt-tip pen
- Torch (for the best results, use a torch with a beam that can be focused)

1 Blow up the balloon and ask an adult to tie the neck. Use the marker or felt-tip pen to draw a line around the middle. This represents the Earth's equator.

HANDY TIP

Try to keep the torch at about the same distance from the balloon as you move it upwards.

Focus the torch so the beam is as narrow as possible

TROPICAL DESERTS

The intense sunlight in the tropics makes them very hot. In dry areas, this leads to the formation of hot deserts of bare rock and sand, where few plants can grow. In wet regions, the heat helps to form huge clouds, which spill tropical rain on to warm rainforests.

2 Darken the room a little, and ask someone to hold the balloon with the equator horizontal. Aim the torch directly at the equator, to make a bright, circular patch of light.

POLAR REGIONS

Near the North and South Poles, the sunlight is spread out, so it is much less intense than in the tropics. It is not strong enough to melt the snow in summer, so the snow builds up into thick ice sheets that cover the land and even parts of the ocean. Nothing grows on ice sheets, so there is no food for animals. These Antarctic penguins get all their food from the open sea beyond the ice.

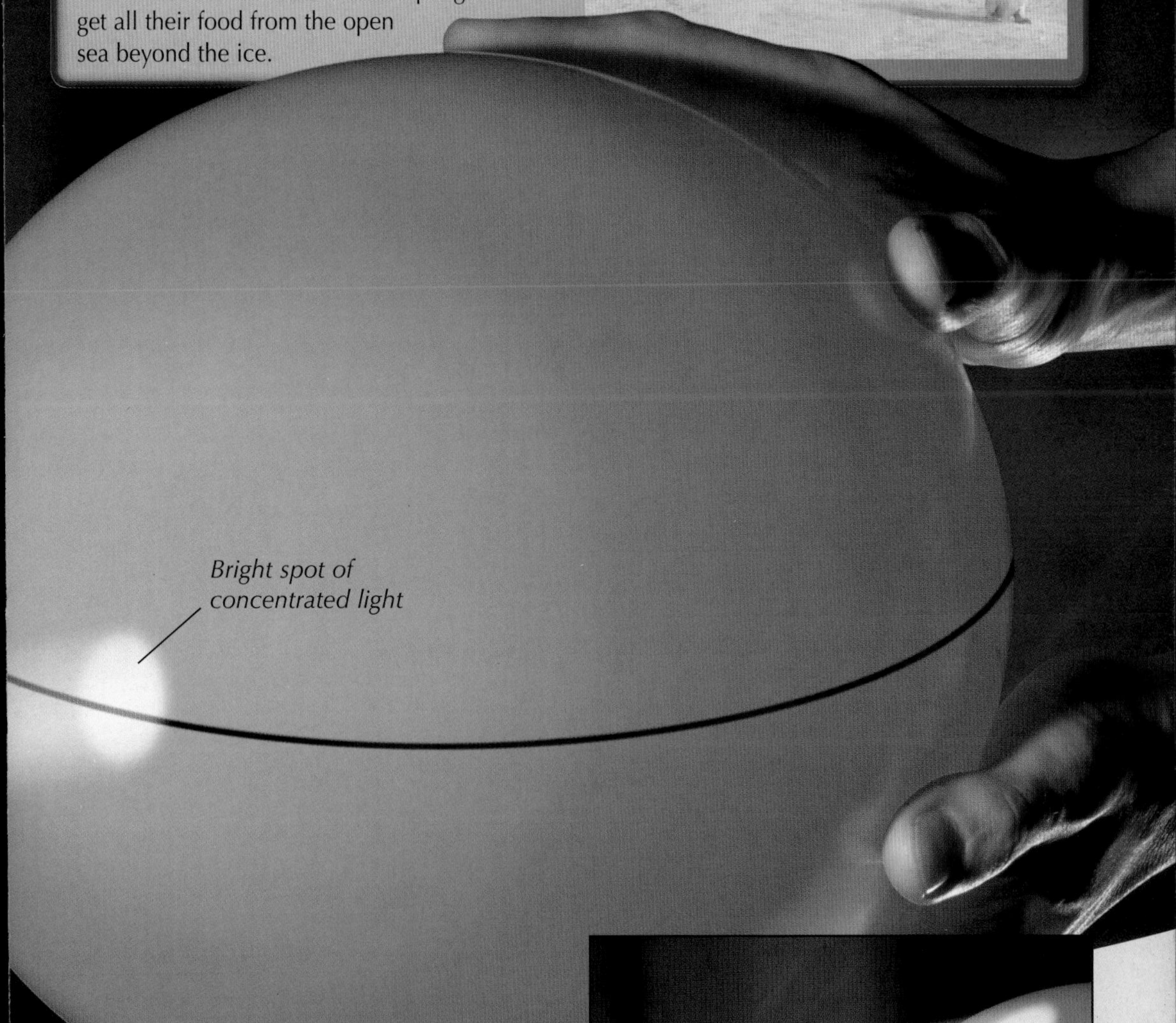

3 **Move the torch upwards**, keeping it horizontal, so the beam lights up the "Arctic" region. The bright spot spreads out because the light strikes the surface at an angle. This spreads the heat energy, making it weaker.

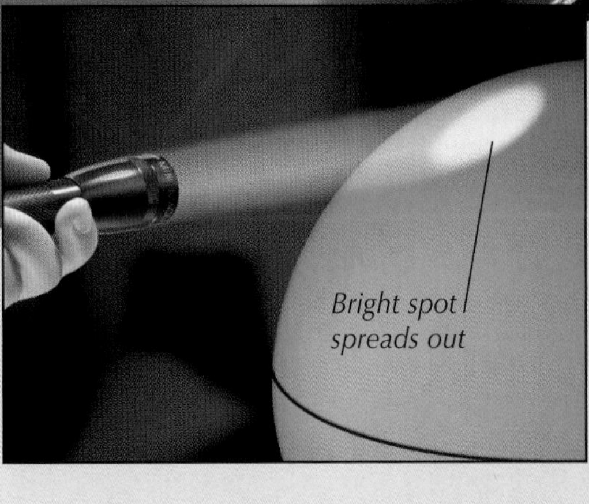

Expanding air

The Sun heats the continents and oceans, especially in tropical regions. Heat rising off the warm ground and sea warms up the air in the lower atmosphere, and this makes it grow in volume, or expand. Expanding warm air usually floats upwards, carrying moisture with it. This air movement leads to the formation of clouds, and powers the world's weather. You can show how warm air expands by using hot water to power a bottle fountain.

MOVING MOLECULES

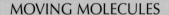

Air is made of gas particles, or molecules. Heating the molecules gives them more energy. The energy makes them move about more, so they need more space. They move apart, so they take up more room. This makes warm air expand. If the air is cooled again, the air molecules lose energy and move closer together, so cooled air contracts.

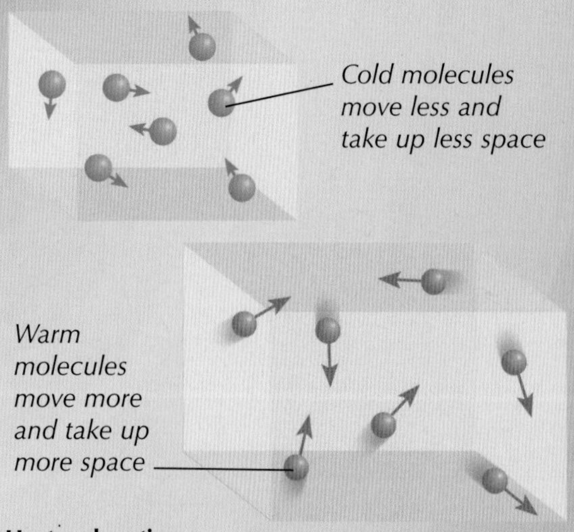
Cold molecules move less and take up less space
Warm molecules move more and take up more space

Heat and motion ▲
Heat is a form of energy. When an air molecule is heated, some of the heat energy is turned into motion. So warm air molecules move about more than cold ones, and move further apart.

1 **Place the pebbles** in the bottle and then, using the funnel, half-fill it with cold water. Add a few drops of food colouring to the water. Dry the neck of the bottle if it is wet.

2 **Place the straw** in the bottle, making sure the bottom end is well underwater. Seal the straw in place by fixing a ball of putty around the straw at the neck of the bottle.

WHAT YOU WILL NEED

- Small plastic bottle
- Some pebbles
- Funnel
- Cold and boiling water
- Food colouring
- Sticky putty
- Drinking straw
- Needle or safety pin
- Large heatproof jug

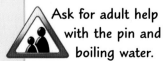

Ask for adult help with the pin and boiling water.

THERMOMETER

You can see how heat makes things expand by watching a thermometer. The liquid in a thermometer expands when it gets warmer, making the liquid rise up the tube. When the temperature falls, the liquid contracts and sinks back down again. The liquid expands at a fixed rate as its temperature goes up, so the height it reaches in the tube gives an accurate measure of temperature.

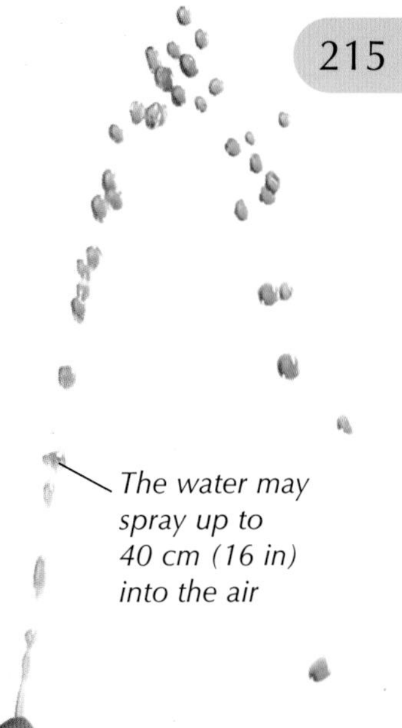

The water may spray up to 40 cm (16 in) into the air

HANDY TIP

The smaller the hole in the plug of putty, the higher the jet will squirt. Stand back!

3 **Plug the end** of the straw with another piece of putty. Pierce this plug with the needle or pin to make a tiny hole.

4 **Pour boiling water** into the heatproof jug. You need enough to cover most of the bottle. Carefully place the bottle into the hot water. The heat will make the air in the bottle expand, pushing coloured water up the straw and squirting it into the air.

IMPORTANT

Be very careful with food colouring as it stains everything. It's best to do this experiment in the kitchen sink, and mop up any spills straight away.

Rising warm air

When warm air expands, its gas particles move apart, so the air is less dense. This makes it lighter than cool air. The lighter warm air rises through the heavier cool air in a convection current, or thermal. Air is invisible, so you can't see this happening. But since water behaves in the same way, you can make a thermal using hot and cold water and some food colouring.

WHAT YOU WILL NEED

- Small cup
- Hot and cold water
- Food colouring
- Cling film
- Rubber band
- Large glass jar with wide mouth
- Long, sharp kitchen knife or skewer

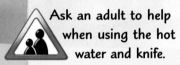

Ask an adult to help when using the hot water and knife.

1 **Fill the cup** to the brim with hot water, and add some food colouring. Cut a circle of cling film and spread it over the top of the cup. Stretch the rubber band over the film to hold it in place.

2 **Carefully put** the cup of hot, coloured water in the bottom of the glass jar. The cling film should stop it from spilling. Then gradually fill the jar with cold water, almost to the top.

3 **Cut the cling film** with the sharp point of the knife or skewer. You need a single, fairly large gash. Then take the knife out and watch as the warm, coloured water starts to appear through the gash.

AIR POWER

Hot air balloons are filled with ordinary air that is heated up with a gas burner. As the air is heated it expands, becoming less dense and lighter than the cool air outside the balloon. This makes it float upwards, carrying the balloon with it. Thermals of warm air rise through colder air in the same way, but you can't see them because the air itself is invisible.

◀ **Extra heat**
The balloon is held up by hot air, not by gas from the gas burner. It starts to sink as the air cools, so the pilot has to fire up the gas for a few seconds to warm it up again.

WARM AIR CURRENTS

If you blow bubbles across the top of a warm radiator or electric heater, they will be caught up in the rising currents of warm air – thermals – and float up with them. Soaring birds, such as eagles, float upwards on thermals in the same way, circling in the rising warm air to gain height.

4 **A plume** of hot water will rise through the cold surrounding water and float above it, just like a thermal of warm air.

The coloured water slowly cools and sinks

5 **If you leave** the cup and jar for long enough, the warm, coloured water at the surface will cool down. As it cools it becomes more dense and heavy, and starts to sink towards the bottom of the jar. Cool air sinks in the same way.

HANDY TIP

Put the cup in the kitchen sink while you are filling it with hot water and covering it with cling film.

Measure air pressure

WHAT YOU WILL NEED

- Wide-neck jar or bowl
- Large balloon
- Scissors
- Sticky tape
- 2 drinking straws
- Coloured card
- Marker pen
- Ruler

When warm air expands and rises, it reduces the weight and pressure of air on the ground below. This creates what weather forecasters call a low-pressure zone – an area of warm, light air. Cool air is heavier, so it sinks and puts more pressure on the ground below, creating a high-pressure zone. Pressure changes show how weather is changing and moving. You can measure them using a home-made barometer.

1 Cut the neck off the balloon, together with part of its body. You should have just over half the balloon left. Stretch this tightly over the top of the bowl as if you are making a drum. Tape the balloon in place.

2 Make a short slit in the end of one straw and push this end inside the other straw. Tape them together. Tape one end of the extra-long straw to the middle of the balloon, so it rests on the rim of the bowl.

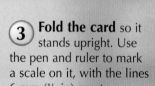

3 Fold the card so it stands upright. Use the pen and ruler to mark a scale on it, with the lines 6 mm (¼ in) apart.

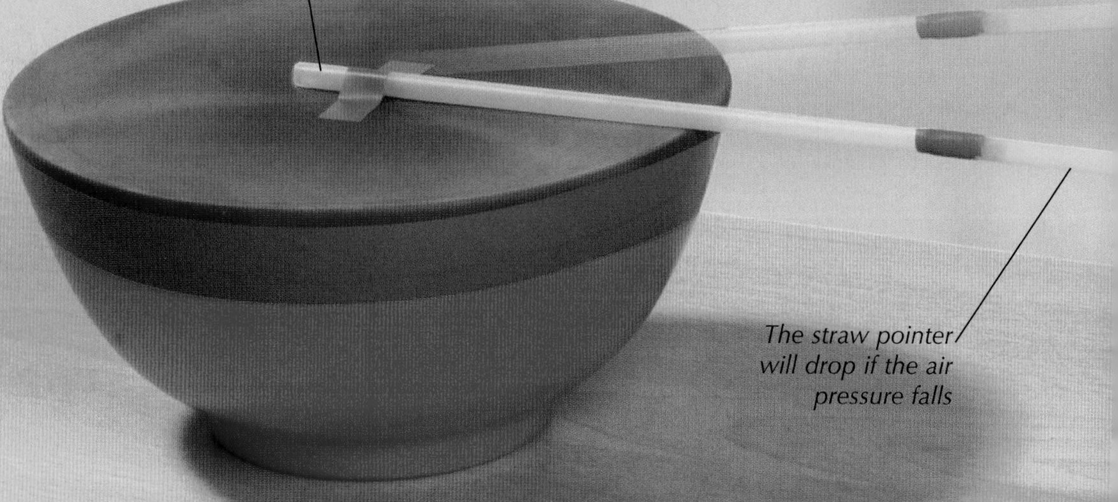

High air pressure pushes the balloon down, moving the pointer

The straw pointer will drop if the air pressure falls

MAPPING AIR PRESSURE

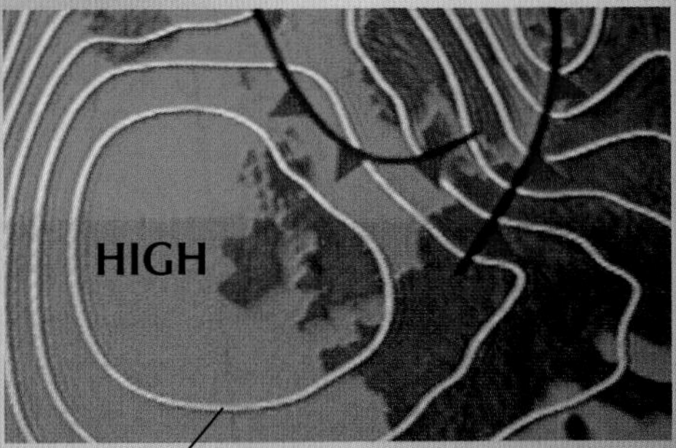

Barometers are used to measure air pressure at many different locations. The pressures are marked on maps, and any pressures that are the same are linked with lines called isobars. The result is a map of pressure zones, with areas of high and low pressure marked by the isobars. These highs and lows indicate what the weather is like on the ground.

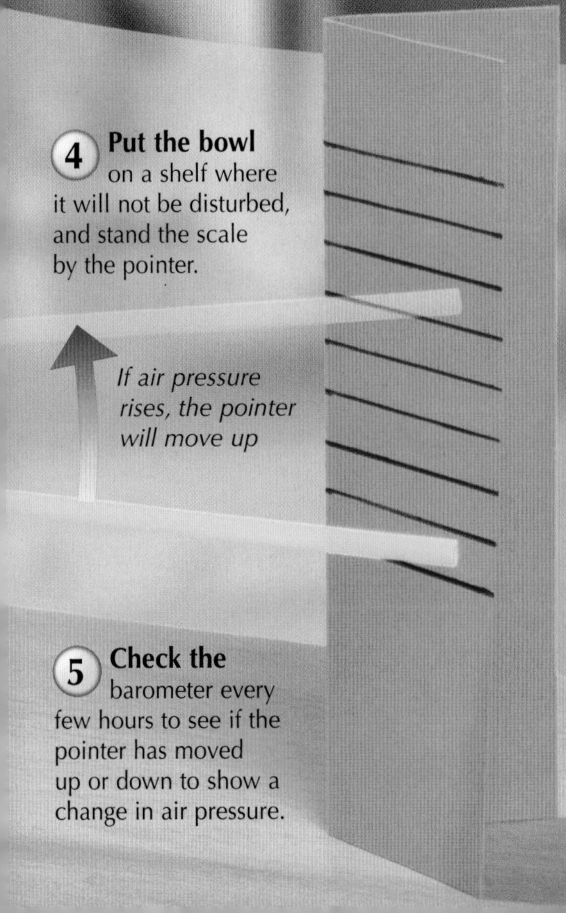

If air pressure rises, the pointer will move up

4 Put the bowl on a shelf where it will not be disturbed, and stand the scale by the pointer.

5 Check the barometer every few hours to see if the pointer has moved up or down to show a change in air pressure.

HIGH AND LOW PRESSURE

Weather forecasters can work out what the weather is like simply by looking at maps of pressure zones. Where warm air is rising, causing low pressure, it often creates clouds and rain. Where cool air is sinking, causing high pressure, it often creates clear, sunny skies. The wind blows from high-pressure zones to low-pressure zones, so forecasters can work out wind directions, and also how strong the wind might be. The pressure zones usually move from day to day, taking their weather with them.

Low-pressure weather ▲
Rising warm air in low-pressure zones carries moisture up into the sky with it. The air cools as it rises higher, and this makes clouds form. Tiny water droplets inside the clouds come together to form big drops that may fall as rain. This is why low-pressure weather is usually cloudy and rainy, with grey skies that block out the sunshine.

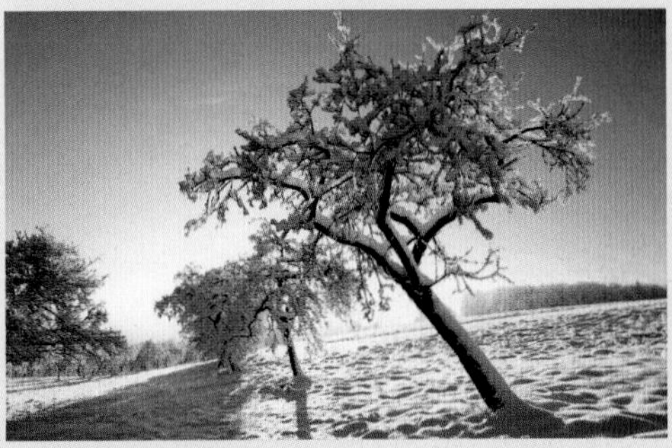

High-pressure weather ▲
Sinking cool air in high-pressure zones stops moisture rising into the sky. This prevents clouds from forming, so there is no rain. The sky is blue, and summer high-pressure weather is sunny and warm. High-pressure weather in winter can be sunny, too, but at night there is no cloud to stop heat escaping into space, so it can also get very cold.

Creating a breeze

Air flows away from high-pressure zones, where cool air is sinking, towards low-pressure zones, where warm air is rising. This creates wind. Some winds blow over great distances, but others, such as sea breezes, are local. Using ice and hot sand, you can see how a breeze works by observing how smoke is blown from a tiny high-pressure zone to a tiny low-pressure zone.

WHAT YOU WILL NEED

- 2 metal baking trays
- 2 heatproof mats or boards
- Oven gloves
- Large cardboard box
- Dry sand • Ice
- Incense stick
- Scissors
- Matches

Ask an adult to help when using the oven, and to light the incense stick.

THE SEA BREEZE

On warm summer days, the land heats up more quickly than the sea. It warms the air above and causes it to rise. Cooler air from above the sea is drawn into land, creating a sea breeze. Meanwhile, warm air flows out to sea at a high level. This cools and sinks to replace the air that has blown onshore.

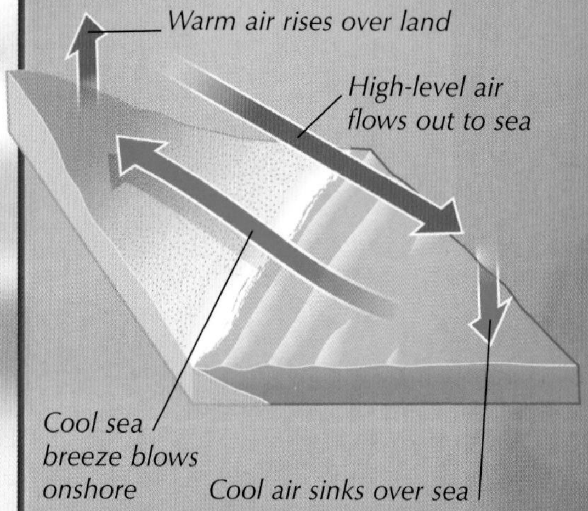
Warm air rises over land
High-level air flows out to sea
Cool sea breeze blows onshore
Cool air sinks over sea

Circulating air ▲
Rising warm air over the land forms a small low-pressure zone. Sinking cool air over the sea forms a small high-pressure zone. Since air flows from high to low pressure, this creates a breeze.

IMPORTANT

Use insulated oven gloves to hold the hot tray.

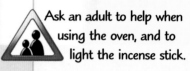

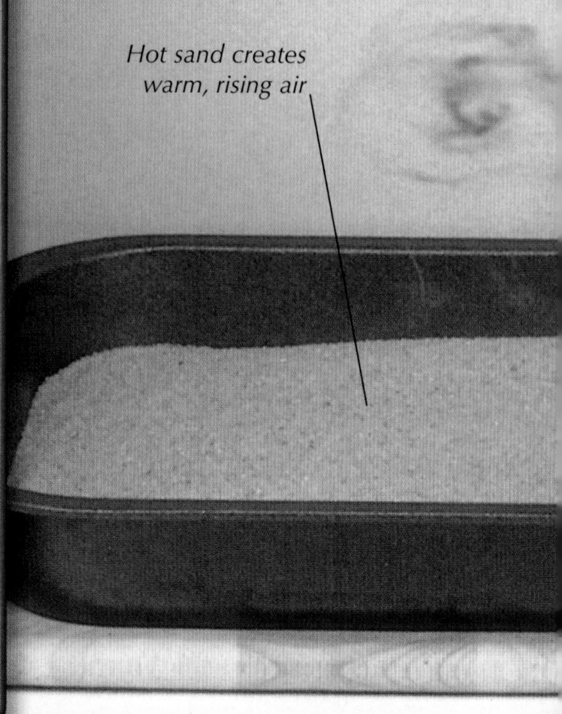
Hot sand creates warm, rising air

1 **Fill one tray** with sand, and ask an adult to place it in the oven on low heat to warm up.

2 **Use the scissors** to cut the front off the cardboard box – the box acts as a screen to block out draughts. Put the mats in the bottom of the box.

3 **Fill the second** baking tray with ice from the freezer, and put it on one of the mats. Ask your adult helper to take the warm tray from the oven and place it on the other mat, so the two trays are side by side.

TRADE WINDS

In tropical oceans, hot sunshine near the equator makes warm air rise high into the atmosphere. The rising air is replaced by air blowing in over the sea from subtropical regions, where cool air is sinking. This giant version of a sea breeze creates the trade winds.

◀ **A power supply for ships**
In the past, sailing ships relied on the steady, predictable trade winds to carry them across the oceans.

4 **Light an incense stick** and hold it between the two trays. As the warm air rises off the warm tray, it creates a low-pressure zone. The smoke will be blown towards the warm tray from the high-pressure zone above the cold tray.

Ice creates cool, sinking air
Smoke drifts in a light breeze

Make a wind vane

The wind doesn't blow straight from high-pressure zones to low-pressure zones. It spirals around them, like water swirling down a drain. So when a moving low-pressure system is approaching, the wind changes. As it passes overhead, the wind keeps changing, then finally settles when the weather system has moved on. You can watch for these shifts using a wind vane.

WHAT YOU WILL NEED

- A4 sheet of stiff card
- Pencil
- Scissors
- 2 small coins
- Pen top
- Sticky tape
- Kitchen or barbecue skewer
- Long garden cane
- 4 clothes pegs (1 a different colour)
- Compass

Ask an adult to help when using the skewer.

1 Score down the centre of a piece of stiff card and fold it in two. Draw two diagonal lines from the bottom corners of the card to the top of the central fold. Cut along the lines to make a long folded triangle.

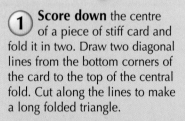

2 Tape two small coins inside the triangle, on one side near the tip. The weight of the coins will help balance the wind vane when it is finished.

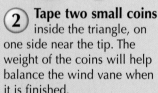

3 Fold the triangle together and tape it up. Balance the triangle on a pencil and make a mark at the balance point. Tape the pen top to the card at the mark. This will form the pivot of the wind vane.

INTO THE WIND

When light aircraft take off they head into the wind, because this lifts them off the runway quicker. That is why small airfields have wind indicators. The runway is usually built so it faces the prevailing wind, but if the wind changes dramatically the aircraft may have to take off from the other end.

◀ **Windsock**
Airfields use windsocks as wind indicators. They show the strength of the wind as well as its direction.

MOVING WEATHER SYSTEMS

Satellite images of moving weather systems show how the wind swirls around them in giant spirals, carrying cloud with it. As different parts of the spiral system move overhead, the wind at ground level keeps changing direction.

◀ **Low-pressure spiral**
This low-pressure system in the Northern Hemisphere is swirling anticlockwise and moving from west to east. The wind keeps changing as the low-pressure system approaches and passes overhead.

HANDY TIP

Site the vane well away from buildings or trees that could interfere with the wind.

5 Put the vane on the skewer and make sure it spins freely. Push the cane into soft ground or tie it to a post. Using a compass, turn the cane so the coloured peg points north.

4 Tape the skewer to a long garden cane, with the pointed end at the top. Attach the four clothes pegs to the cane in a cross, near the top.

6 The vane points towards the direction from which the wind is blowing. Note the wind direction over a week or two. Does it usually blow from one direction? This is the prevailing wind, which blows unless upset by a moving weather system.

The red peg indicates north

Measure wind speed

Air is squeezed out of high-pressure zones and flows to nearby low-pressure zones. This creates the wind. A big difference in air pressure between the two zones makes the wind blow faster. If the two zones move closer together, this also increases the wind speed, and the faster the wind blows, the stronger it is. Wind speed is measured using an instrument called an anemometer. You can make your own simple version using four paper cups.

1 Mark one of the paper cups by sticking coloured tape around the outside.

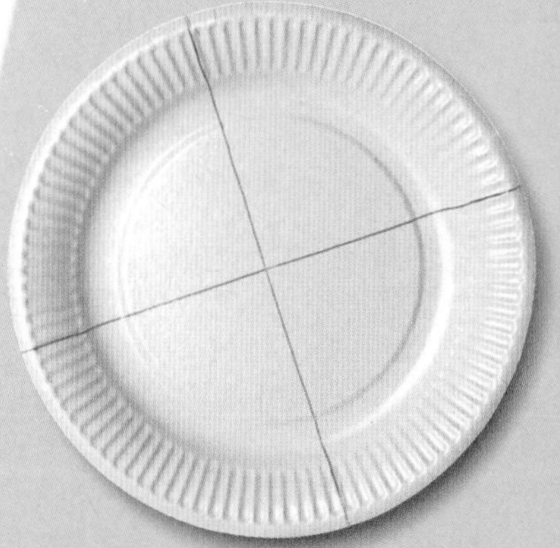

2 Using the pencil, draw a cross on the plate to find the centre. This will be the pivot point for the anemometer.

3 Stick a short length of double-sided tape to the side of each cup. Attach one cup to the nearest edge of the paper plate, so its open end is on the left. Turn the plate and attach the other cups in the same way.

WEATHER MAPS

The isobar lines on a weather map surround zones of high or low pressure. Each line marks a different level of air pressure. In some places lines are close together, while in other places they are further apart. The closer they are, the steeper the pressure difference between the high-pressure and low-pressure zones, and the stronger the wind.

Mapping the wind ▲
On this weather map of Europe, the tight isobars over northern France show that it is very windy there. The widely spaced isobars over Sweden show that the wind is light. The wind blows along the isobars, around the pressure centres.

WHAT YOU WILL NEED

- Paper plate
- 4 paper cups
- Coloured sticky tape
- Pinboard pin with plastic end
- Eraser-tipped pencil
- Double-sided sticky tape
- Stopwatch

Ask an adult to help with the pin.

A PROFESSIONAL ANEMOMETER

The anemometers used in weather stations are similar to the home-made version. The main difference is that the spinning cups are linked to an electronic device that counts the turns, and converts them into a display of the wind speed.

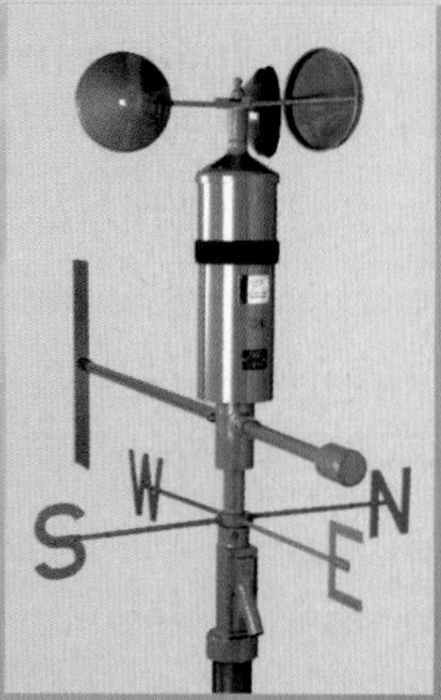

Speed and direction ▶
This anemometer is mounted above a wind vane, to show the wind direction as well as the wind speed.

Pin through the centre of the plate

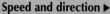

4 **Pin the plate** to the eraser on the end of the pencil, so that the pin passes through the centre of the cross. Hold the anemometer up so it spins in the wind.

5 **Using the stopwatch**, count how often the marked cup passes around in 30 seconds. Write down the number next to the local wind speed, which you can find on a website. Do this for several days and make a chart in which you translate the numbers into wind speeds.

Watch the marked cup and count how many times it spins in the wind

Invisible water

Water that is warmed by the Sun turns to water vapour, a gas that is carried upwards by rising warm air. It is invisible, unlike steam, and it forms at quite low temperatures. Huge masses of water vapour rise off tropical oceans, which have surface temperatures of about 20°C (68°F). This is the level at which your central heating is likely to be set. Try creating water vapour at home using a radiator.

WHAT YOU WILL NEED

- Large glass jar
- Cool water
- Cool glass bowl with curved base that will sit in the mouth of the jar
- Warm place such as the top of a radiator or the warm vent at the back of a refrigerator

HUMIDITY

The amount of water vapour in the air is referred to as its humidity. Warm air can hold more water vapour than cold air. This means that warm, wet places are very humid, creating that tropical sticky feeling.

A hygrometer ▸
Humidity is measured with a hygrometer, which uses a modified thermometer to detect water vapour in the air.

Condensation
When it is cold outside and warm inside, the low temperature of a window can cause water vapour in the warm air to turn back into water. Droplets form on the inside of the window in a process called condensation. It is the opposite of evaporation, which turns liquid water into vapour.

EVAPORATION

The water of oceans and lakes is always turning to water vapour. The process is called evaporation. It also happens on land, and this is why wet things dry out in hot sunshine. As the water turns to vapour it leaves everything else behind, including any substances such as salt that were dissolved in the water.

◀ **Salt Lake**
In deserts, lakes form like giant puddles after rare rainstorms, and then dry out in the desert heat. As the water evaporates, it leaves any dissolved salt behind, so the remaining water gets more and more salty. White salt crystals form on rocks on the lake shores, like these at the edges of the Great Salt Lake in Utah, USA.

1 Put some cool water into the glass jar. A depth of about 5 cm (2 in) is plenty.

2 Stand the jar in a warm place. Put the cool glass bowl on top, so the base of the bowl seals the mouth of the jar.

3 Over time, water droplets appear on the bottom of the glass bowl. Water is evaporating in the jar, and then condensing on the cool base of the bowl to form liquid water again. The water vapour itself is invisible.

HANDY TIP

Put the glass bowl in the refrigerator to cool it down before placing it on the jar.

Winter frost

The soft white hoar frost that forms on plants, fences, and windows in winter is dew that has settled on freezing cold objects, and turned into ice crystals. The water vapour in the air turns directly to ice, without passing through the liquid water phase. You can see this happening by using ice cubes and salt to make your own frost.

WHAT YOU WILL NEED

- A tall glass
- Crushed ice
- Salt

1. **Fill the glass** with ice and add some salt. The salt makes the ice melt, and when it does this it draws in heat from the surrounding air. This lowers the air temperature and cools the glass.

BLACK ICE

Very cold rain falling on freezing cold roads at night can form glassy sheets of ice called glaze. It is often referred to as black ice because you can see the dark colour of the road through the ice. Since it looks like water and is very slippery, black ice is far more dangerous than hoar frost or even snow. It causes a lot of accidents in winter.

Melting the ice ▲
In northern countries where black ice is a regular problem, special mobile heaters are used to melt it and make the roads safer.

2 **Frost crystals** grow on the outside of the chilled glass, just like hoar frost forming on an ice-cold leaf. The crystals have formed from invisible water vapour in the air, which turns directly to ice when it contacts the glass.

STEAMING FROST

Frost often forms on clear, cold winter nights. If the sky is still clear in the morning, the warm sunshine can turn the ice straight back into water vapour. This is hoar frost formation in reverse.

Sublimation ▲
As frost turns to water vapour in the morning sunshine, it often looks like steam rising off the trees. This process of ice turning to vapour without becoming liquid water first is called sublimation.

FROST AND ICE

The frost that forms on cold objects in winter can be very beautiful, creating wonderful feathery patterns of ice crystals. But thick layers of ice can add so much weight to trees and cables that they sometimes collapse under the strain.

Frost patterns ▶
If dew forms on a smooth surface, such as glass, and then freezes, it forms leafy, fern-like patterns as the ice crystals grow.

Hoar frost ▶
When water vapour freezes on to leaves, the first ice crystals form at the edges, which are the coldest parts of the leaf.

Rime ▶
Water droplets in very cold freezing fog can freeze on to cold objects, forming thick layers of white ice crystals called rime.

Heavy ice ▶
Power lines can become thickly covered in rime, glaze, or hanging icicles. These can be so heavy that they cause the lines to snap.

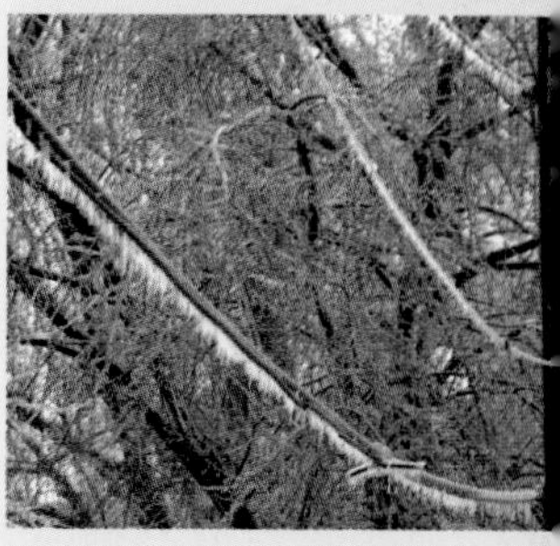

Ice storms ▶
Places such as Canada sometimes suffer ice storms of heavy glaze that can break tree branches.

Clouds and fog

As warm air rises, it cools, and any water vapour in the rising air cools, too. Eventually, it gets cool enough to condense into the tiny droplets of water that form clouds. But the vapour needs something to condense on to, such as microscopic dust or smoke particles in the air, called condensation nuclei. These allow cooled water vapour to turn into clouds. You can show how this works using warm water, ice, and smoke particles from a smouldering match.

FOG

If water vapour in the air condenses into cloud droplets at ground level, it forms the low-lying clouds we call fog. This often happens on cold, clear nights when the ground cools down quickly, cooling the air above it so any water vapour condenses into radiation fog. It also happens at sea when warm, moist air moves over cold water, cooling the vapour so it turns into sea fog.

Pacific coast fog ▲
Off the coast of California, USA, moist air is cooled by the cold Californian current that flows south from Alaska. Water vapour condenses into sea fogs that roll in under the Golden Gate Bridge in San Francisco.

1 Tape the black paper or card to the back of the jar to create a dark background. This will make your cloud more visible. Fill around a third of the jar with warm (but not steaming) water.

2 Light a match, and then blow it out. Wait for a second or two before dropping the smoking match into the jar. Quickly put the bag of ice on top of the jar, so it forms a cold lid over the opening.

WHAT YOU WILL NEED

- Large, wide-neck glass jar
- Warm water
- Black paper or card
- Sticky tape
- Plastic sandwich bag filled with ice cubes
- Matches

Ask for adult help with the match.

3 Water vapour rising from the warm water condenses on to the smoke particles and forms a cloud. Lifting off the ice bag releases the cloud.

HANDY TIP

Don't drop the match in too quickly after blowing it out, or you'll get too much smoke.

Make sure the ice bag won't fall into the jar

BIRTH OF A CLOUD

Clouds seem to form out of nothing, because the water vapour that becomes cloud droplets is an invisible gas. Cloud droplets are so tiny that it takes a million of them to form a raindrop, but they are big enough to be visible.

Cloud droplets form ▶ Invisible water vapour carried upwards in warm air currents gets cooler as it rises. As it cools, the water vapour starts to form cloud droplets around microscopic condensation nuclei.

White haze ▶ As more cloud droplets form, the young cloud starts to become visible as white haze or wisps of white against the blue sky.

Floating water ▶ The cloud droplets are so tiny that they are able to float on the rising air currents even though they are made of liquid water.

White and grey ▶ The cloud becomes thick enough to stop the sunlight shining through it, so the thickest parts are in shadow and appear grey.

Clouds and rain ▶ Eventually, the cloud droplets may join together to make much bigger, heavier water drops, and these then fall as rain.

Weather fronts

When warm air flowing from the tropics meets cold air from nearer the poles, the warm air rises above the cold air. As it rises, it cools, resulting in clouds and rain. The boundary between the two air masses is called a front. It is invisible in air, but you can create a "front" between warm and cold water, using food colouring to show the separate layers.

WHAT YOU WILL NEED

- Large glass jar
- Jug
- Very hot water (but not boiling)
- Very cold water
- Food colouring
- Thermometer

Ask for adult help when using the hot water.

The warm, coloured water stays at the top

1 Fill the jug with the hot water and add some of the food colouring. Pour the cold water into the big jar so it is more than half full.

2 Tip the jar of cold water so the water is close to the rim. Very slowly and gently, pour the hot coloured water from the jug down the neck of the jar, so it trickles into the cold water. The coloured water should stay near the surface.

A WARM FRONT

When warm air pushes against cold air, the warm air rides up over the cold air at a shallow angle. The angled boundary between the air masses is known as a warm front. Steeper boundaries caused by cold air pushing beneath warm air are called cold fronts.

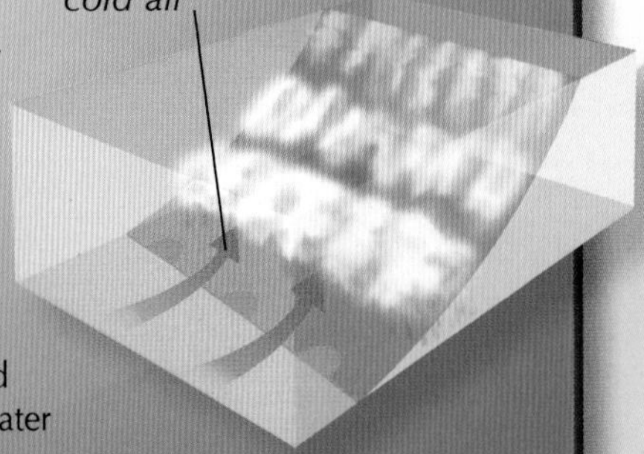
Warm air rides up over cold air

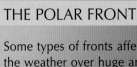

Rising warm air ▶
As the warm air slides up and over the cold air at the front, it gets cooler. This makes water vapour in the air turn to clouds and rain.

3 **If you get it right**, the warm, coloured water will lie in a layer above the heavier cold water, just as warm air lies above cold air. The boundary between the two is like a weather front. You can test the difference in temperature using a thermometer.

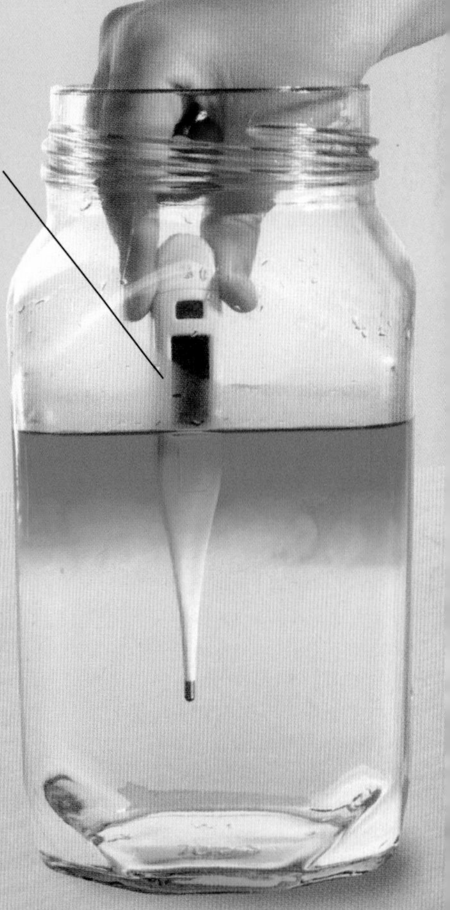
Dip the thermometer below the "front" and see the temperature fall

THE POLAR FRONT

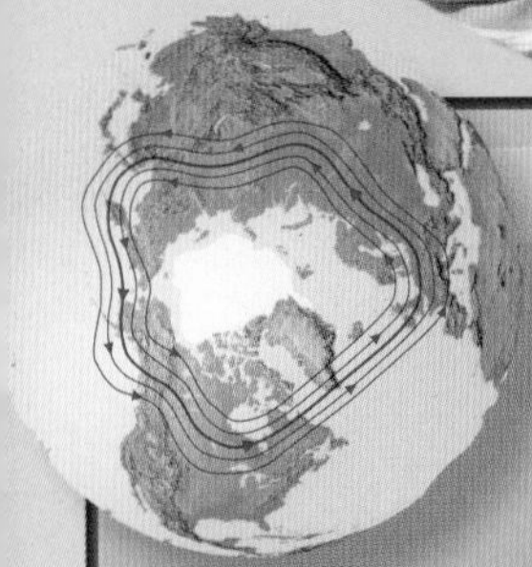

▲ Moving frontier
The winds blow mainly towards the east around the polar front, carrying the weather systems with them. The shape of the front changes all the time, and it is often broken up into separate fronts.

Some types of fronts affect the weather over huge areas. The polar front forms where warm tropical air meets cold polar air over North America, Europe, and northern Asia. It makes a wavy line around the globe, where the warm and cold air masses push into each other. The waves in the polar front cause the mobile weather systems that make the weather so variable in these northern regions.

Swirling air

When a warm air mass rises over a cold air mass at a front, the rising air reduces the air pressure on the ground below. The pressure is lowest where the air is rising quickest. The surrounding air swirls into this low-pressure area and is sucked upwards. The warm and cold air masses swirl around each other, too, separated by warm and cold fronts that bring clouds and rain as they pass overhead. This type of low-pressure weather system is called a cyclone, a depression, or simply a low.

Cloudy weather
The rising warm air in a low-pressure weather system usually creates a lot of cloud. Huge banks of cloud can build up over the weather fronts that separate the warm and cold air masses. They often produce a lot of rain, and big clouds over cold fronts sometimes cause thunderstorms.

ATLANTIC CYCLONE

Cyclones are very common over the north Atlantic, where warm tropical air meets cold polar air at the polar front. The cyclones push eastwards, carrying cloudy, rainy weather over northern Europe. They are marked by spirals of cloud that can be seen from space. Orbiting weather satellites send images of them back to Earth.

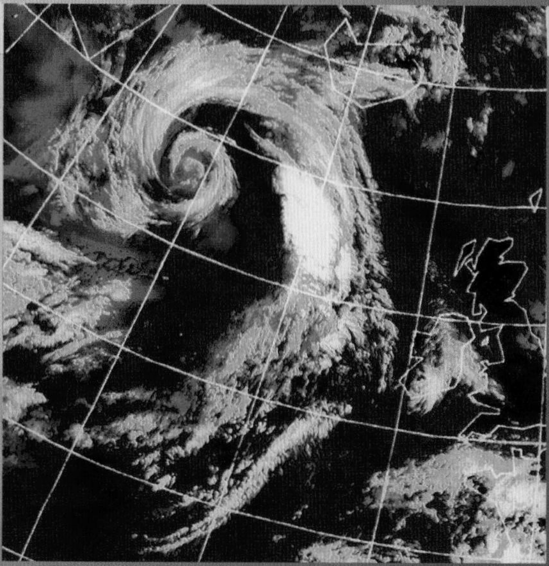

Cloud spiral ▶
This false colour satellite image shows an Atlantic cyclone approaching Britain and Iceland. As with all low-pressure systems in the Northern Hemisphere, it is spiralling anticlockwise.

SWIRLING CYCLONE

If you watch water draining down a plughole you will get a good idea of how air is drawn into a cyclone – but remember that the air rises at the centre instead of sinking. The spinning Earth makes cyclones swirl anticlockwise north of the equator, but clockwise south of the equator. They are balanced by anticyclones, which swirl down and outwards in the opposite direction.

Down the drain ▲
Air swirls into a cyclone rather like water pouring down a drain. It circles in a vortex rather than flowing straight into the centre.

THE LIFE OF A CYCLONE

Temperate northern cyclones normally move from west to east, developing as they go. Warm and cold air masses twist around each other, forcing warm moist air upwards and generating high winds, clouds, and rain.

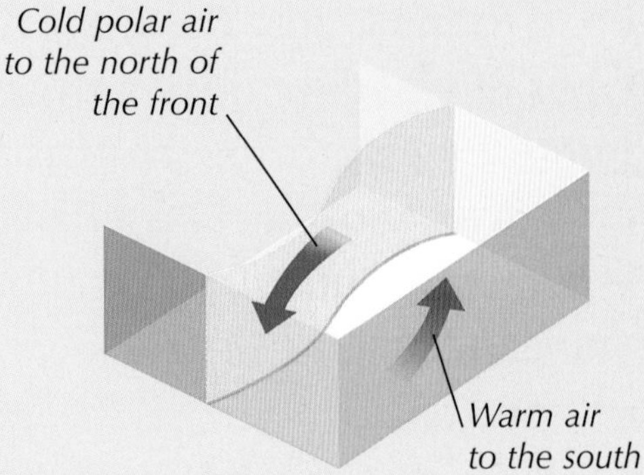
Cold polar air to the north of the front
Warm air to the south

Air masses twist around ▲
A Northern Hemisphere cyclone begins with a mass of warm air pushing north, to the right of a mass of cold air. They are separated by a front.

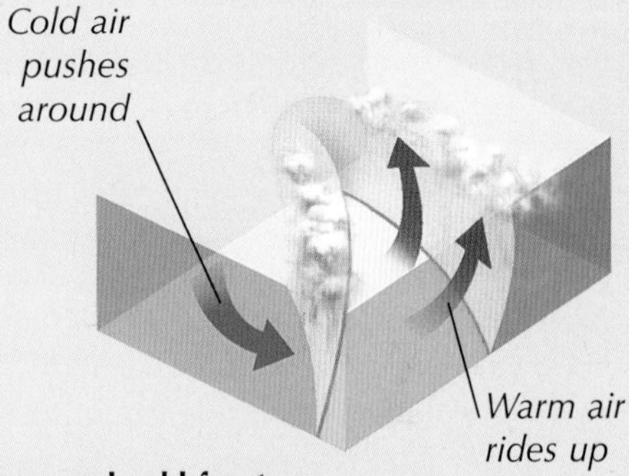
Cold air pushes around
Warm air rides up

Warm and cold fronts ▲
The warm air rides up over cold air to the east at a warm front. Meanwhile, cold air from the west pushes the warm air up at a cold front. Both fronts are marked by clouds and rain.

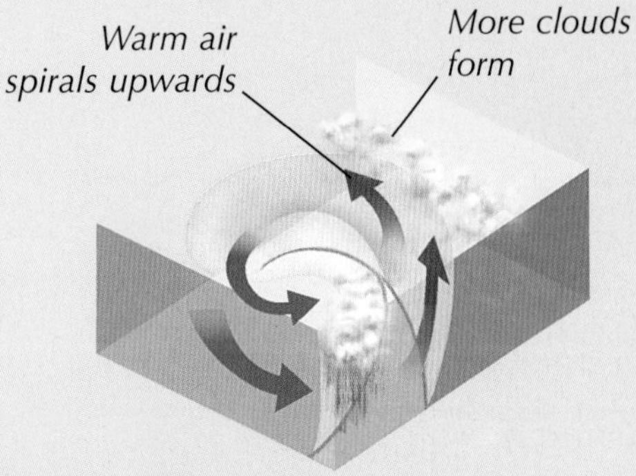
Warm air spirals upwards
More clouds form

Cyclone occludes ▲
The cold air from the west moves faster than the warm air, pushes under it, and lifts it right off the ground. This is called an occlusion.

Track a cyclone

A moving low-pressure weather system, or cyclone, has a warm front and a cold front, with warm air in the middle that is pushed up to form clouds. There are different types of clouds at the warm and cold fronts. By identifying them as they pass over, and checking changes in air pressure and wind direction, you can track the progress of a cyclone.

Moving weather

In the diagram of the cyclone shown below, the cyclone is moving from west to east. At the centre is a zone of warm air. At its leading edge, warm air is sliding up over cold air at the warm front. The rising air forms a sequence of clouds, from high-level cirrus to low-level nimbostratus. As the cyclone passes over, cold air from behind forces warm air up at the cold front, forming big cumulonimbus clouds.

ⓐ Cumulus clouds
Small cumulus clouds often follow the cold front, causing showers. Eventually, they blow away and the sky clears.

ⓑ Cumulonimbus clouds
A narrow band of cumulonimbus clouds can form over the cold front, causing heavy rain.

ⓒ Stratus clouds
Flat, low-level stratus clouds often cover the sky in the middle of the moving cyclone. The weather is dull, but not rainy.

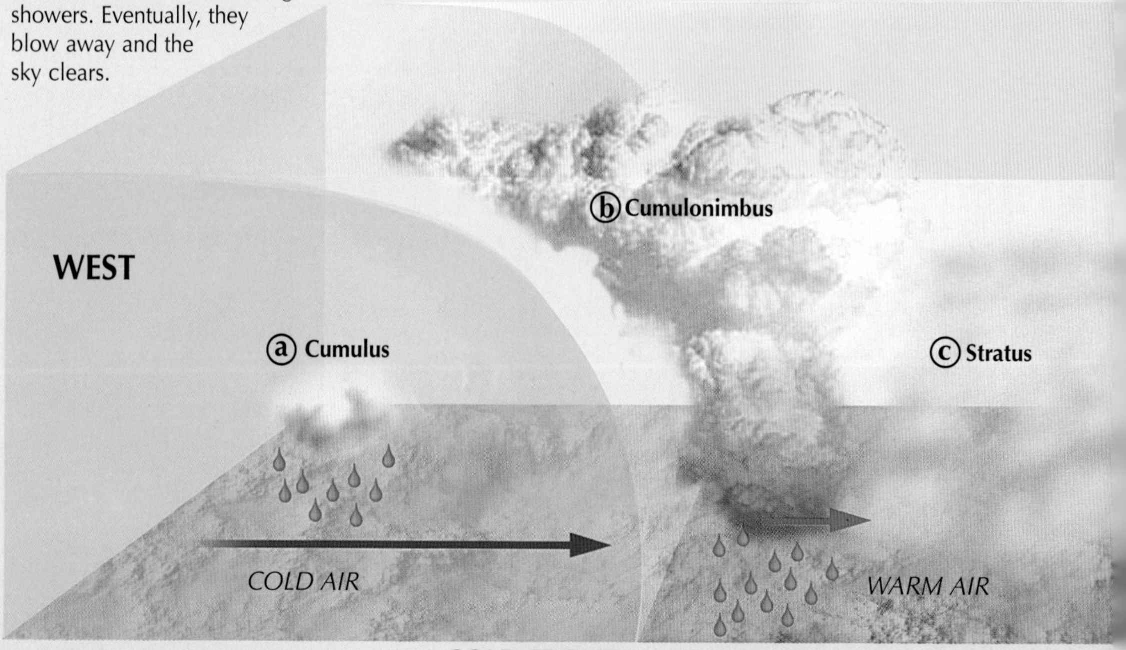

COLD FRONT ▲

PRESSURE AND WIND

As a cyclone passes over, the air pressure and wind direction change. You can use your home-made barometer and wind vane to keep track of these changes. The pressure falls as clouds build up over the warm front, and keeps falling. Meanwhile, the wind swings around to blow from a different direction, which varies depending on where you are. As the warm front passes the pressure stays low, but the wind often changes back to how it was. As the cold front passes the pressure rises again.

ⓓ Nimbostratus clouds
Thick, grey, low-level nimbostratus clouds build up over the warm front. As they pass over they bring steady rain.

ⓔ Altostratus clouds
Thin cirrus and cirrostratus becomes thicker, lower altostratus as the warm front gets nearer, and the air pressure falls steadily.

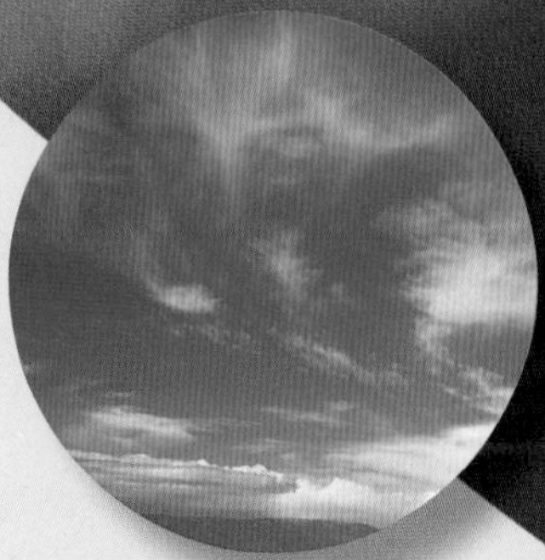

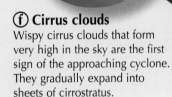

ⓕ Cirrus clouds
Wispy cirrus clouds that form very high in the sky are the first sign of the approaching cyclone. They gradually expand into sheets of cirrostratus.

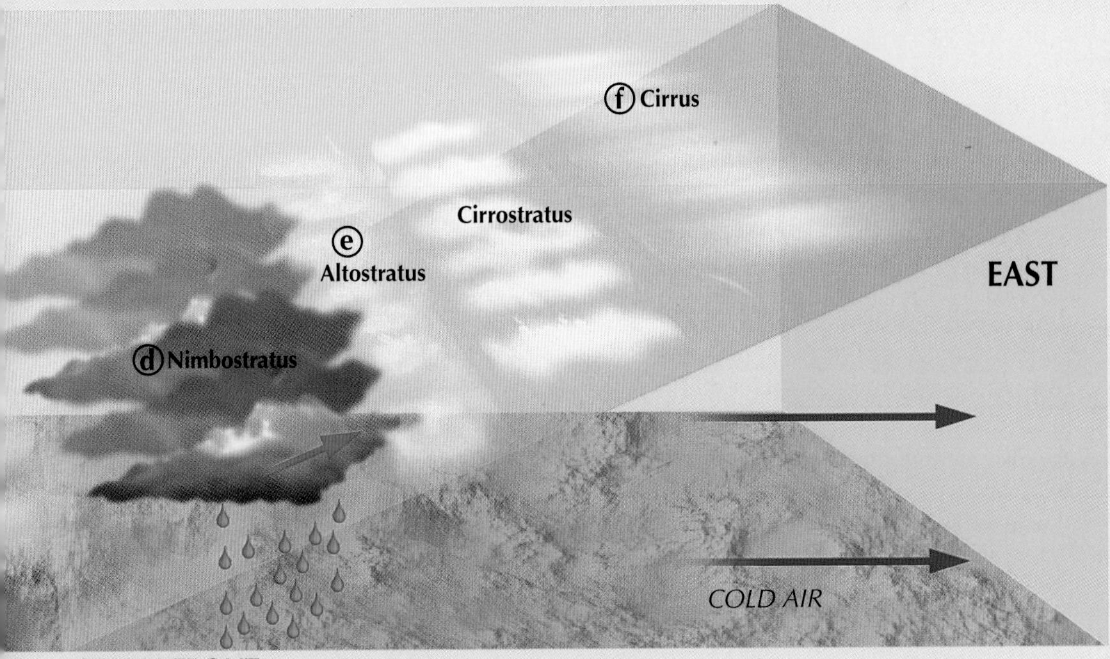

▲ **WARM FRONT**

Measure rainfall

The tiny water droplets and ice crystals that form clouds may eventually grow into bigger raindrops and snowflakes. When these get heavy enough, they fall towards the ground. The snowflakes often melt on the way, turning into rain. Rainfall is measured in centimetres or inches using a rain gauge, and it is easy to make your own.

WHAT YOU WILL NEED

- Large, clear, straight-sided plastic bottle
- Coloured sticky tape
- Handful of pebbles
- Scissors
- Ruler
- Water

Ask an adult to help you cut off the bottle top.

1 **Cut the top** off the bottle at the point where the curved "shoulders" join the straight sides. Try to make a straight cut. Save both parts of the bottle (you can throw away or recycle the cap).

2 **Put the pebbles** in the bottle. Stick some tape to the side of the bottle above the pebbles. Add water until it reaches the top of the tape.

3 **Turn the top** section of the bottle upside-down, and insert it in the lower section of the bottle.

RAIN AND SHOWERS

Rain often falls over quite small areas at a time. Weather forecasters call this type of rain a shower, even though it may be quite heavy. Showers travel across country, so they don't last very long in one place. The steady rainfall caused by broad weather fronts also travels across country, but it extends over such a large area that it can keep falling all day.

Distant rain ▸
You can often see local showers falling in the distance. The rain looks like grey or silver streaks falling from the dark rain clouds.

4 Put the rain gauge outside in a place where it is exposed to the sky. If it rains, measure the amount of water above the tape in centimetres or inches. Then pour water out until it is level with the top of the tape again.

The ruler gives an accurate measure of rainfall in centimetres or inches

HANDY TIP

Measure the rainfall every day at the same time to build up a record of annual rainfall.

Make a snowflake

When clouds rise high in the sky, their temperature falls below freezing, so the tiny cloud droplets freeze into microscopic ice crystals. These may join together to form snowflakes. Each snowflake contains about 200 ice crystals in a six-sided pattern. You can make a giant snowflake using a substance called borax, which forms beautiful crystals of its own.

WHAT YOU WILL NEED

- Large measuring jug
- 3 white pipe cleaners
- White string
- Scissors • Pencil
- Boiling water
- Borax (sugar or salt can be used as an alternative)
- Wooden spoon
- Blue food colouring

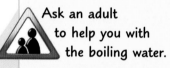

Ask an adult to help you with the boiling water.

CRYSTALLIZATION

The activity on these pages works because cold water cannot dissolve as much borax as hot water. So as the water cools, solid borax collects on the framework of pipe cleaners and string. As it collects, the borax forms glinting crystals. The slower the water cools down, the bigger the crystals.

Crystal faces flash in the light

Borax crystals ▲
Each crystal is built up from borax molecules that were spread out in the hot water. They clump together in a shape that mirrors their atomic structure.

1 **Take the three** pipe cleaners and twist them together in the centre to make a six-pointed star. Make sure the star is small enough to fit in the jug.

2 **Tie the string** around the points of the star to link them together. The result looks like a snowflake.

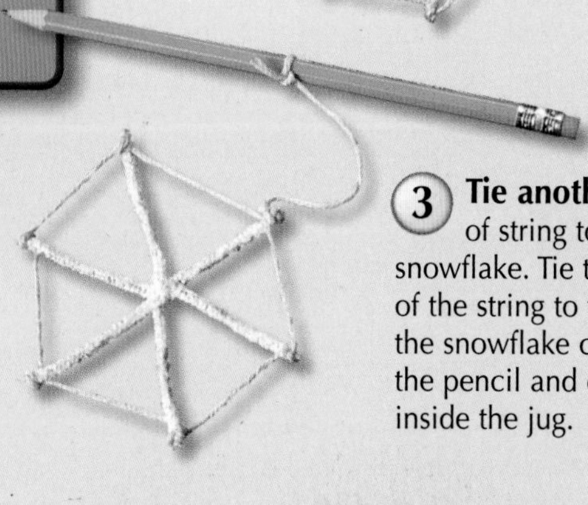

3 **Tie another length** of string to your snowflake. Tie the other end of the string to the pencil so the snowflake can hang from the pencil and dangle inside the jug.

HANDY TIP

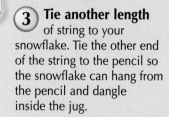

You can buy borax from hardware stores. It should not be ingested.

ICE CRYSTALS

The tiny ice crystals that form high in clouds are shaped like microscopic six-sided rods. They are drawn together by electric forces, along with tiny water droplets. The water freezes and welds the crystals together in an amazing variety of patterns, but since the crystals have six sides, the flakes always have a six-sided or six-pointed form.

◀ Snowflake variety
All snowflakes are shaped rather like six-pointed stars, but every one is different because the ice crystals come together in different ways.

Make sure the snowflake is not resting on the bottom of the jug

4 Pour boiling water into the jug, and add a spoonful of borax. Using the spoon, stir until the borax is dissolved. Keep adding borax and stirring until no more will dissolve. Add a few drops of blue food colouring.

5 Hang the snowflake in the jug so that it is immersed in the liquid. Wait at least overnight, or longer if you are using sugar or salt. Your snowflake will be covered with beautiful crystals.

Storm clouds and hail

The biggest clouds are the black storm clouds known as cumulonimbus clouds. They tower high into the sky, and are much deeper than other clouds. They are made of water droplets at the bottom and ice crystals at the top. Powerful air currents toss the crystals around, making them gather more ice and grow into hailstones. The currents also rub the droplets and crystals against each other, generating static electricity that is eventually discharged as lightning.

Ice crystals collide with water droplets and become charged with static electricity
Powerful currents of air
The bottom of the cloud becomes negatively charged

Charged up

Strong air currents surging through deep storm clouds charge them up with static electricity. The charge is positive at the top and negative at the bottom, just like a giant battery.

GIANT HAIL

Some parts of the world, such as the American Midwest, suffer from huge hailstones that can be as big as tennis balls. They form inside gigantic storm clouds of the type that often turn into tornadoes. The hailstones fall out of the sky like rocks, and can cause a lot of damage.

Crop damage ▲
A big hailstorm can flatten valuable crops, so there is nothing left to harvest.

Treacherous roads ▲
Hailstones on the road roll beneath cars like ball bearings and can cause crashes.

The top of the cloud becomes positively charged
Ice crystals are swept around the cloud and get coated with more and more layers of ice
Eventually, the ice crystals become so heavy that they fall from the cloud as hailstones

HAIR RAISING

You can generate your own static electricity by rubbing an inflated balloon against your clothes for a few minutes. If you rub hard, this will build up an electrical charge in the balloon, just like the charge that builds up in a storm cloud. Stand in front of a mirror and hold the charged balloon above your head. Bring it down slowly, and you will see how the electrical charge attracts your hair, making it stand on end. Luckily, the charge is not powerful enough to produce lightning!

Electrostatic attraction ▲
The static electricity creates a force that attracts your hair. It can also attract the balloon to other objects. Try charging the balloon, then throwing it up against the ceiling. What happens to it?

Shattered glass ▲
Giant hailstones are heavy enough to smash glass and dent steel.

◄ Deadly hailstones
Most hailstones are the size of peas or marbles, but the ones shown here are nearly as big as the golf ball next to them. The largest authenticated hailstone in the world fell in Kansas, USA, in 1970 and weighed 0.77 kg (1 lb 11 oz).

Thunderstorms

The charges that build up in storm clouds can reach 100 million volts or more, making huge sparks leap between the cloud and the ground. These begin as faint, forked, and stepped leaders that zigzag downwards. When one leader approaches the ground, a spark leaps up to meet it, and a massive bolt of electricity lights up the leader as a lightning flash. You can simulate the effect by charging up a metal plate and using it to create a spark.

LIGHTNING AND THUNDER

Lightning heats the air within the flash by up to 30,000°C (54,000°F) in less than a second. That's four to five times the surface temperature of the Sun! The intense heat makes the air expand explosively, causing a shockwave that makes the noise we call thunder. There are usually several lightning strokes within a few fractions of a second, and this is why thunder sounds crackly.

Struck by lightning ▲
Lightning usually strikes tall objects such as trees. The intense heat burns a track down the tree and can completely destroy it. Metal lightning conductors stop this happening to buildings.

Forked lightning
The main lightning stroke flashes along one of the fainter leader strokes that fork down from the thunder cloud.

WHAT YOU WILL NEED

- One rubber glove
- Cloth, preferably one made from artificial fibre
- Metal plate or tray
- Kitchen scissors with plastic handles
- Stopwatch

1 **Lay the cloth** on a table. Put the rubber glove on your hand to insulate it, and rub the metal plate lightly against the cloth for several minutes. This should build up a charge of static electricity.

2 **Darken the room**. Very slowly, lower the tips of the scissors towards the metal plate. If the plate is charged up enough, a spark will jump between the plate and the scissor tips, and you may hear a faint crackle of thunder.

HOW NEAR IS THE STORM?

The speed of light is so fast that you see lightning the instant it happens. The speed of sound is slower, so you hear the thunder after the flash. Since sound travels 1 km in 3 seconds (1 mile in 5 seconds), the time difference between the flash and the thunder tells you how near the storm is.

Use a stopwatch ▲
Time the difference with a stopwatch, and then divide the seconds by three (km) or five (miles) to give the distance between you and the storm.

HANDY TIP

Some types of carpet generate static electricity, so you could try rubbing the plate on the floor.

Glossary

Abdomen The rear part of an insect's body. It contains the insect's digestive system and sometimes ends in a sting.

Air pressure The squeezing effect of the weight of air in the atmosphere (also known as atmospheric pressure). Rising warm air weighs less, so gives low air pressure. Sinking cool air gives high air pressure.

Altostratus Mid-level, sheet-like clouds.

Alum A salt that is sometimes used as a fixative in dyeing. Its chemical name is potassium aluminium sulphate.

Anemometer An instrument for measuring wind speed.

Ant A small insect that lives in a nest and gathers its food on plants or on the ground. Worker ants don't have wings, but they may have a sting.

Antennae Two jointed organs on the head of an insect, which it uses for sensing things.

Aphid A sap-sucking bug that lives on plants. Aphids are also known as greenfly or blackfly, depending on their colour.

Asteroid A rocky body in the solar system that can be as big as 1,000 km (620 miles) wide. Most asteroids lie in a belt between Mars and Jupiter.

Astronomy The scientific study of space.

Atmosphere The blanket of mixed gases that surrounds the Earth.

Atom The smallest unit of matter, which cannot be divided into smaller parts, except in a nuclear reaction.

Barometer An instrument for measuring air pressure.

Basalt The most common type of volcanic rock, formed as lava cools and hardens.

Bee A stinging insect that feeds at flowers. Some types of bees live in large nests, while others live on their own.

Beetle An insect that has thickened forewings, or elytra. When a beetle is on its feet, its elytra are closed up tightly.

Biology The study of living things. Scientists who study biology are called biologists.

Bird of prey A bird that hunts other animals during daylight, catching them with its claws.

Black hole A point in space with such a powerful gravitational pull that nothing, not even light, can escape.

Body feather A feather that gives a bird's body a smooth outline so that it can slip through the air. Body feathers are usually short and overlap like tiles on a roof.

Bug In everyday language, a bug is any kind of insect. To scientists, a "true bug" is a particular type of insect with piercing mouthparts and two pairs of wings. True bugs feed on plants and animals.

Butterfly An insect that has two pairs of wings covered in tiny scales and that usually flies by day. Most butterflies feed at flowers.

Calcite The main mineral in limestone and chalk. Its chemical name is calcium carbonate.

Camouflage Colours or patterns that help an animal to hide by making it blend in with its background.

Carbon dioxide A gas used by plants to make sugar and produced by animals in the reaction that turns sugar into energy. It exists in very small quantities in the atmosphere.

Carnivores Animals, such as wolves, whose diet consists mainly or entirely of meat.

Celestial pole The point at the top or bottom of the celestial sphere. The north and south celestial poles do not move during the night and are always due north or due south.

Celestial sphere This imaginary globe surrounds Earth. Stars move around Earth as if fixed points on this sphere.

Centipede A long-bodied animal with one pair of legs on each of its body segments. Centipedes have a poisonous bite.

Cephalothorax In spiders, the front part of the body. The cephalothorax is usually much bigger than the head, and the spider's legs are attached to it.

Chlorophyll Green pigment that colours plants and traps the Sun's energy during photosynthesis.

Circumference The distance around a circular object.

Circumpolar star A star that does not set, but remains above the horizon, and circles the celestial pole.

Cirrus High, wispy cloud.

Clay Mineral particles that are smaller than about 0.002 mm (0.00008 in) wide, and are common in soil and sediment. Clay forms by the weathering of granite and other rocks.

Climate The average weather in a particular place.

Cold front The boundary between cold and warm air masses, created when the cold air pushes under the warm air.

Comet A comet's body is made of ice and rocky dust. When a comet nears the Sun, its surface evaporates and releases gas and dust in glowing tails.

Condensation The process of gas turning into liquid. When water vapour turns into liquid water, it condenses.

Condensation nuclei Tiny particles in the atmosphere that attract water vapour and make it turn into droplets of liquid water.

Conifers Plants, mostly tall forest trees, that produce their seeds in cones.

Constellation A pattern of stars in the sky, often named after a mythological person or creature.

Coriolis effect The effect of the spinning Earth on the way air masses and weather systems, for example, move across the Earth's surface.

Crab spider A spider that catches insects by lurking in flowers. Unlike most spiders, crab spiders are often brightly coloured.

Crater This bowl-shaped depression can be formed by a meteorite impact or by a volcanic eruption.

Crust The outer layer of the Earth that lies over the mantle. There are two main types of crust: continental and oceanic.

Crustacean An animal with a hard body, lots of pairs of legs, and two pairs of antennae. Apart from woodlice, most crustaceans live in the sea.

Crystal A geometric form of a mineral or other solid, with naturally formed plane faces that reflect the arrangement of the atoms that make it up.

Cuckoo A migratory bird that tricks other birds into raising its young. Female cuckoos lay their eggs in other birds' nests.

Cumulonimbus Very deep storm clouds that rise from low level to high level, and produce heavy rain, lightning, and hail.

Cumulus Heaped, often fluffy-looking, low-level clouds.

Cyclone A weather system with low air pressure at its centre, and warm and cold fronts that create wind, clouds, and rain.

Damselfly An insect with a long, slender body and two pairs of transparent wings. Like dragonflies, damselflies grow up underwater.

Deciduous Describes trees, such as oak and maple, that shed their leaves at a certain time of year, often in the autumn.

Degree A unit used in measuring angles or distances across a sphere or globe.

Depression *See* **Cyclone**.

Dew Drops of water produced by water vapour condensing on to cold surfaces overnight.

Dinosaur A member of a prehistoric family of reptiles that lived from 230 million years ago up to 65 million years ago. Their closest living relatives are birds and crocodiles.

Dove Doves are close relatives of pigeons. Some of them feed on fruit in trees, while others feed on seeds on the ground.

Down feather A fluffy feather that helps to keep a bird warm. Young birds often have thick down, particularly if they grow up in cold places.

Dragonfly A fast-flying insect with a long body and two pairs of stiff, transparent wings. Dragonflies grow up underwater.

Entomologist Someone who studies insects.

Equator The imaginary line around the centre of the Earth that marks its widest point. Equatorial regions are very hot.

Erosion The wearing away and removal of exposed land by water, wind, and ice.

Evaporation The process of liquid turning into gas, or vapour. When water turns into water vapour, it evaporates.

Evergreen Describes trees, such as pine and holly, that shed and replace their leaves constantly, so are always in leaf.

Fangs In spiders, a pair of sharp mouthparts that stab into the prey, injecting venom.

Finch A small bird with a wedge-shaped beak that is specially shaped for cracking open seeds. Many finches live in large flocks.

Flight feather A feather from a bird's wings or tail. Flight feathers have a wide blade and a strong shaft, or quill.

Fly An insect that has only one pair of wings.

Forewings An insect's front wings. The forewings are often bigger than the hindwings, and in some insects they are thick or leathery.

Fossil The remains, traces, or impressions of organisms, such as plants and animals, that have been preserved in rock.

Fossil fuels The remains of ancient plants and animals that have been turned into energy-rich coal, oil, or gas.

Fruit A structure produced by flowering plants that contains and protects seeds.

Galaxy A group of millions or billions of stars held together by gravity.

Gall A plant growth used as a home by insects. The insects give off chemicals that make the galls grow.

Gall wasp Tiny wasps that grow up inside plant galls.

Gannet A large seabird that catches fish by diving into the sea from high up in the air. Gannets' faces are specially protected against the impact of the dive.

Geode A stone containing a crystal-lined cavity.

Germination The start of growth of a seed into a seedling.

Glaze Glassy ice.

Grasshopper An insect with strong back legs and leathery forewings. Grasshoppers are very good at jumping and feed on plants.

Grub A young insect or larva. Grubs look very different from adult insects and they often live inside their food.

Habitat The kind of surroundings that an animal normally lives in. For example, insect habitats include forests, deserts, and freshwater.

Herbivores Animals, such as deer, that feed exclusively on plants.

Hindwings An insect's back wings.

Honeydew The sugary liquid that aphids produce when they feed.

Hoverfly A fast-flying insect that feeds on nectar. Hoverflies get their name because they often hover over flowers.

Humidity A measure of the amount of water vapour in the air. Warm air can hold more water vapour, so is often more humid than cold air.

Hummingbird A small, nectar-eating bird that hovers in front of flowers to feed. Hummingbirds are found only in the Americas.

Hydrogen The most common chemical element in the universe. Hydrogen is the main component of stars and galaxies.

Hyphae The tiny filaments or threads that make up a fungus, and through which it feeds.

Igneous rock A type of rock that forms as magma or when lava cools and hardens. Intrusive igneous rock forms underground from magma; extrusive igneous rock forms on the Earth's surface from lava.

Isobar A line on a weather map that joins places with the same air pressure.

Jay A colourful member of the crow family that lives in woods and forests. Jays often bury nuts as winter food.

Jumping spider A spider that has large eyes and that catches its prey by jumping on to it instead of by making a web.

Kestrel A small bird of prey that spots its food by hovering high up in the air.

Kingfisher A colourful bird that swoops down on its food. Many kingfishers eat fish, but some catch animals on the ground.

Larva A young insect that looks very different from its parents and that changes shape as it grows up. Grubs, caterpillars, and maggots are all examples of larvae.

Latitude A measure of the distance north or south of Earth's equator. Latitude is measured in degrees and shown on globes as lines parallel to the equator.

Lava Molten rock that is forced out of a volcano during an eruption on to the Earth's surface.

Leaf miner An insect grub that feeds by chewing or mining its way through the inside of a leaf.

Light pollution The glow in the sky caused by street lights and atmospheric pollution. Light pollution makes stargazing difficult in cities.

Light-year The unit of astronomical distance based on the distance light travels in a year – 10 million million km (6 million million miles).

Macaw The largest type of parrot. There are more than ten kinds of macaws. Many of them are in danger because they are caught and sold as pets.

Mammal A warm-blooded animal, such as a mouse, with fur that feeds its young on milk.

Mantle The layer of the Earth between the outer core and the crust. The mantle is made of solid rock that is very hot and slightly viscous, allowing it to flow and circulate over long periods of time.

Merganser A kind of duck that has a slender beak and dives underwater to catch fish.

Metamorphic rock A type of rock that forms when other rocks are subjected to intense heat and/or pressure, causing chemical changes and the recrystallization of its minerals.

Meteor shower A period when the rate of shooting stars rises as Earth passes through the trail of dust left by a comet.

Meteorite A rock from space that falls to the Earth's surface without completely burning up.

Micrometeorite A microscopic meteorite.

Migration Moving between summer and winter quarters.

Milky Way This is the galaxy in which we live. It can be seen as a pale, milky band across the sky on dark nights.

Millipede A long-bodied animal with two pairs of legs on each of its body segments. Millipedes have hard bodies and often coil up into a spiral if they are touched.

Mineral A naturally occurring mixture of chemicals that has certain regular characteristics, such as atomic structure and chemical composition. Minerals are the building blocks of rocks.

Monsoon A seasonal wind pattern that brings heavy rain for part of the year, especially in southern Asia.

Moth An insect that has two pairs of wings covered in tiny scales and that usually flies by night. Most moths feed at flowers.

Moulting Shedding old feathers and replacing them with new ones. Most birds moult their feathers gradually once or twice a year.

Mustelids Group of mammals that includes weasels, polecats, otters, and badgers.

Naked eye Human vision that is not enhanced in any way.

Nebula A vast cloud of gas and/or dust in space.

Nectar A sweet liquid produced by flowers to attract pollinating animals.

Nesting colony A large group of birds nesting together.

Nightjar A night-flying bird that catches insects on the wing. Nightjars have large mouths and they use them like scoops as they fly.

Nimbostratus A sheet-like rain cloud.

Nimbus A rain cloud.

Nocturnal Describes an animal that is active at night.

Occlusion When a mass of warm air is pushed off the ground by a cold front catching up with a warm front.

Omnivores Animals, such as bears, whose diet consists of a mixture of meat and plants.

Open cluster A loose cluster of young stars.

Opposition The point in the orbit of a planet when it is on the opposite side of Earth from the Sun, making viewing easy.

Orbit The path in which one object travels around another, more massive, object.

Organism A living thing.

Ornithology The study of birds and the way that they live.

Owl A predatory bird that hunts at night. Unlike birds of prey, owls are very good at seeing in the dark, and they have keen hearing as well.

Oxygen A gas found in air that is taken in by living things to release energy from food.

Parasite An animal that feeds on the living body of another one.

Parrot A colourful bird with a hooked beak. Most parrots live in warm places. They eat food from plants, including nectar, fruit, nuts, and seeds.

Period A division of geological time during which an arrangement of rocks is formed.

Photosynthesis The process by which plants make food from simple substances using sunlight energy.

Pigeon A fast-flying bird that feeds on the ground and normally lives in a flock.

Planet A large, spherical body that orbits a star.

Planisphere A star chart with a rotating window that shows which stars are visible at particular times and dates, based on your latitude.

Plate A large fragment of the Earth's crust, also known as a tectonic plate.

Polar regions The regions around the North Pole and South Pole, where freezing winters and cold summers create permanent ice.

Pole Star The star Polaris that marks the north celestial pole, and around which the northern sky appears to rotate. The Pole Star is always due north.

Pollen The dust-like substance that plants produce.

Pollination The transfer of pollen from the male part of a flower to the female part of the same or a different flower.

Predator An animal that hunts others for food.

Preening Cleaning and rearranging feathers to keep them in good condition. Birds preen their feathers with their beaks and sometimes their feet.

Prey An animal that is hunted by a predator.

Pupa The resting stage in the life cycle of many insects, when the young insect's body is broken down and an adult one is built in its place.

Quadrillion The number equivalent to one thousand million million.

Quill The shaft that runs down the middle of a feather.

Red giant A star that has swollen in size and becomes red as it nears the end of its life.

Resident A bird that stays in the same area throughout the year.

Rime Thick deposits of ice crystals caused by freezing fog.

Rock A solid mixture, or aggregate, of minerals. Rocks are divided into three main groups: igneous, sedimentary, and metamorphic.

Rodents A large group of small- to medium-sized mammals with gnawing teeth that includes rats, squirrels, and beavers.

Saddle In adult earthworms, a smooth band around the body, about one-third of the way down.

Sedimentary rock A type of rock that forms when sediment is compressed and cemented over long periods of time. The sediment may consist of eroded rock debris or of organic remains, such as the mineral shells of sea organisms.

Seed A structure containing an embryo (baby) plant and its food store, produced by plants when they reproduce.

Shooting star Another name for a meteor.

Shrike A small bird with a hooked beak that catches lizards and other small animals.

Silica A hard mineral that is the main component of sand. It occurs naturally as quartz, and its chemical name is silicon dioxide.

Skeleton A framework made of bone or other material that supports an animal's body and enables it to move.

Solar system A sun and its surroundings, including planets and asteroids.

Songbird A small bird that often sings to attract a mate. There are more than 5,000 kinds of songbirds.

Spore A tiny package of cells released by fungi, mosses, and ferns when they reproduce.

Stalactite An icicle-shaped deposit of calcite hanging from the roof of a cave.

Stalagmite A deposit of calcite shaped like an upside-down icicle that rises from the floor of a cave.

Star A gigantic globe of glowing gas, lit up by nuclear fusion reactions in its core.

Starling A noisy flock-forming bird with a sharp beak.

Static electricity The electric charge that builds up as a result of friction in storm clouds and causes lightning.

Strata Layers of sedimentary rock.

Stratosphere The layer of the atmosphere that lies above the lowest layer.

Stratus Sheets of cloud.

Sublimation The process in which a solid turns directly to a gas without passing through a liquid phase, or the other way around. For example, ice turning to water vapour.

Succulents Plants, such as cacti and spurges, that survive in dry places by storing water in stems or leaves.

Sunspot A relatively cool, dark spot on the Sun's surface.

Supernova A huge explosion that happens when a star dies.

Swallow A migratory bird with a forked tail that feeds on insects in mid-air. Swallows often nest near houses.

Swift A migratory, insect-eating bird with crescent-shaped wings. Swifts catch their food in the air and sleep on the wing.

Temperate Neither too hot nor too cold. Used to describe the regions to the north and south of the warm subtropics.

Tern A fish-eating bird with small legs and a sharp beak. Terns often flutter above the water before splashing down to catch their food.

Thermal A warm, rising air current.

Thorax The middle part of an insect's body. The other two parts are the head and the abdomen.

Thrush A ground-feeding bird that eats snails and worms. Many thrushes have attractive songs.

Tit A small, acrobatic bird that feeds in trees and bushes. Tits feed mainly on insects and often live in small flocks.

Transpiration The loss of water vapour by evaporation from a plant's leaves.

Tree A large, woody plant with a single main stem (trunk).

Tropical rainforest A forest that grows near the equator and is wet and warm all year round.

Tropics The hot regions of the world that lie between the Tropic of Cancer and the Tropic of Capricorn.

Troposphere The lowest layer of the atmosphere, where all the weather happens.

Tundra The treeless lands surrounding the polar ice sheets, which are frozen in winter but thaw in summer.

Universe Everything that exists – planets, stars, galaxies, and all space in between.

Volcano A vent or fissure in the Earth's crust through which molten rock and hot gases escape. The molten rock typically piles up around the vent, forming a mountain.

Vortex A swirling funnel of water or air, as seen when water swirls down a plughole.

Warm front The boundary between warm and cold air masses, created when the warm air slides up over the cold air.

Wasp A stinging insect with two pairs of wings. Wasps are often coloured yellow and black to show other animals that they are dangerous, so they leave them alone.

Water vapour The invisible gas that is formed when liquid water evaporates.

Woodpecker A bird that pecks holes in trees with its sharp beak. Woodpeckers live in woods all over the world, except for Australia and New Zealand.

Worker An insect that lives in a nest and that carries out the daily tasks needed to keep the nest thriving. Unlike the queen, workers do not breed.

Index

Q, R

S

T

U, V, W

Acknowledgements

The publisher would like to thank the following for their kind permission to reproduce their photographs:
(Key: a-above; b-below/bottom; c-centre; f-far; l-left; r-right; t-top)

Jacket images: *Front:* **Ardea:** Pascal Goetgheluck cb. **Getty Images:** Stock Image/Martin Ruegner bl; Stone/Catherine Ledner fbl; Stone/Peter Hince cl; Taxi/Gail Shumway fbr. **Robert Harding Picture Library:** Travel Pix (sky). *Back:* **Corbis:** Gabe Palmer cr.; **Getty Images:** Riser/Chad Ehlers clb. Spine: **Getty Images:** Stock Image/Martin Ruegner bc; Taxi/Gail Shumway ca.

Alamy Images: Alaska Stock LLC 1bc, 241tl; Andrew Darrington 181tl; David R Frazier Photolibrary, Inc 237cr; Danita Delimont 204bl; David Hoffman 34bl; IPS 72tl; K-Photos 240–241; Alan Mather 186–187; Renee Morris 187tc; Rosey Pajak 186tr; Troy and Mary Parlee 237c; Phototake Inc 235cla; Robert Pickett/Papilio 59cra, 59fcra; David Tipling 40–41; Genevieve Vallee 184br. **Ardea:** Piers Cavendish 19cr; Steve Hopkin 68br; B Moose Peterson 33b, 203tl; Geoff Trinder 201ca; M Watson 26c, 199br. **Avpix/Hugh W Cowin:** 222clb. **Peter Chew:** Brisbane Insects and Spiders 65tr. **Collections:** Peter Wilson 134bl. **Corbis:** 81r; James L Amos 158–159; Ron Austing/Frank Lane Picture Agency 8bl; Tom Bean 137clb; Lester V Bergman 240cl; Annebicque Bernard 41tr; Bettmann 149tr; Ralph A Clevenger 84–85 (background); Philip James Corwin 217tr; Bennett Dean/Eye Ubiquitous 136br; Duomo 216bl; FLPA/Michael Callan 173br; Natalie Fobes 42tl; Patrik Giardino 137r; David Gray/Reuters 242br; Farrell Grehan 18–19 (background); Annie Griffiths Belt 165br; Derek Hall/Frank Lane Picture Agency 134–135; Angela Hampton/Ecoscene 52tr; Lindsay Hebberd 137tc; Kit Kittle 209cb; Matthias Kulka 222bl; William Manning 40crb; Don Mason 131b; George McCarthy 29, 32, 66–67b; Joe McDonald 41clb; Roy McMahon 243cr; Marko Modic 176cl; Eric Nguyen/Jim Reed Photography 243bc; Gabe Palmer 106–107 (family); Chris Rainier 10–11; Anthony Redpath 209clb; Roger Ressmeyer 136tr; Lynda Richardson 29tr; Galen Rowell 168–169; Scott T Smith 227tl; Joseph Sohm/ChromoSohm Inc 155cla; Chase Swift 40clb; Brenda Tharp 130bl; Thinkstock 237cl; Roger Tidman 234–235; Onne Van Der Wal 230bl, 230–231 (background); Sandro Vannini 137cb; Maurice Walker/Frank Lane Picture Agency 41bc; Ron Watts 130br; Michael S Yamashita 242–243. **David Tipling Photo Library:** Windrush Photos 23tr. **Dorling Kindersley:** The Ivy Press Limited 28c; Howard Rice 192bl; Stephen Oliver 183cb, 193fcra; Kim Taylor 37bl. **Thomas R Fletcher:** 68–69. **FLPA:** B Borrell Casals 71cra; S Charlie Brown 179cl; Robert Canis 181cb; Christiana Carvalho 209crb; Arthur Christiansen 198bl; Tim Fitzharris/Minden Pictures 181c; Michael & Patricia Fogden/Minden Pictures 208cb; Michael Gore 30bc; Derek Hall 126–127; Holt Studios International/Nigel Cattlin 75clb; Mitsuhiko Imamori 180; J C Allen and Son 242bc; Frans Lanting/Minden Pictures 169tl, 185cr; S & D & K Maslowski 16tr, 189cla; Derek Middleton 173cr; Maurice Nimmo 173crb; Silvestris Fotoservice 174–175; John Watkins 17tl; Martin B Withers 23br; Martin B Withers 172–173; Steve Young 31fbr. **Getty Images:** AFP 209tr; Photographers Choice 208–209; Stone/Alan R Moller 206–207, 236c, 236tl. **Mike Jordan:** 172bl. **Moviestore Collection:** 163tr. **NASA:** 98clb, 168bl; JPL 95tr, 104cb, 107r, 108–109, 109bc, 109tr; STScI/AURA 89cr. **The Natural History Museum, London:** 180cb, 181ca. **naturepl.com:** Ingo Arndt 48bc; Juan Manuel Borrero 168tr; Adrian Davies 181crb; Geoff Dore 56bl, 63clb; John Downer 61tr; David Kjaer 170–171; Brian Lightfoot 72cr; George McCarthy 173cla; Duncan McEwan 72bl, 75tr; Dietmar Nill 16cr; Rolf Nussbaumer 187cr; Premaphotos 64cl, 81tl. **NHPA/Photoshot:** Anthony Bannister 55tr, 70–71; George Bernard 59cl, 71tl; N A Callow 73cla; Laurie Campbell 24, 35cl, 202bl; Bill Coster 31fcr; Stephen Dalton 25t, 35bl, 46–47, 54–55 (background), 77br, 77tr; Manfred Danegger 34cr, 36–37; Daniel Heuclin 60bc; Ernie Janes 33t, 35cr, 78–79; Mike Lane 37c, 166–167, 173cra; Roger Tidman 11tr; Alan Williams 35tl, 35tr, 38bl; David Woodfall 9tl. **Photolibrary:** OSF/Claude Steelman 205 (starfish); OSF/IFA-Bilderteam Gmbh 186bc; OSF/Richard Packwood 175tr; OSF/Roland Mayr 179br. **Andrew Purcell:** 82bl. **rspb-images.com:** Gerald Downey 41br; Bob Glover 21tl; Mark Hamblin 40bc; George McCarthy 17; Roger Wilmshurst 16bl. **Science & Society Picture Library:** 97tr. **Science Photo Library:** 224bl; P G Adam/Publiphoto Diffusion 208crb; Mike Agliolo 151cra; David P Anderson, SMU/NASA 103cr; Bill Bachman 133br; Celestial Image Co. 119cra, 121cr; Lynwood Chase 189cr; David A Hardy, Futures: 50 years in Space 123cr; Luke Dodd 123bc; European Southern Observatory 100tr, 119cl, 124cr; Mark Garlick 94bl, 111cra; Tony & Daphne Hallas 118cl; David A Hardy 92bl, 124b; Larry Landolfi 106tr; Lawrence Lawry 144br; Damien Lovegrove 226cr; MPIA-HD/BIRKLE/SLAWIK 124cla; David Nanuk 189br; NASA 102clb; National Otical Astronomy Observatories 119crb; NRSC LTD 223tl; David Nunuk 86–87, 88–89t, 110–111; Pekka Parviainen 102–103, 112–113; Paul Rapson 225tr; Jim Reed 243bl; Royal Observatory, Edinburgh/AAO 120–121; Rev Ronald Royer 107clb; John Sanford 98bl, 98–99 (background), 103c, 118–119, 122clb; Francoise Sauze 66clb; Alan Sirulnikoff 135cr; Eckhard Slawik 1cr, 98–99 (Moon), 101cra; Space Telescope Science Institute/NASA 105tr, 119br, 119cr; Barbara Strnadova 48–49; Joe Tucciarone 122–123; University of Dundee 234br; Detlev Van Ravenswaay 92–93; VVG 49b; Dirk Wiersma 128c, 128–129; Frank Zullo 93cr, 110bl, 124–125. **Still Pictures:** 141tr, 161cra; Jeremy Woodhouse 25br. **SuperStock:** Age Fotostock 200l. **Warren Photographic:** 168cr, 176cr, 176–177; Kim Taylor 9br, 15b, 17bc, 18–19 (owl), 30–31, 57tl, 65cl, 67tr, 69tr, 70l, 76–77, 79cla, 80b; Mark Taylor 42–43.

The publisher would like to thank Jackie Brind for the index, and Charlotte Webb for proofreading.

All other images © Dorling Kindersley
For further information see:
www.dkimages.com